Hampton and Newport News in the Civil War

War Comes to the Peninsula

1st Edition

This series is dedicated to the State of Virginia and all of her people who lived during the War Between the States. It is the purpose of this series to preserve, as a part of our heritage, the deeds and sacrifices of these Virginians. Your support of this project is greatly appreciated.

Number 123 of 1,000

John V. Quarstein

Copyright 1998 H. E. Howard, Inc.

Manufactured in the United States by
H. E. Howard, Inc., Lynchburg, Virginia

Printed by H. E. Howard, Inc.

ISBN-1-56190-109-1

Hampton and Newport News in the Civil War

War Comes to the Peninsula

1st Edition

John V. Quarstein

Introduction

I came to the Peninsula in 1960 when my father, then a captain in the U. S. Army, was assigned to Fort Monroe. I was almost seven years old, and my first visit to Fort Monroe hooked me forever on the Civil War. The fort was fascinating and its history enthralling. I just could not learn enough about the ironclads, the cannons, and the great leaders — all of which I could feel when I stood on the Fort's bastions. I knew then I wanted to be a historian and would one day write about the Peninsula's role in the Civil War.

Some twenty-six years later I realized that it was time to write this book. I regrettably witnessed the destruction of a redoubt at Lee's Mill; it was a dreadful scene. This open season on earthworks, I thought, was all based on greed, and perhaps more importantly, on the general lack of knowledge by local residents about the Peninsula's tremendous Civil War legacy. That day in 1986 transformed me into a dedicated Civil War preservationist, determined to do whatever was necessary to insure that the remaining sites, like Young's Mill, were effectively preserved and interpreted. My completion of this text also coincides with the acquisition by the Virginia War Museum, where I have worked for the past twenty years, of three major Civil War sites: Endview Plantation, Lee Hall Mansion, and Lee's Mill battlefield. These nationally recognized historic sites place in a visual context part of the Peninsula's Civil War experience.

The Peninsula's role in the Civil War is really confined to the war's first year. Nevertheless, between May 1861 and May 1862 some of the conflict's most meaningful events occurred on this land bordered by the James and York rivers. Ben Butler's arrival in May 1861 brought the Civil War a step closer to becoming a war about freedom, which would forever change America, when he issued his "Contraband of War" decision. Unfortunately for the Union, Butler was not much of a general and he blundered his way shortly thereafter to Big Bethel. At Bethel, known as the

Civil War's first land battle, Butler encountered John Bankhead Magruder and suffered defeat. The short-lived Butler-Magruder relationship resulted in some fanciful legends, but sadly, also in the burning of Hampton by Magruder's troops. Hampton was the first town laid to waste in such a manner during the Civil War.

Beginning in March 1862 the Peninsula became the stage for what is undoubtedly one of the Civil War's most pivotal events: The Peninsula Campaign. Major General George Brinton McClellan's plan to strike at Richmond by way of the Peninsula was a sound concept enabling the Union to utilize its naval superiority to protect his army's flanks and carry his troops. Even before McClellan began moving his army to Fort Monroe to begin his campaign, the emergence of the powerful ironclad ram C.S.S. Virginia (Merrimack) disrupted his plan. The ensuing battle between the ironclads, the U.S.S. Monitor and C.S.S. Virginia on March 9,1862, in Hampton Roads, forever changed naval warfare. No longer would wooden ships rules the waves — ironclads became the key to naval superiority. Of even greater strategic impact, nonetheless, was that the Virginia continued to block the James River and forced McClellan to concentrate on the York River. His path to Richmond, however, was also blocked by Major General John B. Magruder's fortifications at Yorktown and along the Warwick River, Magruder's bluff of strength prompted McClellan to besiege the Confederate defenses. The ensuing month's delay was critical and contributed to the campaign's ultimate downfall.

When the Confederate army retreated from its defenses along the Warwick River, it ended the year-long saga along the rivers, forts, marshes and fields of the lower Peninsula. "Sic transit gloria, Peninsula," Magruder was reported to have said before he left Lee Hall Mansion enroute to Richmond; indeed, the Southerners had abandoned the Peninsula to Union occupation. Yet, the Peninsula events had had a profound impact. The Civil War had changed from a war of limited purpose into a war of attrition that would eventually define the meaning of freedom to all Americans.

Acknowledgments

I am indebted to many people for their help with this book. I especially must express my appreciation to my friends Dewey Stinson and Joe Gutierrez for their constant encouragement which gave me the fortitude to complete this volume. Natalie Ann Merry also is due great credit for her research assistance while serving as a Virginia War Museum intern. Mary LaPrade Kayaselcuk must also be thanked for her preparation of the maps which accompany the text. I must certainly laud Tim Smith and J. Michael Moore for all of their assistance selecting photographs to illustrate the book. Michael Moore, along with Jon Gates, Elisa Finneran and my father, Colonel Vernon A. Quarstein, Ph.D. assumed the mammoth chore of editing and deserve my heartfelt gratitude for accomplishing this task.

I would be most remiss if I did not thank my wife, son and parents for all of their constant support which enabled me to write this book. Martha, a descendant of several Southern soldiers who served on the Peninsula and who are all mentioned in this book, diligently deciphered and typed my text, while my son John Moran brought the laughter of a four-year old into my study which kept me in touch with the 20th Century. My parents, Mary and Vernon Quarstein, first introduced me to the Peninsula's Civil War experience in 1960 and have advocated my study of these events ever since. This book is an oblation in return for their love, patience and constant support.

Finally, I must honor men like Franklin Buchanan, John Bankhead Magruder, George McClellan and Dana Greene, among many others, for making such dynamic history for me to document. The Peninsula At War: Newport News and Hampton in the Civil War is a tribute to all the people who participated in the Peninsula events that defined the Civil War as America's greatest turning point.

Table of Contents

Introduction	....	i - ii
Acknowledgments	....	iii
Chapter 1	Forts and Fleets	1
Chapter 2	The Ante-bellum Peninsula	9
Chapter 3	Our Peaceful Life is Ended	17
Chapter 4	Every Inch a King	31
Chapter 5	A Sacrifice to the Grim God of War	47
Chapter 6	Beyond the Pale	61
Chapter 7	The Gathering Storm	74
Chapter 8	"Give 'Em A Broadsides Boys, As She Goes"	82
Chapter 9	Battle of the Ironclads	96
Chapter 10	Drums Along the Warwick	112
Chapter 11	Burnt Chimneys	128
Chapter 12	Siege	141
Chapter 13	Occupation and Surrender	153
Endnotes	....	167
Bibliography	....	180
Index	....	189

Chapter 1

Forts and Fleets

Today's cities of Hampton and Newport News are twentieth-century communities that grew rapidly out of the ashes of the Civil War. Before the war, these cities were the apparently idyllic communities of Warwick and Elizabeth City counties. Only one true town had developed: Hampton, and it was a small, fading port overshadowed by Norfolk and Portsmouth across the Hampton Roads.

Water dominated the Virginia Peninsula. The Peninsula is almost surrounded by the Chesapeake Bay, York River, Hampton Roads, and James River, and dissected by numerous creeks and rivers such as Deep Creek, New Market Creek, Back River and the Warwick River, these bodies of water provided residents with excellent avenues of transportation and bountiful harvests of oysters, crabs, fowl and fish. The counties had flourished in the tobacco society prompting an agricultural decline caused by overproduction of tobacco. However, the land was rejuvenated in the 19th Century to provide a wide variety of truck crops. In many ways the lower Peninsula was an Eden; but another factor was clearly evident: it was a place of extreme strategic value.

One of the first landfalls made by the English when they arrived in Virginia in 1607 was at a spit of land which would eventually be called Old Point Comfort. Even though the colonists moved on to Jamestown, they recognized the site's military importance. Located twenty miles from the Chesapeake Capes and commanding the entrance to Hampton Roads, as well as the lower James River, Captain John Smith considered it a "little Ile fit for a Castle."[1] The fortifications, or lack thereof, on Old Point Comfort would dominate the region for the next four centuries.

The colonists soon followed John Smith's advice. Fearing

excursions by Spanish or French fleets and leery of the native inhabitants, Old Point Comfort was first fortified in October 1609 by Captain James Davis and a company of sixteen men. The earthwork was named "Algernourne Fort." The work was named by President of the Colonial Council George Percy in honor of his ancestor, Lord Algernon, who had come to England with William the Conqueror. Fort Algernourne was soon reinforced with Captain John Ratcliffe's company from Jamestown.[2]

The death of Humphrey Blunt, on July 16, 1610, by the hands of the Kecoughtan Indians made the colonists more alert to the native threat. Thus, other fortifications were built to defend the Peninsula's Hampton Roads' frontage and the entrance to the James River. Fort Henry and Fort Charles were constructed in 1610 to guard the entrance to the Hampton (then called Southampton) River, and a three-gun earthwork was built on Newport News Point to guard the entrance to the James River. Fort Algernourne was stockaded in 1611 and armed with seven heavy cannon.[3]

The Spanish finally came into Hampton Roads in late June 1611. No attack was made and three Spaniards were captured.[4] One of these men, Diego de Molina, wrote a description of the colony's Hampton Roads fortifications upon his return to Spain:

> At the entrance is a fort [Algernourne] or, to speak more exactly, a weak structure of boards ten hands high with twenty-five soldiers and four iron pieces. Half a league off is another [Charles] smaller with fifteen soldiers, without artillery. There is another [Henry] smaller than either, half a league inland from here for a defense against the Indians. This has fifteen more soldiers.[5]

The colony's defenses appeared in disarray. When Fort Algernourne burned in 1612, it was rebuilt shortly thereafter; yet it too was poorly maintained. A more permanent and extensive fort was built in 1630. It took two years to construct under the able supervision of Captain Samuel Matthews.[6]

Despite the brief periods of military awareness which prompted a flurry of work to enhance Virginia's defenses, there were continual reports of these forts falling into disrepair. No funds were available for upkeep until 1632 when a tax was passed by the House of Burgesses called "castle duties." All new immigrants were levied a fee of 60 pounds of tobacco and incoming ships were charged powder and shot to help arm the forts. This revenue appears to have either been squandered or misapplied because the forts continued to deteriorate.[7]

When the 2nd Anglo-Dutch Naval War broke out in 1665, the Peninsula was virtually defenseless. Colonel Miles Cary abandoned the work at Old Point Comfort describing the fort as "useless." The House of Burgesses awoke in 1667 to the danger and appropriated funds to rebuild the fort. Before work commenced, a Dutch fleet passed through Hampton Roads and destroyed several tobacco- ladened ships in the James River. Colonel Cary was killed while trying to stop the Dutch raiding party.[8] The colonial government then detached Colonel Leonard Yeo to mount eight guns at Old Point Comfort. The project was unsuccessful as a hurricane struck on August 27, completely destroying the fort and its fortification.

Once again the Old Point Comfort fortifications were rebuilt and in 1670 were called "the most important military work within the colony." Yet, again it fell into such disrepair that during the 3rd Anglo-Dutch Naval War the result was the same as in 1667: the Dutch destroyed several vessels at anchor in the James River in 1673.[9] This pattern would continue into the 18th Century. In 1711 Old Point Comfort was reported to mount a battery containing 70 cannon, but by 1728 repairs were once again declared necessary. Finally, a more permanent work was erected in 1736. Named Fort George and commanded by Captain Samuel Barron, the colony's governor, reported that "no ship could pass it without running great risk." Fort George was demolished by a hurricane in 1749. The fort was never effectively rebuilt.[10]

Peninsula citizens had by now become somewhat complacent, enjoying the wealth of the tobacco economy. Their enemies seemed so far away that forts were forgotten and militia training languished.

Events at Lexington and Concord in April 1775 stirred Virginia into action. Enthusiasm for the patriot's cause led to the royal governor's defeat at the battles of Great Bridge and Crickett Hill. Lord Dunmore and his loyalist followers fled the colony. The Peninsula appeared safe from British excursions until 1780 when the subjugation of the southern colonies became the focal point of English grand strategy. The Royal Navy, using a fleet of 30 vessels, established a blockade which stretched in a line from Newport News Point to the Nansemond River while turncoat Benedict Arnold led raids up and down the James River. Hampton was captured in October 1780, and by late spring 1781 Lord Cornwallis brought his main army into Tidewater. The "badly armed" militia was hard pressed to defend the Peninsula, no effective fortification was available to stem the invader's tide. Even so, there were several small engagements that sprang up between the marauding British and the patriots. One action at Waters Creek was a victory for the local militia despite the death of their commander, Colonel Francis Mallory, who was "pierced with shot, saber and bayonet."[11] Even the fledgling Virginia State Navy sent help to limit British excursions., The *Patriot*, a sixty-ton brig mounting eight two-pounder swivel guns, moved into the lower James River under the command of Lieutenant James Watkins. During a battle with a British sloop in April 1781, the Patriot was captured.[12] The entire Peninsula suffered serious deprecations as the British roamed the countryside virtually at will throughout the spring and summer of 1781. The British had cowed the countryside into submission. One militia unit of 400 men was defeated in May 1781 by a small reconnaissance patrol commanded by Lieutenant Colonel Banistre Tarleton. Cornwallis' control was so complete that he was able to order the Warwick County militia to give up their weapons, parole themselves and provide provisions for "his Majesty's troops."[13]

Sir Henry Clinton, overall commander of the British forces in North America, ordered Cornwallis to seek winter quarters for his troops suggesting Old Point Comfort as the best alternative. Cornwallis believed that Old Point Comfort was "poorly situated for defense" and moved his army to Yorktown.[14] Soon he found himself trapped in his defenses as the French fleet defeated a British squadron during the September 13-14, 1781 Battle of the Capes. A little more than a month later, on October 19, 1781, Cornwallis surrendered his army thus virtually ending the Revolutionary War.

During the Yorktown siege the French naval commander, Admiral Comte de Grasse, used local militiamen to build a French artillery battery at Old Point Comfort. Hospitals were established in several Hampton public buildings for sick sailors and soldiers. After the Yorktown victory, Hampton was used as winter quarters for the French army. They were all gone by the next spring and the Peninsula was vacant of all military activity.[15]

Peace had come once again to the Peninsula but there were still concerns about harbor defense. The area's economic importance had greatly diminished since the colonial era. It was, however, still an avenue of approach to Virginia's James River hinterland, thus, some thought was given to refortifying Old Point Comfort. Nothing other than talk had been accomplished when the new nation found itself embroiled in another war with Great Britain over issues of free trade and westward expansion. Often called the Second Revolution, the War of 1812 disrupted the pastoral quiet of the Peninsula as the British sought to "chastise the Americans into submission." Control of the Chesapeake Bay was one of Britain's primary strategic aims. In February 1813, Admirals Sir John Borlase Warren and Sir George Cockburn sailed into Hampton Roads and positioned their fleet off Newport News Point. Local defense was in the weak hands of the 115th Virginia Militia Regiment and these men, many of whom were often "too sick to bear arms," were unable to stop British raiding parties from looting homes and farms throughout the Peninsula.[16]

On June 22, 1813, the British attempted to capture Norfolk but were unexpectedly defeated during the Battle of Craney Island. Cockburn was enraged by this repulse and sought vengeance against Hampton. The town was defended by a small earthwork mounting four 12-pounders and three 6-pounders at the head of Sunset Creek and manned by Major Stapleton Crutchfield's 436 strong militia detachment. Cockburn, on the morning of June 25, feigned an attack with barges using rockets and Royal Marines. This feint against Blackbeard's Point deceived Crutchfield's militia into believing it was the main British assault. Meanwhile, the main British force of 2,500 men commanded by General Sir Sidney Beckwith landed at Newport News Point and Celey's Plantation just east of Salter's Creek and marched toward Hampton virtually unopposed. This movement unhinged the militia's defensive plans and quickly forced their rapid retreat. Hampton was occupied by Beckwith's troops, then sacked and burned by the marauding soldiers promised "Booty and Beauty" by Admiral Cockburn. It was later reported by Lieutenant Colonel Sir Charles Napier that "every horror was committed with immunity — rape, murder, pillage, and not a man punished." The blame for the "rape" of Hampton was laid on the shoulders of French ex-prisoners of war serving in the Chasseurs Britaniques and the Americans protested the town's destruction but to little avail. The British continued their blockade of Hampton Roads until the war was over.[17]

The primary lessons learned from the War of 1812 was the obvious need for a more effective defensive system to protect Hampton Roads and the surrounding communities. This prompted Congress to upgrade the entire coastal defense system and to approve construction of a masonry fortification on Old Point Comfort.

Named for President James Monroe and designed by the distinguished French military engineer and former aide-de-camp to Napoleon, Brigadier General Simon Bernard, Fort Monroe would become the largest moat encircled masonry fortification in America. The fort would eventually cover 63 acres with the circumference of its walls being over a mile in length. The eight-foot deep moat varies in width from 60 to 150 feet at the Main Sally port. Fort Monroe was designed to mount 412 guns and house a wartime garrison of 2,625 officers and men. The fort's design featured seven fronts with several large bastions to maximize direct, flank and cross fire. Extensive outer works, including a redoubt and redan, were built to protect it from land attack. It also featured a Water Battery containing 40 guns to concentrate fire at vessels before they could enter the channel. Construction on the fort began in earnest in 1819 and it was virtually complete in 1834.[18]

Old Point Comfort's one weakness, which was recognized by Lord Cornwallis in 1781, was that its guns could not totally command the main shipping channel leading into Hampton Roads. Complete control of the channel could only be achieved by building a companion work to Fort Monroe on the Rip-Raps, a shoal almost a mile from Old Point Comfort in the middle of the entrance to Hampton Roads. This required engineers to first create an artificial island of stone upon which a tower battery, with three tiers of casemates, was to be built. Designed to mount 232 guns and a wartime garrison of 1,130 officers and men, the work was named Fort (also referred to as Castle) Calhoun in honor of then Secretary of War John C. Calhoun. Construction began in 1823, but foundation problems caused numerous delays. It was not until 1860, under the able direction of Colonel Rene E. DeRussy, that Castle Calhoun neared completion, though greatly modified from its original design.[19]

Fort Monroe, nevertheless, soon became one of the most important military installations in the south. In 1824 it was selected as the location of the Artillery School of Practice. During the Seminole War, Nat Turner's Rebellion, the Black Hawk War, and the Mexican War the fort was used as an assembly, training, and embarkation site for units designated for combat. Many individuals who later gained rank and acclaim during the Civil War served at Fort Monroe prior to the war. The young engineer Robert E. Lee helped supervise the moat's construction in the early 1830s. His first son, George Washington Custis Lee, was born on Fort Monroe. Others include John B. Wool, Robert B. Anderson, Silas Casey, Samuel Cooper, Joseph E. Johnston and Jubal Early.[20]

The fort soon became a popular resort. President Andrew Jackson used Fort Monroe and the Rip-Raps as a Summer White House in 1829, 1831, 1833, and 1834. President John Tyler, who owned a home in Hampton, was a frequent visitor to the fort and used the Rip-Raps as a retreat following the death of his first wife in 1842. He returned to Old Point Comfort with a new wife in 1844 and once again in 1845. The Hygeia Hotel was built outside the fort's walls in 1822 and soon became one of the leading hotels in America.[21]

Fort Monroe would dominate the Peninsula and Hampton Roads region socially, economically and politically. The fort's existence made the surrounding communities secure, but soon would become a major thorn in the local citizenry's effort to forge a separate nation.

Chapter 2

The Ante-bellum Peninsula

Fort Monroe and the partially completed Fort Calhoun provided the Hampton Roads region with one of the most extensive defensive systems in America. The forts, however, did not provide the Peninsula with any great stimulus for economic or industrial enhancement. The colonial era's tobacco prosperity just had not continued into the nineteenth century. Time was virtually at a standstill; life was good for the gentry but there were few other opportunities available in the quiet and stable agricultural society found on the Peninsula.

Elizabeth City County and especially Warwick County had become backwater communities. Tobacco had depleted the soil and this circumstance coupled with agricultural depressions and the lure of western lands caused a population decline. The 1820 census details that Warwick County had only 1,621 residents: 628 whites, 959 slaves and 34 free blacks. Only 14 taxed residents were pursuing non-agricultural occupations; by 1860 Warwick County had only two doctors and one lawyer.[1]

With more than 67 percent of Warwick County property owners holding less than 200 acres of land, the lack of a major cash crop turned most farmers to truck crops. As George Ben West of Newport News Point remembered:

> Corn, oats, wheat and sweet potatoes were the principal crops raised. The land was particularly adapted to sweets and this was the chief money crop, and every farmer cultivated from four to forty acres. They [were] sold by the bushel and shipped in schooners in bulk . . . In 1860 when the New York steamships from Richmond stopped to take trucks direct to New York . . . Irish potatoes, tomatoes, and other trucks were raised and the sweets were then shipped in barrels . . . Only the

larger farmers raised wheat and oats . . . and they shipped in pungies to Baltimore and Richmond.[2]

The West family and their neighbor, R. E. Bennett, constructed wharves to handle all of this produce. West reported that sometimes as many as a hundred or more sailing ships could be seen at anchor along the James River bank. It was an agrarian wonderland, as described in 1861 by Ben Butler:

> We landed at a little jetty at Newport News and climbed the banks. Here there burst upon my sight one of the finest scenes I ever beheld. At the point nearest the river was a farmers house shaded by some very fine elms, and a field of some sixty or seventy acres, a perfect plain, covered with a beautiful growth of spring wheat waving in a light wind.[3]

Another soldier serving at Fort Monroe in the late 1850s could only concur and described the Peninsula as "a veritable Garden of Eden with numerous fine homes and beautifully cultivated lands."[4]

New agricultural techniques made the Peninsula soil rich and again fertile. Crop rotation, deep plowing and soil fertilization were part of the new scientific "system of farming." Daniel Prentis Curtis of Waterview on Mulberry Island's Pleasant Point noted that "Those who have adopted the four-field system . . . look forward with great expectation of success, both in improvement and profit. Our crops of corn are very promising."[5]

Improved agricultural practices during the ante-bellum period brought even greater wealth to the small gentry class as seen in the construction of Richard Decauter Lee's Italianate mansion Lee Hall, which was financed by a bumper crop of tobacco in 1848. The Young family home, Denbigh Plantation, was described as:

> A large, tastefully built brick house . . . bearing in all respects, the agreeable look of being the seat of the county squire in easy, if not affluent circumstances. Horses, cows, sheep, etc., grazing about the premises gave a lively touch of the rural picturesque to the lawn and domicile.[6]

The gentry elite also controlled local politics. This class is perhaps best illustrated by Humphrey Harwood of Endview Plantation. Each generation of the Harwood family had served as local militia officers, justices of the peace, sheriffs, tobacco inspectors and as members of the House of Burgesses/Delegates for Warwick County since 1629. "Big Humphrey" also represented the county in the General Assembly, and this description of his person helps to define the lives of the Peninsula gentry:

> [He] never spent anything, but saved all the money he made. People had no use for money then, except to pay taxes, doctor's bills, and children's schooling. They made everything for themselves. He used to wear homespun clothes, and brogan shoes . . . as everybody else did. He was a member of the House of Delegates . . . and when there wore a red velvet, double-breasted waistcoat, with buttons made of ten cent pieces.[7]

Big Humphrey typified the gentry's control over local society. He was the fifth generation of the Harwood family to serve as Warwick's representative and would, according to Warwick County resident Benjamin H. Green, "vote, in Warwick, and then ride to James City to vote again."[8] Property ownership in two counties gave Big Humphrey this self-believed right to vote wherever he owned land. Such control over local politics and, in turn, the court and educational systems, enabled the gentry to maintain their power.

If the gentry comprised the upper end of society, their wealth rested on the slaves who toiled on their farms. The largest segment of the Peninsula's population was slaves. This unfortunate system was the mainstay of rural Southern economy, yet George Ben West thought it was somewhat idyllic as he wrote:

> The slaves were notably well treated, well fed and well housed, they were seldom bought or sold. They married either their master's slaves or those of their neighbors. . . . To show how contented they were, not a single one left his master, tho' they had every opportunity of doing so, in the vessels that traded up the James River . . .[9]

Slaves were one of the major cash income sources for poor farmers. Rental to other farms or commercial ventures could bring a handsome profit. Slaves, rented from Elizabeth City County landowners, were actually used alongside convict labor during Fort Monroe's construction. Slaveholders also generated much needed revenues through the sale of their bondsmen to the cotton plantations of the Deep South. William B. Hayes wrote to his son James advising him that "Your uncle Mat. Wills is gone to New Orleans with five of his Negroes to sell, leaving not more than that number at home."[10] The sale of eight of Colonel Harwood's slaves netted his estate the tidy sum of $6,080.[11]

Nat Turner's Rebellion in 1831 in nearby Southampton County caused the Commonwealth to enact more restrictive slave codes. This opened the debate to abolish the institution in Virginia. Both Elizabeth City and Warwick delegates in the General Assembly voted for emancipation, yet the measure failed by a narrow margin.[12]

The Peninsula included a small free black population. Even though there were several restrictive laws requiring these individuals to be registered, and to maintain a certificate of freedom on their person at all times, there was some room for these freedmen to prosper. These families obtained their freedom either by purchase, manumission by their owner, or, like Cesar Tarrant, as a reward for military or otherwise meritorious service to the Commonwealth. Warwick County had a total of 59 free blacks in 1860. One example is Thomas Wright, Sr., who purchased his freedom in 1810 at the age of twenty. Wright served as Warwick County's miller earning $10.00 a month plus a portion of the grain he ground, which enabled him to acquire 60 acres as well as to maintain a family of twelve and three slaves.[13] It is apparent that the citizens of Hampton generally ignored existing laws prohibiting the teaching of slaves and freedmen. Mrs. Mary Peake, a free mulatto, operated a school for slaves in her home near the Hampton Academy. Peake was described as a "gifted teacher."[14]

Hampton, Elizabeth City County's seat, was the lower Peninsula's social, commercial and educational focal point. Rebuilt following the War of 1812 (the damage had not been that severe, but stories of the "sack" of Hampton made good propaganda), Hampton was a town of over two thousand inhabitants in 1860. The port, while still active, had faded from its colonial eminence since Norfolk and Portsmouth had deeper channels and railroad connections. Yet Hampton still prospered in its own way. Many prominent farmers, like Parker West of Newport News Point, maintained homes or businesses in the town.

Hampton was one of the few communities in the Commonwealth which had created a public or "free" school system under an 1845 Act of the General Assembly. Hampton Academy was the main school in Elizabeth City County and had been established in 1805 when Syms Free School and Eaton Charity School were merged. Several other schools within the public school system, such as Fox Hill Academy, operated during the 1850s but few could vie for the educational excellence provided by William and Mary graduate John Baytop Cary. Cary served as principal of Hampton Academy until he established Hampton Military Academy and a school for girls in 1855. He was known as a strict disciplinarian but with the ability to teach almost anyone. The curriculum included Greek, Latin, mathematics and music. Another private school, Chesapeake

Female College, was opened in 1857 by local Baptists. While education flourished in Hampton and Elizabeth City County, Warwick County was too poor and sparsely populated to maintain a consistent free school so the more well-to-do Warwick parents sent their children to either Hampton or Williamsburg for schooling.[15]

Churches were the mainstay of faith and social life on the lower Peninsula. The Episcopal Church, long the leading religious force in Virginia, had been in decline since the Revolutionary War. St. John's Church in Hampton, built in 1728, served the Elizabeth City Parish. The parish is the oldest Episcopal parish in continuous service in the United States. St. John's supported the establishment of the first church on Fort Monroe, the Chapel of the Centurion. The chapel was built following an explosion in the arsenal on June 22, 1855, that killed two soldiers. The one survivor, Lieutenant Julian McAllister, was so moved by his miraculous escape that he headed an effort to build a church which was consecrated on May 3, 1858. The Episcopal Church, however, had not fared well in Warwick County where the old brick Mulberry Island Church was taken over by Methodists. In Hampton, the Methodists had organized in 1772 and built their first church in 1789. However, the strongest denomination was the Baptist Church, creating "a great stir of religion" on the Peninsula. The first Baptist congregation was organized in 1791 in Hampton and by 1861 it claimed 600 black and 200 white members. The religious revival of the 1820s spawned new denominations and churches began to dot the landscape. One such denomination was called the Disciples of Christ, having split off "from both the Presbyterians and Baptists." Their first church, Lebanon Church, was built on Yorktown Road in Warwick County in 1836 and later rebuilt in 1859. Religion was a primary strength of the agricultural society on the lower Peninsula and in some cases, such as Big Bethel, small communities began to grow around the new churches built on important crossroads.[16]

Other than Hampton, towns did not grow on the lower Peninsula. Warwick County had only one so called town, Warwick

Court House, and it was described in 1835 as:

> Besides the usual county buildings, there are only 2 dwelling houses, 1 of which is a house of private entertainment, 1 general store, and 1 common school. Population 21.[17]

The county government complex consisted of a small court house built in 1810, a clerk's office and tiny jail. The community was not an impressive sight and was called by Dr. Edward Rush Young as being "certainly the most dilapidated forsaken place in Virginia."[18]

Elizabeth City and Warwick Counties were virtually devoid of industrial and commercial growth. Improved agricultural profits and fine riverine avenues of transport did not translate into economic expansion. The major problem facing the lower Peninsula was transportation. There were no railroads and only two main roads, the stage road known as the Hampton-York Highway and the Great Warwick Road, leading north toward Williamsburg. These roads were simply terrible. They were not much more than old paths zig-zagging their way through the countryside passing by various plantations but often making circuitous turns to avoid swamps or creeks. Unfortunately there was no effective system of maintenance, and aside from sections filled with oyster shells or planked with wooden boards by nearby landowners, the roads were rutted and difficult to traverse.

The renewed agricultural output in the 1850s did spur some commercial ventures. As local cotton production increased (988 pounds in 1840) it prompted the construction of a cotton mill in Warwick County which housed 1,644 spindles and employed forty-five people. The mill, however, failed due to competition from the Deep South. The Peninsula's vast timber resources enabled the operation of several saw mills. William D. Macy's mill on the Warwick River employed twenty-nine workers and produced 12,000 board feet of oak in 1860. However, tide mills were the most constant industry. Young's Mill, for example, produced 3,840 bushels of meal and Lee's Mill produced 1,000 bushels in 1840.[19]

Even though the waters surrounding the Peninsula teemed with seafood, oystering and other types of harvesting were just a fledgling industry. Warwick County produced 5,300 barrels of pickled fish in 1840 which was the second highest total in Virginia. Oystering would not blossom into a major industry until the post-war era, but still fishermen came from outside the area to dredge the abundant local beds. The oysters were described as being as long as seven inches. The General Assembly was petitioned in 1839 and again in 1858 to protect local oyster beds from harvesting by non-residents and to set seasonal limits. Yet, the plentiful seafood supported the local population with an excellent food source.[20]

The lower Peninsula did not appear to regret the lack of industry. It was, as noted by George Ben West, an earthly paradise for many:

> No one could desire to live in a more favored place with its mild climate, its delightful and health giving sea breezes, its accessibility both by land and water, made it a most desirable section for a home. It was settled by a happy and contented company of prosperous farmers, with comfortable homes, loving families, well tilled and fertile lands, and loyal slaves, everything to make them free from care.[21]

This peaceful and perfect world would soon be disrupted by the clouds of war. The Civil War would destroy this peaceful agrarian life leaving behind financial ruin.

Chapter 3

Our Peaceful Life is Ended

John Brown's raid on Harper's Ferry aroused Virginians to the darkening clouds of war over sectional differences. Yet, by Abraham Lincoln's election in 1860, most Virginians were markedly Unionist in sentiment. Peninsula resident, former President John Tyler, led one of several efforts to reach a compromise that would avoid war. Hampton's delegate to the Secession Convention, Charles K. Mallory, was a strong Unionist as were many residents. Families were divided as to what course Virginia should follow until the fall of Fort Sumter on April 13, 1861. Lincoln's subsequent call on April 15 for 75,000 volunteers from all the states to put down the rebellion, however, ended any hesitation. Warwick County voters, during the Denbigh Court Day, April 17, proclaimed the county to be the "Free State of Warwick." The citizens adopted an advance resolution to leave the Union declaring that if Virginia did not follow suit, Warwick County would do so anyway thus becoming a "free state."[1] This independence movement was brief. The Commonwealth, including the Warwick County delegates, voted to pass the Ordinance of Secession on the very same day.[2]

Independence may have been declared, but local residents had much to do to defend their homeland against the Union hosts that were sure to come to the Peninsula. Both sides recognized the Peninsula as an extremely strategic location, being one of two major approaches to Richmond. The James and York rivers that bordered the Peninsula provided excellent avenues of advance as well as strong defensive opportunities. Control of these rivers would be the focus of Northern and Southern efforts during the next year. The Union, however, had two major advantages: the U. S. Navy and Fort Monroe.

While local Confederates were striving to forge a new nation, the Federals quickly acted to consolidate their hold on Fortress Monroe. The fort, often called the "Key to the South," had already proven itself as an operations base for points farther south. Soldiers from the garrison had been sent by U. S. Army Commander-in-Chief Lieutenant General Winfield Scott to reinforce Fort Sumter and Fort Pickens.[3] This troop movement had seriously depleted the fort's garrison; however, major improvements completed in the year prior to the war under the direction of Lieutenant Colonel Rene E. DeRussy made both Fort Monroe and Fort Calhoun strong enough to thwart any effort to capture them. The Confederates, anyway, were ill-prepared to make any attempt.

Fort Monroe's commanding officer in spring 1861 was Lieutenant Colonel Justin Dimick, an 1819 West Point graduate. Forty years of military service, including brevets for gallantry in the Seminole War and the Mexican War, had well prepared him for the emergency at hand.[4] Dimick, under orders from Winfield Scott, sent the 3rd Massachusetts Regiment to attempt to secure Gosport Navy Yard from capture by local Confederate volunteers. The expedition failed to achieve its primary objective but assisted in the yard's destruction.[5] Dimick now concentrated on strengthening Fort Monroe, requesting troops, rations and ordinance. By mid-May the fort had been reinforced with the 3rd and 4th Massachusetts and the 1st Vermont regiments, numbering over 2,100 men and officers. Winfield Scott wrote that:

> Fort Monroe is by far the most secure post now in the possession of the U.S., against any attack that can be possibly made upon it, independent of the War Vessels, the *Cumberland* and the *Niagara*, at hand, and approaching you.[6]

With his troop strength rapidly increasing, Colonel Dimick informed the local militia commander, Colonel Charles K. Mallory, on May 13 that he intended to take possession of a well on the Elizabeth City County side of Mill Creek. That day elements of the recently arrived 4th Massachusetts Regiment occupied both the Mill Creek Bridge and the Clark Farm.[7] Local volunteers serving as pickets were outraged by the Union advance and swore "vengeance on Massachusetts troops for the Invasion of Virginia."

Southern patriots had not been totally idle on the Peninsula during the Federal troop buildup at Fort Monroe. One of Robert E. Lee's first acts upon being appointed commander of the Virginia forces on April 23 was to order Colonel Andrew Talcott of the CS Engineers to "proceed up James River to the vicinity of Burwell's Bay (across the James River from the mouth of the Warwick River), and select the most suitable point, which in your judgement, should be fortified in order to prevent the ascent of the river by the enemy." Lieutenant Catesby ap R. Jones of the Virginia State Navy was also dispatched on April 29 to fortify Jamestown Island and began to arm a water battery under construction with eight 32-pounder Columbiads captured at Gosport Navy Yard.[8]

As soon as Virginia had left the Union, Benjamin Stoddert Ewell, president of the College of William and Mary and an 1832 graduate of the U. S. Military Academy, offered his services to Governor John Letcher. On April 27, 1861, State Adjutant General Robert S. Garnett commissioned Ewell as a Major and ordered him to begin organizing volunteers from James City, York, Elizabeth City and Warwick counties for the defense of the Peninsula. While Ewell mustered the pre-war volunteer unit, the Williamsburg Junior Guard, into state service on April 28, events on the lower Peninsula drew his attention momentarily away from recruitment. A Federal gunboat, the *Yankee*, shelled members of the Richmond Howitzers as they began to fortify Gloucester Point on May 3. Ewell marched what few troops he had available to support the defense of Confederate works at Jamestown and Yorktown.[9] Fearing further Union aggressive steps up the Peninsula, Ewell quickly moved south to Hampton to muster local volunteers. He arrived just after the Federals had occupied the Clark farm to improve Fort Monroe's water supply. After an interview with Colonel Dimick on May 14, Ewell ordered local volunteers to withdraw a half mile from Fort Monroe to avoid any violence.[10]

The local citizens were in an uproar over this decision. Ewell reflected, "It is difficult to manage Hampton. The people are excitable and brave even to rashness, and are unwilling to give way. It might, on the approach in force of Federal troops, be executed by the military, and the remaining citizens ought to make terms, unless, indeed, it is made a second Saragossa. I doubt if, from the nature of the buildings, this could be done." Ewell had no other option but to establish some kind of no man's land between Hampton and Fort Monroe to give him time to recruit troops to counter the rapid Federal buildup on Old Point Comfort.[11]

More than 2,100 men were on duty within the fort by May 13. The fort was apparently safe from attack by Southern forces and Winfield Scott recognized Fort Monroe as the best available base of operations to mount expeditions to recapture forts along the Atlantic coast. Scott decided to first expand Union control around Old Point Comfort and dispatched more troops to Fort Monroe. He also selected Major General Benjamin Franklin Butler, then in charge of the Union Department of Annapolis, to assume command of the fort effective May 18. Butler had already achieved instant fame during the conflict's first days when he thwarted the secessionist movement in Maryland following the April 19 Baltimore riot. His actions had secured the safety of Washington, D.C., and Butler protested his new command at Fort Monroe as a lesser assignment. This prompted Winfield Scott to establish the Department of Virginia, which included sixty miles of territory around Fort Monroe. Butler, now recognizing the assignment as another opportunity to further his political ambitions, accepted the command.[12]

Butler, a cocked-eyed, corpulent yet astute criminal lawyer and pre-war Democratic politician from Massachusetts[13], was ordered to work in conjunction with the U.S. Navy and move aggressively against local Confederates. His immediate objectives were to disrupt and capture any enemy batteries within a half day's march of Fort Monroe as well as to threaten or recapture batteries on Craney Island and Gosport Navy Yard.[14]

Major General
Benjamin Franklin Butler
Library of Congress

Lieutenant Colonel
Justin Dimick
City of Hampton

Colonel
Charles K. Mallory
City of Hampton

Colonel
Benjamin Stoddert Ewell
Museum of Confederacy

Federal reinforcements continued to arrive at Fort Monroe. The fort, however, was becoming overcrowded. By May 20 Butler's entire command numbered 4,451 men and officers.[15]

Union troops had already expanded their position on the Hampton side of Mill Creek. Massachusetts troops converted former President John Tyler's summer home, Villa Margaret, near Hampton into barracks. Tyler had recently died and his wife Julia attempted to rid her home of "these scum of the earth." Her protestations to Northern authorities to protect her property were in vain and various Union units continued to use Villa Margaret as housing during the next few months.[16] The Federals established a large camp on the Segar Farm at the Hampton end of Mill Creek Bridge. The camp was first called Camp Troy, but soon renamed Camp Hamilton in honor of Lieutenant Colonel Schuyler Hamilton, Winfield Scott's military secretary. The 2nd New York and 1st Vermont were billeted at Camp Hamilton upon their arrival on the Peninsula.[17]

Butler decided to break the informal truce and on May 23 ordered Colonel J. Wolcott Phelps to march his 1st Vermont into Hampton. A Confederate camp was located just outside the town and was commanded by Major John Baytop Cary. This "camp of instruction" contained only 130 poorly armed men, obviously unable to block any Federal advance. Cary had accordingly made plans to burn the Hampton Creek Bridge in case of such a Union movement. When the Vermonters approached the bridge Cary could not locate either the firing party or the combustibles. He somehow was able to start a small fire, but it was slow to set the span into flames. Phelps, as he watched the wisps of smoke rise up from the bridge, ordered his men to the double quick to capture the bridge. At that moment, Cary sent a volunteer, Lieutenant Cutshaw, to ascertain the Union force's purpose. Cutshaw spurred his horse through the flames across the bridge and met with Colonel Phelps. Phelps informed Cutshaw that his troops had no hostile intent "but simply . . . to reconnoiter." With these assurances that neither the town nor its population would be molested, Cary, some citizens and the Vermonters joined together to extinguish the flames. The Confederate troops retreated from Hampton as the 1st Vermont marched into town. The town was in an uproar, despite most of its citizens being Unionist in sentiment prior to the war, as the Federal troops congregated at the intersection of King and Queen streets. it was an unusual coincidence that the Hamptonians were voting that very day to approve the Ordinance of Secession. Phelps closed the polls, thinking this might end the secessionist movement in Hampton, and then marched his men back to Fort Monroe. As Cary's men returned to Hampton, the polls were reopened and the Ordinance of Secession was passed 360 to 6. The gauntlet had now been tossed at the enemy.[18]

Phelps' "reconnoitering expedition" achieved little beyond stopping the Confederate destruction of Hampton Creek Bridge and proving that the Union could march virtually at will wherever and whenever it wished through the countryside of the lower Peninsula. Ewell, recently promoted to Lieutenant Colonel, rushed toward Fort Monroe to ascertain Butler's intentions but was captured enroute by Federal pickets. Major Cary also travelled to Fort Monroe to learn from Butler "how far he intended to take possession of Virginia soil, in order that I might act in such a manner as to avoid collision between our scouts." Cary was advised that the Federals merely needed more land for their encampments and inferred that they would not act aggressively unless molested by Confederate troops. Cary then obtained Ewell's release and was immediately ordered by Ewell to destroy the Hampton Creek Bridge.[19] The May 23 expedition, however, also had far reaching political implications that forever disrupted the pre-war life of the ante-bellum Peninsula.

Abraham Lincoln viewed the war in 1861 as a conflict to preserve the Union. His objective, politically motivated because of the Border States, was not to disrupt slavery where it existed, but to keep the Fugitive Slave Law in force. Regardless of this official policy, local slaves on the Peninsula viewed the troops in blue immediately as men of freedom, saying to the soldiers as they marched into Hampton, "Glad to see you, Massa." This first encounter between bondsmen and Unionists prompted three slaves to escape to Fort Monroe (soon to be called "Freedom's Fortress") which led to an eventual change in the Civil War's purpose. These slaves were owned by Colonel Charles K. Mallory, former commander of the 115th Virginia Militia and a pre-war Hampton lawyer, and had taken "advantage of the Terror prevailing among white inhabitants . . . and in the night came into our pickets" so to secure their freedom.[20]

The next day, May 24, Major Cary went once again to Fort Monroe to endeavor to obtain the return of Mallory's slaves, citing the Fugitive Slave Act as justification. Butler, realizing that the Negroes were at the very core of the conflict and that such laborers were being used to build nearby Confederate fortifications, denied his request. Cary was advised by General Butler that since Virginia now considered itself an independent nation and that Virginia was technically at war with the United States, his "constitutional obligations" under the Fugitive Slave Law to deliver up the slaves were null and void. He would give up the slaves only if Mallory would come onto Fort Monroe and take the oath of allegiance to the Union. Failing this, Butler reiterated that he intended to take possession of whatever property his troops required. Since slaves were considered "chattel property" Butler called the escaped bondsmen "contraband of war" and began using them to support Union operations.[21] It was the Civil War's first step towards becoming a war about freedom. Soon the term contraband would become another word used for runaway slaves.

Butler immediately recognized the political and economic implications of his contraband decision. The slave manpower which made the Southern economy function was now being depleted. Consequently, instead of these slaves working on Confederate fortifications, the contrabands now were building Union batteries.[22] Butler believed that the work of contrabands was a good return for the food and shelter provided them; however, the arrival of young children posed a separate problem. The Union commander felt compelled, for humanitarian reasons, to provide the same support for children without any "profit." Ben

Butler questioned the political ramifications and asked for an opinion from the Secretary of War as to the propriety of accepting non-productive slaves as contrabands. He also noted in his May 27 dispatch to Winfield Scott that the number of contrabands was rapidly increasing. Twelve slaves had escaped from Sewell's Point to become contrabands, bringing the value of contrabands in Union hands to $60,000.[23]

Ben Butler had been instructed by Winfield Scott to act with "boldness" in his operations against the local Confederates. The Southerners had been very aware of the Federal buildup at Fort Monroe and its threat to Hampton Roads. They constructed batteries to defend Norfolk at Sewell's Point on the Elizabeth River, two and a half miles from the Rip Raps and four miles from Fort Monroe as well as at Pig· Point at the entrance to the Nansemond River. The Sewell's Point Battery had been especially troublesome to the Federals. On May 18 and 19, 1861, Confederate cannon fire had driven off Union gunboats. Sewell's Point moreover gave the Southrons an advance vantage point from which they could observe and disrupt Union activities in Hampton Roads. Butler strove to contest these fortifications, threaten Norfolk, and gain control of the James River channel. On May 27 he sent three regiments of New York, Massachusetts and Vermont volunteers with a detachment of U.S. Regulars and two 6-pounders on the steamer *Pawnee* to occupy Newport News Point in order to blockade the James River. The Confederates, alert to this movement, strove to block the expedition with cannon fire from Sewell's Point, yet all their shots fell short. Union forces then landed without opposition as there were only a few Confederate pickets stationed at Newport News. The Federals immediately began building an "entrenched camp." Butler considered Newport News Point to be a very strategic site, as he advised Winfield Scott:

> The expedition to Newport News . . . landed without opposition. I have caused an intrenched camp to be made there, which, when completed, will be able to hold itself against any force that may be brought

against it, and afford an even better depot from which to advance than Fortress Monroe.

> The advantages of the News are these: There are two springs of very pure water there; the bluff is a fine, healthy location. It has two good, commodious wharves, to which steamers of any draught may come up at all stages of the tide; it is as near any point of operation as Fortress Monroe . . . a force there is a perpetual threat to Richmond.[24]

Newport News Point, now named Camp Butler and armed with four 8-inch Columbiads, soon became a major Union fortified encampment as Private William Osborne of the Fourth Massachusetts Volunteers recounted:

> As soon as Colonel Phelps arrived, he began the erection of earthworks. These were of semicircular form, terminating at either extremity on the bank of the river, and were nerely a half mile long. In the ditch in front of the works were placed obstructions . . . On the main works commanding the plain and forest were mounted a number of heavy guns, while on the bluff facing the river was a battery of five large pieces and among them a Sawyer and James rifle. Upon these works the men . . . labored for many days, and at a time when the weather was extremely hot.[25]

Butler believed that from his new base at Newport News Point he could easily capture the Confederate batteries at Pig Point and Suffolk, thereby severing Norfolk's railroad ties to Richmond, causing that port to surrender. Before Butler could put his plans against Pig Point into action, over 4,000 men were transferred from Fort Monroe to Washington, D.C., to counter the Confederate buildup at Manassas.[26]

The day before the arrival of the Union troops, George Benjamin West had returned from Hampton to his father's farm. He and other Newport News Point residents enjoyed watching the war from afar as a Union gunboat exchanged fire with Confederate batteries at Sewell's Point. That Sunday, according to West, "was the last happy day spent in our pleasant house" as the Union troops built Camp Butler around his family's farm. The 303-acre West property, including house, outbuildings and storehouse, stood on the very bluff that the Federals selected to fortify. The wharf built by Parker West in 1860 now became the scene of the debarkation of Union troops by the thousands and all the accompanying materials of war. "War seemed to have come in the midst of perfect peace," West recounted, as his family was forced to request that their home be protected by a "Yankee" guard (of Vermont Volunteers) to prevent their possessions from being looted by "the roughs and jail birds of Boston." Befriending the Vermonters with food, the Wests appeared safe from harm, while other Federal troops plundered surrounding farms and homesteads despite strict orders against pillaging.[27]

The Wests may have lived in fear but the local slaves were "in a state of great excitement and jollification."[28] West noted that two of his family slaves ran away and others refused to do any work. The entire Peninsula was now in disarray and pro-Confederate citizens began escaping toward Williamsburg, Yorktown and Richmond.

The Federals were on the move as Confederate pickets noticed Union troops marching toward Newmarket Creek Bridge. An alarm was sent to Major Cary in Hampton. Cary, in turn, reported to Colonel John Bankhead Magruder, now in command of the Confederate forces on the Peninsula, that five Federal steamers were moving up the James River. Fearing that his troops would be flanked, Cary abandoned Hampton. Magruder reported later that day from Yorktown that:

> The women and children have been passing here all day from Hampton, and Major Cary is also

retreating on this place with about sixty-five men, out of two hundred, which he had a day or two since — the remainder of his men being occupied attending to their families . . .[29]

As Confederate troops retreated from Hampton many lower Peninsula residents decided to abandon their homes and refugee westward. The Hawkins, Marrow and West families of Newport News Point had lived in constant fear, shut in their homes and surrounded by the enemy. While others, like the Parrish family, hoped the war would quickly pass them by, the Wests placed their belongings in several carts and a buggy and set out for Williamsburg. They took their house servants with them and intended to return for their field hands and furniture. The family would not return until 1865 and then all was lost. A pass from Colonel Phelps, commander of Camp Butler, enabled them to pass through the lines. As the Wests travelled up the Great Warwick Road they found most of the fields abandoned until they reached the Confederate pickets the next day at Persimmon Ponds Bridge. The war had taken a turn for the worse for the citizens of the Lower Peninsula.[30] Some, like Robert Scott Hudgins II, a member of the Old Dominion Dragoons, remembered that his father had warned his family from his deathbed on March 31, 1861, that the war was inevitable and that his wife should sell their property and take the girls to Europe. Hudgins' father also knew that his sons would stay behind and fight for the Southland.[31]

Despite the exodus of troops and civilians up the Peninsula, Butler's aggressive moves had stimulated local recruitment. On the very day of Butler's occupation of Newport News Point, the enlistment of troops in Warwick County had proceeded under the leadership of twenty-nine year old Dr. Humphrey Harwood Curtis of Endview Plantation. Eighty men, including four officers and nine NCOs, recruited into the "Warwick Beauregards" from Upper Warwick County and Mulberry Island.

The Warwick Beauregards were a rural company and typified the image of a deferential Southern society led by plantation owners. The company leaders were all wealthy men, led by 1st Lt. William G. Young of Denbigh Plantation who had over $33,000 in real estate and personal property worth $85,000 including his 137 slaves. "Timber Getter" Virginius Nash followed in wealth with a net value of $39,000. Curtises dominated the roster, with 9 family members serving in the company. Captain H. H. Curtis had real estate holdings valued over $8,000 and personal assets of $21,000. His brother, 2nd Lt. Thomas Glanville Harwood Curtis was worth over $7,000. Other Curtises included 3rd Sergeant Robert G. Curtis, worth $9,000, and 4th Corporal William H. Curtis, worth $16,000. But not all members of the company claimed the title of landed gentry; most of the sixty-seven privates enlisting held property valued between $100 to $300, with few exceptions. The men of the Beauregards averaged 27.12 years of age with occupations mainly as farmers, although the roster also included three merchants, eleven laborers, one lawyer, one sailor, one coachmaker, and one constable. Ralph Copeland, age fourteen, was the drummer boy.[32]

The Warwick Beauregards entered Confederate service following a gala at Captain Curtis' Endview Plantation. On May 27, 1861, the Beauregards marched to Camp Page in Williamsburg where they joined several other lower Peninsula units, including the Peninsula Artillery, the Lee Artillery and Wythe Rifles. Lieutenant Colonel Benjamin Ewell unified these troops with his existing forces into an organization that would eventually become the 32nd Virginia Volunteer Infantry Regiment. Ewell immediately put these troops to work, supported by local slave labor, on constructing the series of fortifications which would eventually become the Williamsburg line.[33]

Six weeks after the capture of Fort Sumter by Confederate forces the war on the Peninsula had turned from euphoria into fear for Southern patriots. The bold step toward independence had been stymied by the Unionists' hold on Fort Monroe. The fortress dominated the lower Peninsula and had enabled Ben

Butler to move aggressively against Hampton and Newport News Point. The Yankees had come to stay; and, worse, it appeared that their momentum and overwhelming force might carry them westward to Richmond before spring ended. Benjamin Ewell confirmed this situation on May 29 when he wrote to Robert E. Lee in Richmond: "I beg to call the attention of the Commanding General to the fact that the force now here is insufficient to repel a serious attack. If Yorktown, Jamestown, or the defenses below Williamsburg fall, the way will be open to Richmond."[34]

Chapter 4

Every Inch a King

Robert E. Lee, then Commander of the Provisional Army of Virginia, recognized that the rapidly increasing Union forces at Fort Monroe and Camp Butler posed an immediate threat to Richmond. On May 21, 1861, Lee ordered Colonel John Bankhead Magruder to assume "command of the troops and military operations on the line to Hampton." Magruder was instructed to establish his headquarters at Yorktown and to "take measures for the safety of the batteries at Jamestown Island and York River, and urge forward the construction of the defenses between College and Queen creeks, in advance of Williamsburg."[1]

Prince John, as he was known by many of his old army friends for his lavish dress and entertainments as well as for his fondness of drink and amateur theatrics, was born in Port Royal, Virginia in 1809. He attended the University of Virginia for two years and then obtained an appointment to West Point. Magruder graduated 15th in the class of 1830. Initially assigned to the infantry, Magruder secured a transfer, thanks in part to the support of his uncle Colonel James Bankhead, to the artillery branch in 1831. He saw service during the Second Seminole War and on the Canadian border during the minor border dispute known as the Aroostook War. Promotions were slow for Magruder until he achieved his first real rise to fame in the war with Mexico. Captain Magruder commanded Company I of the First Artillery as part of Winfield Scott's advance against Mexico City. Even though he was slightly wounded twice during the assault on Chapultepec, his brilliant handling of light artillery units helped foil the Mexican attempt to repulse the American attack. The fall of Chapultepec basically ended the war and placed Magruder on center stage in a glorious fashion.[2] One of his soldiers, Corporal George Ballentine, called Magruder "a dashing officer . . . distinguished for his skill in light artillery maneuvers,"[3] and Colonel William S. Harney reported that "Captain Magruder's gallantry was conspicuously displayed on several occasions".[4] Reports of his fame and daring spread throughout the army, prompting many, like the young Lieutenant Thomas J. Jackson to comment, "I wanted to see active service, to be near the enemy and in the fight; and when I heard that John Magruder had his battery, I bent all of my energies to be with him, for I knew if any fighting was to be done Magruder would be on hand."[5] Magruder was breveted lieutenant colonel for his gallant actions and was awarded a gold sword by the Commonwealth of Virginia.

These honors were indeed a fitting tribute to Magruder, the so-called "El Capitan Colorado." Magruder, according to William Booth Taliaferro, had "gained that sobriquet from the flashy uniform which we wore which rivalled that of Murat in the gold lace and red stripes with which it was decorated."[6] In occupied Mexico City Prince John became the toast of the town, reverting to his "gay, rollicking, devil-may-care "habits."[7] He was one of the organizers of the socially elite Aztec Club and served as its vice-president until he left Mexico in November 1847.[8]

The secession crisis found Magruder stationed with his battery in Washington. He was still a captain and had spent the last decade serving in California, Texas, Kansas and Rhode Island. A fellow officer, Captain Edward C. Boynton, wrote of Magruder that he was "ambitious, unscrupulous, treacherous, and dissolute, he had one good quality at least — he was a dashing fearless soldier."[9] The ante-bellum era had not been kind to John Bankhead Magruder. His marriage to the wealthy Baltimore heiress, Henrietta Von Kapff, had fallen apart. Mrs. Magruder had left America in 1850 and moved to Italy with their three children.[10] He was able to obtain leave to visit them once, but, upon his return Magruder continued to be the social lion, especially while on duty at Fort Adams, near Newport, Rhode Island. There, according to Armistead E. Long, "he enjoyed a fine field for exercising his high social qualities and fondness for military display."[11] Magruder's "princely hospitality and brilliant show-drills" achieved him little reward.[12] Plagued by his heavy drinking, his army career seemed destined to go nowhere.

The fall of Fort Sumter placed Magruder, momentarily, once again on center stage. Before Virginia left the Union, Prince John was called upon to escort Abraham Lincoln in the capital city and met with him to discuss security matters. At that time he confided to the President that he "very much regretted secession," but he felt compelled to fight with "those among whom I was born and bred, my relations, and friends all of whom believe they are right."[13] Magruder resigned his commission on April 20 and, with all the flourish of a grand knight on parade, proclaimed to the Governor's Advisory Council that "I have just crossed the Long Bridge, which is guarded by my old Battery. Give me 5,000 men and if I don't take Washington, you may take not only my sword, but my life."[14] Lee demurred the thought, but Magruder was commissioned a colonel in the Provisional Army and after a brief stint training raw recruits in Richmond, he was ordered to the Peninsula. His new assignment would far better serve the needs of the new Confederacy, which was grappling to find the means to organize its defense, than any other glorious action.

Magruder arrived in Yorktown aboard the steamer *Logan* on May 24 and immediately began his sometimes bothersome habit of daily correspondence with Richmond. As with most of his subsequent letters and reports, he demanded reinforcements writing: "I shall need at least four companies of cavalry to operate against the advance of troops against Hampton, to cut off their parties, to harass them on the march, and to beat up their quarters at night."[15]

Magruder quickly set himself to the enormous task of organizing troops and fortifications on the Peninsula. He ordered Ewell to continue work on the Williamsburg Line and sought a more forward defensive position as he later wrote:

> When I took command there were no works on the James River below Jamestown, no fortifications at Williamsburg, Yorktown or Gloucester Point, with the exception of one gun at Yorktown and perhaps two at Gloucester Point. I had to defend a Peninsula

90 miles in length and some 10 miles in width, enclosed between two navigable rivers, terminated by fortresses impregnable as long as the enemy commanded the waters.

I . . . made a tour on horseback of the lower part of the Peninsula, in order to get some knowledge of the country. Seeing at a glance that three broad rivers could not be defended without fortifications, and that these never could be built if the enemy knew our weakness and want of preparation, I determined to display a portion of my small force in his immediate presence, and forthwith selected Bethel as a place at which a small force could best give him battle should he advance.

Returning to Yorktown, I called upon Mr. R. D. Lee, who had mills on that stream, to show one the line of the Warwick River, which rises near Yorktown, flows across the country, and enters James River a little below Mulberry Point, where there is now a fort. Having made this exploration, I determined to adopt this line to Mulberry Point as the true line of defense whenever its right flank, of James River, could be protected by water batteries.[16]

Magruder believed that with 25,000 men arrayed along fortifications built defending the York River at Yorktown and Gloucester Point and "at the mouth of Warwick River, and at Mulberry Island Point, and the redoubts extending from the Warwick to James River,"[17] he could hold off the advance of any enemy force.

What Magruder needed most of all was time and men. He was anxious to begin work on his primary line before the Federals could flank this yet unbuilt position. Magruder recognized the major threat posed by the ever growing Union force at Fort Monroe and the Federal naval presence. He decided to play for time by baiting Butler into attacking an advance position. Magruder advised Richmond:

> Deeming it of vital importance to hold, for a time Yorktown, on York River, and Mulberry Island on James River, and to keep the enemy in check by an intervening line, until the authorities might think proper to take such steps as should be deemed on the Peninsula, I felt so composed to dispose my feeble forces in such a manner as to accomplish these objects with the least risk possible.[18]

Prince John selected Big Bethel Church, a crossroads behind a bend in the northwestern branch (known as Brick Kiln Creek) of the Back River, thirteen miles below Yorktown and eight miles from Hampton, as the place to provoke an attack. Robert E. Lee agreed with Magruder's decision to create a forward position against the aggressive Federal forces, writing: "I take pleasure in expressing my gratification at the movements that you have made, and hope you might be able to restrict the advance of the enemy and securely maintain your own position."[19]

Magruder sought more troops to man his brave front. He reported to Richmond that:

> As to calling out the militia, this country is so thinly populated that it cannot be depended on. Colonel Ewell, who is with me now, thinks it will amount to one hundred and fifty men, all told, and these not effective, and not to be relied on. The reason of this, Colonel Ewell says, is that there are many disaffected men in Elizabeth County . . . many also being obliged to stay at home on account of the occupation of the country by Federal troops . . .[20]

Fortunately, reinforcements were by now arriving on the Peninsula which would increase Magruder's force to almost 4,000

Major General
John Bankhead Magruder
Library of Congress

Major General
Daniel Harvey Hill
Museum of the Confederacy

Private Henry L. Wyatt
15th North Carolina
City of Hampton

Lieutenant John T. Greble
City of Hampton

effectives. John Bell Hood arrived on the Peninsula on May 31. Magruder promoted him to Major to give him the rank necessary to command the Confederate cavalry.[21] Hood was ordered to make "judicious disposition of pickets and videttes"[22] and began probing the Federal positions near Fort Monroe, Hampton and Newport News Point.

Late May also witnessed the arrival of the First North Carolina Volunteers. Commanded by West Point graduate Colonel Daniel Harvey Hill and recruited from the ranks of the North Carolina Military Institute, of which Hill had been superintendent, this well trained unit mustered over 1,400 men. These troops solved Magruder's immediate manpower problems.[23] Hill's arrival, however, caused some questions to be raised as to who actually held the highest rank and would command the Confederate troops on the Peninsula. D. H. Hill wrote his wife that "Colonel Magruder in command is always drunk and giving foolish and absurd orders. I think that in a few days the men will refuse to obey any order issued by him."[24] Magruder, meanwhile, recognizing the Presbyterian Hill's ambition for advancement and command, wrote Richmond that , "I think I rank him, but am of the impression that it is the subject of some feeling on his part. He has, however, obeyed my orders so far, and I presume will continue to do so."[25]

Magruder, overlooking this problem, placed Hill in second-in-command of his little army and then ordered Hill's regiment forward on June 6 to join a small force of three companies and two howitzers under the command of Major Edgar B. Montague at Big Bethel. Additional units were also sent to Bethel including Major George W. Randolph's artillery battalion and Lieutenant Colonel W. D. Stuart's command of four companies of the 3rd Virginia Infantry. These reinforcements brought the entire Confederate troop strength at Big Bethel to 1,458 men. Hill, exercising overall command of this advance force, organized the construction of entrenchments around Big Bethel and established a forward position three miles away at Little Bethel.[26]

The Federals, meanwhile, had not been idle. More troops, including Colonel Washington A. Bartlett's Naval Brigade, were arriving at Fort Monroe. Butler, with the support of the U.S.S. *Cumberland*, mounted a Sawyer gun at Castle Calhoun on the Rip Raps to shell Sewell's Point.[27] He also began probing the surrounding countryside to disrupt Confederate cavalry movements. On June 4 elements of the 5th New York marched to the little village of Fox Hill, fives miles away from Fort Monroe, to uncover suspected enemy activity. Nothing was achieved by this advance other than prompting the Confederates to burn Howard's Bridge on the Hampton-York Road on June 6 to protect their York River flank. On June 7 and again on June 9 Federal reconnoitering parties clashed with Confederates near New Market Bridge.[28] D. H. Hill reported to Magruder after the June 9 fight that "reliable citizens reported that two cartloads and one buggy load were taken into Hampton. We had not a single man killed."[29]

Butler now was alert to the increasing Confederate presence near Hampton which threatened communications between Fort Monroe and Camp Butler. Reports of the Confederate outpost at Little Bethel and entrenchments at Big Bethel convinced him that he needed to strike out and destroy their position. The capture of Bethel, situated astride the Hampton - York Road, Butler believed would open the door to Richmond. Thus, Butler conceived a somewhat complex plan, devised by his secretary Major Theodore Winthrop, to utilize troops from Camp Butler, Camp Hamilton, and Fort Monroe to converge on the Bethel area before dawn on June 10. The night march was planned to give the Union force an element of surprise which, it was hoped, would help ensure victory.[30]

The Union strike force was placed under command of Brigadier General Ebenezer W. Pierce, commander of Camp Hamilton. Duryea's Zouaves (5th New York) led the march across Hampton Creek from Camp Hamilton at midnight with orders to intersect the Confederate positions between Little Bethel and Big Bethel. The Zouaves were then followed a hour later by

Colonel Frank Townsend's 3rd New York Regiment with two howitzers. Lieutenant Colonel Peter T. Washburn organized a battalion of handpicked men from the 1st Vermont and 4th Massachusetts who were to march from Camp Butler to make a demonstration in front of Little Bethel. Colonel John E. Bendix's 7th New York with two field guns was to follow Washburn from Newport News Point. The plan dictated that Bendix and Townsend should juncture about a mile and a half from Little Bethel Church and then continue their march toward the Confederate positions. The entire force numbered 4,400 men.[31]

One key element of the Union assault plan was the night march; and to avoid confusion caused by converging troops, Federal soldiers wore white armbands to distinguish themselves from the enemy. Another precaution, the password "Boston" which was to be announced when unrecognized troops approached, was implemented to limit confusion.[32]

Meanwhile the Confederates were bracing themselves for an attack that they knew would be launched against Big Bethel. J. W. Ratchford, an aide to D. H. Hill, noted the Confederates' precarious position when he wrote: "It looked as if Magruder was only sending down to the vicinity of the fort as a dare to General Benjamin F. Butler. He no doubt thought that we would have sense enough to get out of his way."[33] Magruder, however, wanted to precipitate a fight, perhaps as a dramatic way to throw down his gauntlet against the enemy to see who could achieve the first accolades of glory. On June 8 and 9 Magruder had inspected the Big Bethel defenses and was satisfied with Hill's arrangements. Hill had constructed earthworks across the Back River to defend his right flank which was also protected by the river and a marsh. One howitzer was added to strengthen this advance position. On the north side of Brick Kiln Creek Hill's men constructed earthworks which commanded the bridge and encircled the road to defend the position's flanks. Three artillery pieces were placed to control access to the bridge: a Parrott gun and one howitzer from the Richmond Howitzer Battalion were placed in the main battery in front of the church; a howitzer commanded by Captain Brown was placed to defend the western flank; and a howitzer was positioned on the left side of the bridge. Also, outside the redoubt a rifled howitzer manned by cadets from the North Carolina Military Institute was positioned to guard a ford. Hill filed his men into this position; however, Magruder had other ideas. At 3 a.m. on June 10, he gave Hill orders to advance toward Hampton. This order was superseded by the events that were about to unfold.[34]

The Union advance from Camp Hamilton was led by Captain Judson Kilpatrick with two companies of Duryea's Zouaves (5th New York). Duryea followed shortly thereafter with the rest of his command, after crossing Hampton Creek in scows. Kilpatrick's advance guard crossed the New Market Bridge at 1 a.m. on June 10. His force continued on the road to Little Bethel where his men encountered Southern pickets just before dawn, capturing one officer and two soldiers.[35]

Meanwhile Bendix's force had marched from Newport News Point and arrived at a crossroads near Little Bethel after Duryea's's troops had passed but before the arrival of the rest of Pierce's column from Camp Hamilton. As the 3rd New York approached the 7th New York, Bendix's men, unable to see the white armbands and alerted by the sound of horses (the Federals did not use any cavalry in the advance against Bethel), nervously fired into the ranks of the 3rd New York before Townsend's troops could identify themselves. Two men were killed and sixteen wounded during the confusion.[36]

This fifteen-minute skirmish also alerted the Confederates to the Union advance. They abandoned Little Bethel and fell back on to their entrenchments at Big Bethel to await the anticipated Union assault.

General Pierce now held a council of war. Even though the Federals realized that the element of surprise had been lost, Pierce decided to proceed with the attack. Pierce discovered that Little Bethel chapel had been abandoned by Confederate pickets and ordered the small church to be burned. While the Federals reorganized themselves, Hill deployed his men. Lieutenant Colonel William D. Stuart, with elements of the 3rd Virginia Regiment and one howitzer, filled the advance redoubt across the creek and sharpshooters from the 1st North Carolina were positioned on the left of the Hampton - York Road on the southern side of Brick Kiln Creek. Randolph's Richmond Howitzer Battalion manned the three guns in the main redoubt facing the bridge; Major Montague's companies and elements of the 1st North Carolina held the flanks and rear of the main redoubt.[37]

The Union attack was slow to develop as the Federal "organization was all broken up,"[38] according to D. H. Hill. Units came on the field in a piecemeal manner. Kilpatrick led the first advance of Zouaves around 9 a.m. and pushed aside the Confederate pickets but quickly came under artillery fire. The Zouaves started to take casualties and fell back behind an orchard. By now a Union battery arrived under the command of Lieutenant John T. Greble and began shelling the Confederate advance redoubt.[39]

A second attack was organized. The 3rd New York moved to envelope the Confederate right as the 5th New York and 2nd New York moved across the field toward the redoubt. The Virginia troops initially held their position, but a malfunction causing a priming wire to break off in the howitzer forced the gun's withdrawal. Soon the 3rd Virginia abandoned the work under pressure by the New Yorkers advance led by Duryea's himself. Simultaneously, a move by the group of Zouaves to cross an old ford downstream was blocked by a company of the 3rd Virginia which had recently fallen back into the main Confederate redoubt.[40]

The artillery duel between Randolph's and Greble's batteries continued to heat up. Colonel Townsend began to urge his men to assault the Confederate right when he noticed a glint of bayonets reflecting the sun through the woods. Believing his troops were about to be flanked by a Confederate force, he

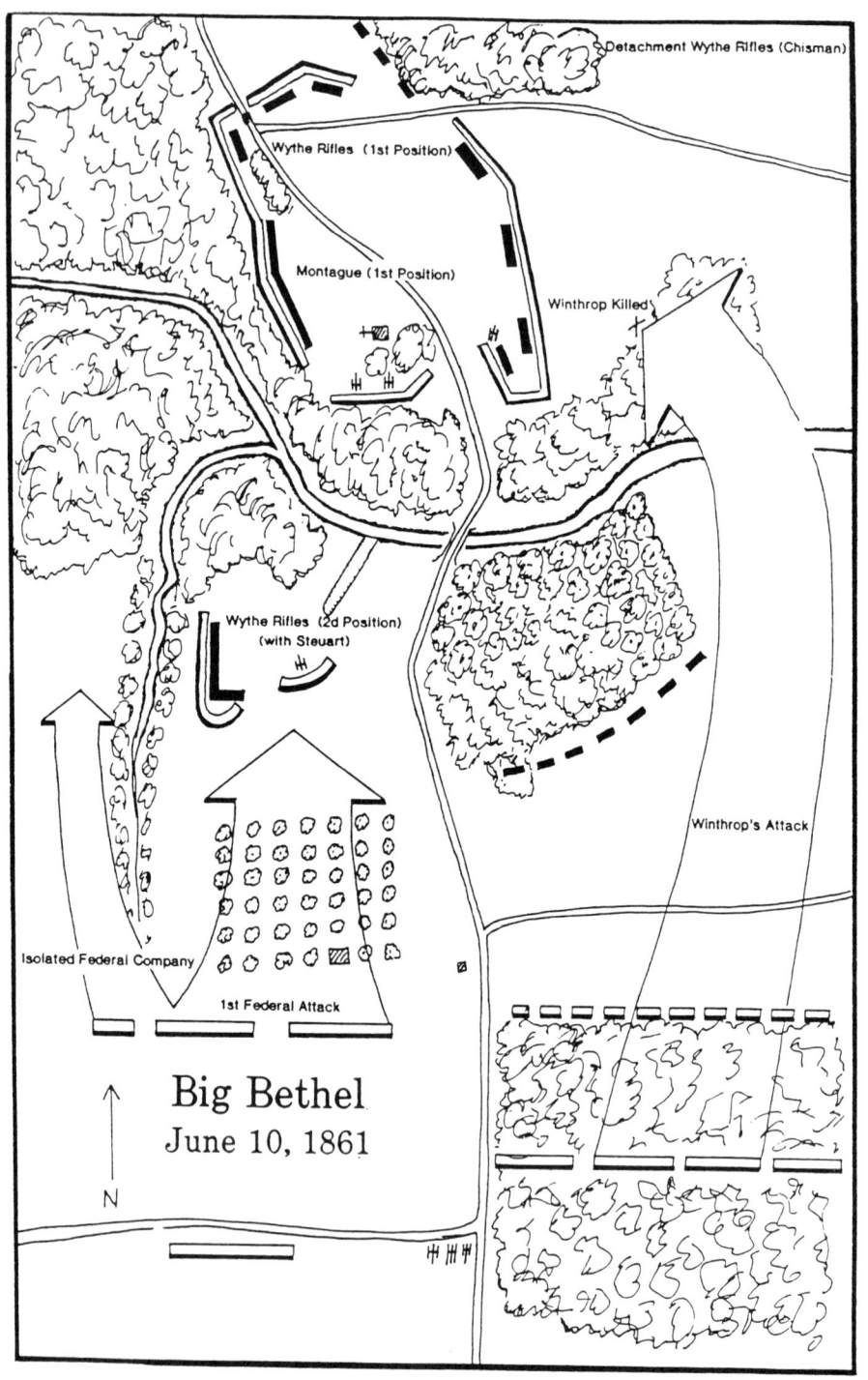

ordered a withdrawal. This left the Zouaves isolated in the Confederate redoubt, and, under pressure from a developing counter-attack by elements of the 3rd Virginia, Wythe Rifles and the 1st North Carolina, they retreated.[41]

While the Federals fell back from the advance redoubt, Major Theodore Winthrop organized an assault on the Confederate left flank using Vermont and Massachusetts troops. Winthrop led his men across the creek with a cheer and advanced toward the main redoubt under a withering fire. Southerners would later claim that Winthrop's men had only been able to gain this advantage by adopting the Confederate recognition badge of a white band around their caps. As Winthrop's men crossed the ford they supposedly displayed the white bands in the Confederate fashion and shouted, "Don't Fire!" which confused the Southerners. The ruse brought the Union troops little gain. Winthrop, striving to rally his men for a final charge that might have carried the day for the Union, stood on a log brandishing his sword and was immediately shot through the heart. His death demoralized his troops and they fell back across the creek. This retreat, wrote D. H. Hill, "decided the action in our favor."[42]

Pierce, according to a New York Times correspondent, "appears to have lost his presence of mind," and ordered a complete retreat toward Hampton.[43] It was 1:30 p.m. and the Union soldiers were exhausted and harried during their retreat by Hood's cavalry until halted by a destroyed bridge blocking their path.[44]

Big Bethel was a complete disaster for the Union. D. H. Hill commented that his soldiers "seemed to enjoy it as much as boys do rabbit-shooting."[45] North Carolinian B. M. Hord remembered that "a Regiment would come up, fire a volley or two, mostly over our heads and precipitately fall back. It seemed that their principal object was simply to get a sight or a shot at a Rebel, then fall back as quickly as possible."[46] The Federals lost a total of 76 men: 18 killed, 53 wounded and 5 missing. The Union ineptitude during the engagement required that a scapegoat be found. Butler was blamed for sending his troops forward with such poor intelligence and for remaining at Fort Monroe during the battle. Pierce, however, took most of the responsibility for the defeat. He was labeled incompetent and was mustered out of the army at the end of his 90-day service. The Northern press tried to salvage some honor out of the defeat. The Union troops were called courageous as "they fought both friend and foe alike with equal resolution and only retired after exhausting their ammunition in the face of a powerful enemy."[47] Winthrop and Lieutenant Greble, who was killed near the end of the battle while serving a cannon, were lionized for their valor and sacrifice. Lieutenant Greble was the first West Point graduate killed during the war. He had commanded his battery with distinction during the battle and was described as possessing "to a notable degree the two qualities most needed at the time, namely, military skill and presence of mind in the face of the enemy."[48] Theodore Winthrop was, according to D. H. Hill, the "only one of the enemy who exhibited an approximation of courage that day."[49] Butler had warned him at the expedition's beginning to "Be bold! Be bold! But not too bold!"[50] Winthrop almost won the day for the Union with his bravery. Several articles he had written for the Atlantic Monthly chronicling events in Virginia during the early days of war were published posthumously which gave him even greater fame for his heroic exploit on June 10, 1861.[51]

Southrons rejoiced over the Big Bethel victory and laurels were spread everywhere. Confederate casualties were only one killed, seven wounded and three missing. The dead soldier, Private Henry L. Wyatt of Company B, 1st North Carolina, achieved martyrdom as he had been killed by a shot through the forehead during a volunteer mission to "burn a house between the lines."[52] He was the first Southerner to die in battle and, as Magruder later wrote, "Too much praise cannot be bestowed upon the heroic soldier who we lost."[53] Magruder was equally praiseworthy of many of his officers, particularly D. H. Hill and George W. Randolph. Hill, who would soon be promoted to Brigadier General for his leadership at Big Bethel, was lauded by Magruder for his "judicious and determined action was worthy of his ancient glory."[54] Randolph, according to Magruder, "has no superior as an artillerist in any county" and the victory was partially credited to the "skill and gallantry" of Randolph's howitzers.[55]

It was Magruder, however, who was accorded most of the glory for the Big Bethel victory. Jefferson Davis announced the battle to be a "glorious victory"[56] while Robert E. Lee took pleasure in expressing "my gratification at the gallant conduct of the troops under your command and approbation of the dispositions made by you, resulting as they did, in the rout of the enemy."[57] Magruder was promoted to Brigadier General exactly one week (June 17, 1861) after the Bethel Battle. Soon myths were being made surrounding his meritorious and courtly actions during the days before and after the battle. Lieutenant Baker P. Lee of Montague's Battalion observed Magruder before the battle and called him a "picturesque figure:"

> He had a fondness for tinsel and tassels. With an irrepressible spirit of restless energy, instinctively susceptible of the charm of danger, full of health and physical force, it was evident that nature made him a soldier . . . it was in the field, in full military array, well mounted, as he always was, with the fire of patriotic ambition and personal pride in his eye, that he was seen at his best.[58]

Baker later noted that it was Magruder "who sighted by his own accurate eye"[59] the first cannon fired at Big Bethel.

Legends even arose lauding Magruder's noble conduct following the battle. Magruder was reported to have said under a flag of truce, to coordinate the return of the body of a slain Union officer, that once he agreed to the corpse's removal, Prince John left the young Federal Lieutenant on the solemn mission with the comment, "We part as friends, but on the field of battle we meet as enemies."[60] He even corresponded with Ben Butler over the return of the four Confederates captured during the engagement. The opposing commanders exchanged pointed comments concerning a Private Carter who had been asleep while on picket duty when captured. Butler made a statement about how quickly Carter's three companions had escaped without awakening him, to which, Magruder replied: "Had Private Carter been awake, perhaps a retreat would not have been necessary." It was even rumored that Prince John challenged Butler to a duel to settle the matter in a gentlemanly manner. Eventually, the four Confederates were exchanged.[61]

The Southern newspapers played upon Magruder's every comment as his actions typified Prince John's reputation as "the picture of the Virginia gentleman, the frank, manly representative of the chivalry of the dear Old Dominion."[62] Magruder was placed in the Pantheon of Southern heroes with Beauregard and called "every inch a King."[63] "He's the hero for the times," one ballad proclaimed, "the furious fighting Johnny B. MaGruder."[64] The fame seemed to fall upon Magruder naturally and in every fashion he lived up to the honor bestowed upon him. He was a vigorous 51 years of age, tall, erect and handsome. Always perfectly uniformed, he appeared magnificently everywhere at a gallop talking incessantly despite his unusual lisp. His impressive nature and dramatic flair would prove useful during the coming year.[65]

Chapter 5

A Sacrifice to the Grim God of War

"I think that this little fight was a feeler, tomorrow in all probability we may have something more serious"[1] wrote Lieutenant William G. Young of the Warwick Beauregards, who had remained in Yorktown during the Big Bethel engagement, to his wife. Young was wrong in his assumption as Butler's defeated men retreated back onto their fortifications. Butler and Magruder were both uninformed as to the plans and resources of their enemy. Each commander feared that his opposition would mount an overwhelming attack against his men's exposed positions.

Butler strengthened the armaments at Fort Monroe. On June 14 the massive 12-inch, 52,005-pound "Union" gun arrived. It was mounted on the carriage that once held the first 15-inch Rodman gun ever built. This gun, weighing 49,100 pounds and capable of firing a shell 5,375 yards, was eventually remounted. Both were intended for service against the Confederates in Norfolk.[2]

Butler continued to be impressed with the Sawyer gun mounted on Fort Calhoun. This experimental gun had been invented by Sylvanus Sawyer and fired a lead-coated shell with six ribs cast to its exterior to fit the weapon's rifling. Although other versions of the Sawyer gun were prone to bursting,[3] the 24-pounder model on the Rip-Raps could shell the Sewell's Point Battery with some accuracy. Butler ordered Fort Monroe's ordnance workshop to rifle two other 6-pound cannon to take the elongated 53-pound Sawyer shell.[4]

Magruder, meanwhile, did not rest on his laurels. He continued to strengthen his forward position at Big Bethel and established a new base at Young's Mill on the Warwick Road. More reinforcements were being sent to his self-styled "Army of the Peninsula." A "Spy Battalion" under Major John Baytop Cary was organized utilizing three companies of cavalry and the Wythe Rifles who were to "act as voltigeurs." Magruder intended to use these troops and his forward fortifications at Big Bethel and Young's Mill to harass the enemy's movements.[5]

The Confederates were beset by numerous problems as they sought to strengthen their defenses. Magruder was dissatisfied by Ewell's progress building the Williamsburg Line. Captain Alfred Rives surveyed the works and then criticized Ewell's efforts commenting that "nothing had been achieved." Rives reported that ". . . no definite selection whatever of points of defense . . . only this: That in the colonel's estimation the lines should rest on Queen's and College Creeks, passing somewhere near Williamsburg . . ." Magruder was perturbed and ordered the recently arrived Colonel Lafayette McLaws to "order all the troops to work on the trenches until they are completed, and press the works forward with the utmost possible vigor . . ."[6]

Magruder also encountered troubles organizing his troops. Local troops were somewhat disjointed with units like the Lee Guards unable to maintain their organization. On July 1, 1861 these lower Peninsula units, including the Williamsburg Junior Guard, Hampton Grays, Nelson Guard, Wythe Rifles, York Rangers, and Warwick Beauregards, were unified into the 32nd Virginia Volunteer Infantry. The James City Artillery, Peninsula Artillery and Washington Artillery were assigned to the regiment, however, later in the summer they would be transferred into the 1st Virginia Artillery. Benjamin S. Ewell was promoted to Colonel and named commander of the regiment. The 32nd remained stationed throughout the Peninsula, and it continued to disrupt the command structure.[7] Other problems were also encountered with troops reinforcing the Peninsula command. The Louisiana Zouaves arrived almost drunk to the man and soon rebelled against their commander Lieutenant Colonel George Coppens. These problems virtually opened the door to further Union aggressions.[8]

Ben Butler was actually concerned about the Confederate intentions. Even though he continued to send his troops to probe the surrounding countryside as a show of force, Butler believed that he was outnumbered by Magruder's force and called for more reinforcements. The Union general wrote Winfield Scott:

> It is among the possibilities and perhaps the probabilities that a concentration of troops may be made at Yorktown via James River, and an advance movement upon this post ensue . . . Newport News, perhaps, can hold out with the three thousand men there against that attack of five thousand or six thousand men, but we have not, as yet, any field artillery here. To defend ourselves outside the fort, we have but about three thousand effective men, and some of them not the best troops . . . The enemy are apparently preparing for an advance movement from Yorktown and the Norfolk troops, should they attack, I should be, to say the least, largely outnumbered.[9]

Despite this call for reinforcements, a litany constantly repeated by both commanders on the Peninsula, continued skirmishing became the norm during the weeks following the Big Bethel engagement. The Federals endeavored to expand their command of territory around Fort Monroe and Camp Butler while Magruder attempted to limit their movements up the Peninsula. A Confederate picket was killed on June 15, and nervous Southerns wounded one of their own cavalry videttes on June 16.[10] Butler sent two expeditions out from Fort Monroe on June 24 to disrupt Confederate activities. The first merely marched toward Big Bethel with orders not to bring on an engagement and drove back the Confederate pickets.[11] The other had a greater purpose. Elements of the 10th New York marched from Fort Monroe to the mouth of the Back River where they met the steamers *Adriatic* and *Fanny*, a steam launch from the U.S.S. *Roanoke* and several bateaux. The New Yorkers were then transported upstream. Their mission was to destroy vessels involved in trade with the Eastern Shore which were providing support for the local Confederate troops. Eight sailing vessels and numerous small boats on the Back River and six schooners found up Harris Creek were destroyed by the expedition. The Confederates were powerless to stop this destructive amphibious movement.[12]

Rumors of a Union march against Warwick Court House prompted Magruder to reinforce his forward position at Young's Mill with the 5th Louisiana and 6th Georgia. Additional entrenchments were constructed. Magruder himself led a force containing North Carolina and Louisiana troops, cavalry and artillery down the Warwick Road on June 28 toward Newport News Point. This strike force advanced within reach of the Federal pickets and then returned to Yorktown. Prince John was distressed by the evidence of Union pillaging and vandalism that he discovered during his expedition. He reported:

> We found a most respectable man [Captain Nelson Smith] and his family still living on their place, but subject to the threats, annoyances, robberies and abuses of these unprincipled foes, who threatened their lives, as well as to burn their property, on the grounds of their being secessionists. After leaving this house I addressed a letter to Colonel Phelps, in command at Newport News, calling his attention to this improper and uncivilized conduct, and stating to him that it was not to be expected that the courtesy and humanity that had characterized our treatment of those who had fallen into our hands would continue if such conduct on the part of his officers and men were longer tolerated.[13]

Magruder resolved to strike back at the marauding Federals. On July 3, Magruder learned that a Federal foraging force planned to march up the Warwick Road toward Young's Mill. He ordered Lieutenant Colonel William D. Dreux to take his Louisiana Battalion, with elements of the Wythe Rifles, and some artillery to ambush the Union excursion. This force surprised the Hawkins Zouaves at daybreak near Captain Nelson Smith's home on July 5. The resulting melee turned out far differently than the Confederates had planned as they were repulsed. Dreux and one Louisiana private were killed in this skirmish.[14] The Confederates immediately sought revenge against the "Lincolnites" as "Colonel Drue's [sic] death was mourned by all who knew him — on account of his bravery and high military genius," noted Lieutenant William J. Stores of York County.[15]

Realizing that the Federals frequented the area near Captain Smith's and the Curtis Store along the Warwick Road, the Southrons sought an opportunity to retaliate. A cavalry force under command of Major John Bell Hood laid a trap, as Hood recounted:

> Soon after the affair at Big Bethel, it became the custom of the enemy to send out every few days scouting parties of infantry in the direction of our position at Yorktown. I determined to go at night into the swamp lying between the James and York River roads, remain quietly under cover, and, upon the advance of such a party, to move out upon its rear, and capture it if possible. In accordance with this plan, I concealed my troops in the swamp several nights, when finally a battalion of infantry came forth upon the James River Road.[16]

The Confederate cavalry struck out at an unsuspecting wood gathering detail of 200 members of the Hawkins Zouaves on July 12 at the very spot of Colonel Dreux's death. The surprised Zouaves were routed, as Hood later reported, with "a great consternation and the enemy ran in all directions through the woods."[17] Four Federals were killed and twelve captured with the loss of only one horse.[18]

Magruder called the skirmish "a brilliant little affair" and commended Hood.[19] "Too much praise cannot be bestowed on

Private Richard Whitaker
3rd Virginia Cavalry
Mrs. Donald C. Adams

Lieutenant William Young
32nd Virginia Infantry
Mrs. Donald C. Adams

Captain
Humphrey Harwood Curtis
32nd Virginia Infantry
Mrs. Elizabeth F. S. Bentien

Jesse Simpkins Jones
3rd Virginia Cavalry
City of Hampton

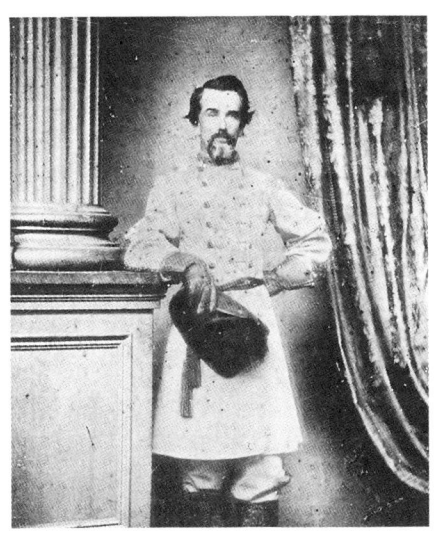

Captain
Jefferson Curle Phillips
3rd Virginia Cavalry
City of Hampton

Corporal Robert T. White
32nd Virginia Infantry
Leslie Dawson

Private Richard Curtis
32nd Virginia Infantry
Museum of the Confederacy

Captain
Francis Lightfoot (Frank) Lee
32nd Virginia Infantry
Virginia War Museum

Major Hood and the cavalry generally for their untiring industry in efforts to meet the enemy, and for their energy with which they have discharged their harassing and unusually laborious duties," wrote Magruder. Despite this embarrassing repulse, the Union continued to maintain a presence along the Warwick Road. Several weeks following the July 12 skirmish, Union troops commented about seeing the "blood pools this side of the opening on which Nelson Smith's dwelling is situated remaining from the fight." Pickets also reported hearing the distinct neighing of horses and "loud cheers from a nearby Rebel camp."[20]

Other small engagements took place in this part of July as both sides exerted pressure on this no man's land that stretched across the Peninsula between the Confederate forward positions at Big Bethel and Young's Mill and the Federals in Hampton and at Newport News Point. Several other incidents occurred during mid-July. On July 19, Federal troops captured the horses of a picket on the Back River Road, and elements of the Warwick Beauregards were sent to Bethel to lay a trap, which was never sprung, for the Federals. Two days later, Union pickets were ambushed outside Camp Butler. One Federal soldier was killed and two Confederates captured. The next day, on July 22, two brief encounters took place during which a Federal quartermaster sergeant was killed while chasing cattle near Camp Butler and four Confederates were captured.[21]

Ben Butler had already realized that his communications with his outlying posts at Camp Hamilton and Camp Butler were subject to interruption by Confederate cavalry. He further felt that his command required a more reliable and quicker means of emergency communication than the two steamers which made daily trips between Old Point Comfort and Newport News Point. A corps of signal officers was organized in mid-June to install a telegraph line between the fort and Camp Butler via Hampton. The line was completed by early July.[22]

Butler was also concerned about his precise knowledge, or lack thereof, of the Confederate positions and troop strength surrounding the Federal enclave. Thus, Butler contacted the aeronaut, John La Mountain, on his own initiative, offering him the position of aerial observer with his department. La Mountain had obtained national fame with his balloon flight covering 1,100 miles between St. Louis and Henderson, New York, but his previous offer to serve the Union had been ignored. The aeronaut arrived at Fort Monroe on July 23, equipped with two balloons. His first flight on July 25 was unsuccessful due to high winds, however, on July 31 La Mountain was able to reach an altitude of 1,400 feet and observed a radius of over thirty miles. La Mountain's observations impressed Butler as he was able to report the existence of concealed camps behind the Confederate batteries at Sewell's Point and Pig Point. Another ascension on August 1 uncovered that the Confederate camp at Young's Mill had between 4,000 to 5,000 men and an advance position on Water's Creek manned by several hundred troops. Butler now knew that the Confederate troop strength was far less than rumored and that there were no signs of Southern effort to move against Hampton.[23]

On August 3, 1861, La Mountain made his first flight from the deck of the gunboat *Fanny*. The *Fanny*, with La Mountain's balloon secured to the ship's deck with a windlass and mooring ropes, steamed into the channel off Sewell's Point. The balloon reached a height of 2,000 feet and enabled a thorough inspection of the Confederate positions defending Norfolk. A second flight was made on August 10 from the deck of the tug *Adriatic*.[24]

La Mountain had by now used up all of his hydrogen gas making materials and needed to leave Fort Monroe to obtain these supplies. Before he departed, La Mountain proposed to Butler that he could return with a balloon that could "shell, burn or destroy Norfolk." He added, "Ballooning can be made a very useful implement in warfare." Butler agreed, forwarding the concept to the War Department with his endorsement.[25]

La Mountain's balloons may have created an expression of Union strength and technological advantage, but, it did little to block the Confederate resurgence in late July. The Federal rout at the 1st Battle of Manassas on July 21, 1861, had repercussions that reached all the way down to the Peninsula. Winfield Scott ordered Butler to send troops to Washington on July 24 to help defend the Capital. Butler quickly complied and on July 26 and 27, the 3rd, 4th, and 5th New York and Baker's California regiment boarded steamers enroute to Washington.[26] Ben Butler himself left Fort Monroe on July 29. He travelled to the Capital to meet with General Scott in order to explain just how precarious the Union position had become on the Peninsula and expressed the need for a more experienced officer to assume command.[27]

The reduction of 4,000 soldiers from the Union command on the Peninsula forced the Federals to abandon Hampton. The Union troops had occupied the town on July 1 and during their withdrawal a third of the town was burned. Union pickets were simultaneously removed from New Market Creek Bridge and repositioned on the Camp Hamilton side of Hampton Creek Bridge.[28]

The hasty Federal evacuation of Hampton on July 25 prompted Magruder to take advantage of the Union retrenchment. He organized a strike force of 1,600 men with cavalry and two artillery batteries. Colonel Robert Johnston was placed in command. Johnston, an 1850 graduate of West Point, had replaced John Bell Hood as commander of Magruder's mounted units with the grand title of "Commander-in-Chief of Cavalry, Army of the Peninsula." He was ordered to proceed to Whitney's Store near New Market Bridge in an effort to sever Federal communications between Camp Butler and Fort Monroe and to suppress any Federal troop activity outside their fortifications. His second duty was to sweep through the lower Peninsula from the Back River to Harwood's Mill to Newport News Point to capture escaping slaves. Magruder added: "If the negroes in the Back River region and on the James River can be surprised and captured at night or by day by small parties of troops who know the country, and they are willing to undertake it, let them do it."[29] More than 150 blacks were apprehended by Confederate troops, including several who were captured near the contraband camp at Newport News Point by members of the Old Dominion Dragoons, who noted that re-enslaved blacks "evinced the strongest dislike to being taken . . . ." These unfortunate individuals were then transported to Williamsburg to work on fortifications. Magruder supported this movement by establishing a supply base at Warwick Court House.[30]

Johnston's raid had provided Magruder with the knowledge that the Federals had removed all but one regiment from Newport News Point. Thus, on July 28 the Confederate commander sent a flag of truce to Camp Butler demanding that the Federals leave within 24 hours or be assaulted. Even though Magruder understood that the strong fortifications on Newport News Point discouraged attack or investment, he continued to demonstrate against the Union position hoping to draw the "invaders" out of their works into battle. While a small engagement fought at Salter's Creek inflicted several Union casualties, Magruder's attention soon shifted to Hampton.[31]

On August 6 Magruder, with a force of 4,000 infantry, 400 cavalry and Randolph's howitzer battalion, marched once again against Camp Butler. His troops penetrated the Union lines the next morning reaching to within a mile and a half of Newport News Point. The Federals refused the bait despite the Confederates now being between the two Federal positions. The telegraph line was cut and Magruder moved his men to within a mile of Hampton.

Magruder obtained a copy of the New York Tribune during the march to Hampton. He learned from its pages which included a report from Butler to Secretary of War Simon Cameron, that Butler intended to refortify the town as "he did not know what to do with the many negroes in his possession unless he possessed Hampton; they were still coming in rapidly; that as their masters had deserted their homes and slaves, he would consider the latter free, and would colonize them at Hampton, the home of most of their owners." Magruder immediately decided to destroy the town, later advising Richmond:

> Having known for some time past that Hampton was the harbor of runaway slaves and traitors, and being under the guns of Fort Monroe, it could not be held by us, even if taken, I was decidedly under the impression that it should have been done before, and when I found from the above report of its extreme importance to the enemy, and that the town itself would lend great strength to whatever fortifications they might erect around it, I determined to burn it.[32]

With an agreement from the local soldiers in his command as to the "propriety of this course," and seeing that Butler had already destroyed a third of Hampton when his troops had evacuated the town,[33] Magruder organized a force under the command of Captain Jefferson Curle Phillips of the Old Dominion Dragoons to complete this "loathsome yet patriotic act" prompted by "the foulest desecrations of these houses and homes of our Virginia people by their former Yankee occupants."[34]

Captain Phillips organized a force of approximately 500 men including the Old Dominion Dragoons, the Mecklenburg Cavalry, the Warwick Beauregards and the York Rangers to destroy the town. Many of these men owned homes in Hampton. After dark on August 7, Phillips' command, accompanied by Colonel James G. Hodges' 14th Virginia Infantry Regiment, marched over the New Market Bridge toward Hampton. Once they had reached the brick wall surrounding St. John's Church, Phillips sent the Warwick Beauregards and the York Rangers to the Hampton Creek Bridge where they engaged Union pickets defending the bridge. The 14th Virginia moved to support the action and soon the Federals were forced to retreat. The Beauregards and Rangers left the 14th Virginia to guard the bridge and returned to the center of the town where they rejoined Phillips and the rest of the Confederate troops. Phillips had already sent soldiers throughout the town to warn residents of the impending doom, and he now sent each company to a quarter of Hampton to begin their destructive task. Once the town was fired, the men reconverged on St. John's Church and then marched out of town toward Big Bethel.[35]

Sergeant Robert Hudgins II of the Old Dominion Dragoons recounted the scene:

> As the smoke ascended toward the heavens I was reminded of the ancient sacrifices on the altar to many deities, and I thought of how my little hometown was being made a sacrifice to the grim god of war.
>
> We raced back to the town to be in at the finish and to participate in the actual work of destruction ere it was too late. By the time we had reached the corner of King and Court Streets the Baptist Church was burning like an inferno — the flames belching out of the steeple like a furnace. The courthouse on the opposite was also in flames though it had not been consumed to the extent as had the church. At the cross streets it seemed as if hell itself had broken loose, and as if all of its fiery demons were pouring fuel upon the flames. The light of the flames in the sky gave nearly the luster as if it was midday.
>
> ... As we filed out of the town, there rested in the hearts of each of us the realization of a great sacrifice nobly made, and the heroic satisfaction of a soldier's duty well performed.[36]

The Confederates had thrown down the gauntlet of total war and appeared determined to block any further Union expansion up the Peninsula. The town's burning was indeed, as Lieutenant William J. Stores of the York Rangers later wrote in his diary, "patriotism as a principal of action."[37]

Ben Butler also recognized Hampton's burning as symbol divining that the war was entering a new phase. "This act upon the part of the enemy seems to me to be a representative one," Butler wrote Winfield Scott, "showing the spirit in which the war is to be carried on on their part, and which perhaps will have a tendency to provoke a corresponding spirit on our part, but we may hope not."[38]

The Federals were shocked by Hampton's destruction as one Northern newspaper called it "a wanton act of cruelty to the resident Unionists, and moreover useless."[39] "Such a picture of war and desolation I never saw nor thought of, and hope I shall not again," wrote Lieutenant Charles Brewster. "I pass through the churchyard round the celebrated Hampton Church, the oldest one in use in the United States, it is completely destroyed all but the walls and they are useless."[40] Ben Butler could not understand the Confederate scorched earth policy, writing to Washington, "A more wanton and unnecessary act than the burning, as it seems to me, could not have been committed, I confess myself so poor a soldier as not to be able to discern the strategic importance of this movement."[41] It was an eerie scene, as one Union correspondent noted, "Nothing but a forest of black sided chimneys and walls of brick houses tottering and cooling in the wind, scorched and seared trees and heaps of smoldering ruins mark the site . . .A more desolate sight cannot be imagined than is Hampton today."[42]

Chapter 6

Beyond the Pale

Hampton's burning was the last major offensive move in the 1861 chess match between the opposing forces on the Peninsula. The Union success in holding Fort Monroe and Camp Butler, thereby ensuring control of the Hampton Roads harbor, had been tempered during the summer by its defeat at Big Bethel. More changes were in store for the Peninsula during the upcoming year, as noted by New York Volunteer Captain Ole Peter Balling from Camp Butler:

> One cannot help reflecting on the change wrought by time and events. Where now crowds of hardy soldiers refresh their tired frames by gambling in the luxuriously fresh waves of the James River, only twelve months ago the nobility and fashion of the South gathered to enjoy the stillness and beauty of the scenery; and so the change ever goes on! Who knows what sorts of guests may be sojourning at Newport News in August 1862?[1]

Northerners and Southerners alike realized by August 1861 that the next year's campaign would prove critical to the control of the Peninsula. Both sides, consequently, appeared content by late summer to concentrate on improving their existing positions and await reinforcements before attempting any aggressive action.

Ben Butler's request to be relieved of command of the Union Department of Virginia was finally fulfilled on August 17, 1861, when Major General John Ellis Wool arrived as Butler's replacement.[2] Butler left Hampton Roads on August 26 with Commodore Silas H. Stringham's seven- vessel fleet enroute to capturing Hatteras Inlet.[3] The seventy-seven-year-old Wool had served in the U. S. Army for almost fifty years. He assumed his command at Fort Monroe with the same vigorous leadership that had earned him honors at Queenstown Heights and Plattsburg during the War of 1812. This service elevated Wool to the rank of colonel and he served as Inspector General from 1816 until promoted to brigadier general in 1841. Perhaps he achieved his greatest fame during the Mexican War when he had rapidly marched his troops 900 miles from San Antonio to reinforce Zachary Taylor at the Battle of Buena Vista. Wool was breveted major general and received the thanks of Congress "for gallant and distinguished conduct" during this action. In early 1861, he commanded the Department of the East until transferred to Virginia by Winfield Scott.[4]

Upon his arrival at Old Point Comfort Wool continued to improve the Union toehold on the lower Peninsula. He advocated strengthening Fort Monroe and Camp Butler as a threat against Richmond as well as other points along the Confederate coast line, writing Winfield Scott that:

> To operate on this coast with success . . . we want more troops . . . If I had 20,000 or 25,000 men, in conjunction with the Navy, we could do much on this coast to bring back from Virginia the troops of North Carolina, South Carolina, and Georgia; but the arrangements should be left to Commodore Stringham and myself. We know better than anyone at Washington attached to the Navy what we require for such expeditions.[5]

Wool recognized that Fort Monroe's command of Hampton Roads not only limited the Confederate riverine communications between Norfolk and Richmond, and blocked these ports' access to the sea; but, more importantly, it provided a valuable springboard for Federal expeditions against other Southern ports.

Fort Monroe's existence as the only Union strategic fortified position in the upper South began to pay dividends by late 1861. Butler's expedition was successful in capturing Hatteras Inlet on

August 29, 1861. This effort as a model, Old Point Comfort, Camp Hamilton and Camp Butler became useful staging areas for other major amphibious operations. Flag Officer Samuel F. DuPont launched his Port Royal campaign from Hampton Roads in October 1861. Brigadier General Ambrose E. Burnside's command was ordered to Fort Monroe to unite with Flag Officer Louis M. Goldsborough's fleet for an expedition against the North Carolina coast. This operation left Hampton Roads on January 8, 1862, and would eventually result in the capture of Roanoke Island, New Bern, Fort Macon and Beaufort. Another expedition, Farragut's New Orleans campaign, left Hampton Roads in February 1862.[6]

Fort Monroe also became a transfer point for Confederate soldiers and sympathizers captured by Union forces. Political prisoners from Baltimore arrived on September 15 and were confined in casemates. The Rip Raps was used for POWs captured during the Hatteras expedition and other military prisoners awaiting transport. Wool was decidedly against using these exposed fortifications as prisons, as he wrote to Secretary of War Cameron:

> The crowded state of this fortress which from the great number of stores and supplies within it has obligated me to place these prisoners in very close quarters where they cannot obtain even the necessary conveniences of health and must suffer seriously for the want of air and ventilation, and to detail a strong guard for their safe-keeping which with the reduced force now at my disposal has necessarily interfered with other important duties of the men . . . At the Rip Raps they could not be accommodated from the great number of prisoners waiting there for conveyance to the Tortugas.[7]

The political prisoners were transferred northward three days later. The fort, however, would later serve as an exchange point on November 14, 1861, for Confederate prisoners captured at Hatteras.[8]

All the Union positions on the lower Peninsula became a lure for area slaves seeking their freedom as the result of Ben Butler's "contraband of war" decision. Despite the Confederate efforts to stop this exodus, local slaves continued to contraband towards the Union lines. George Ben West wrote that two of his family's slaves left his farm as soon as the Federals arrived. When the West family refuged to Richmond their slaves refused to leave. George Ben West hoped to come back for them later, but he was never able to do so. Before he left the Peninsula, West noted that hundreds of runaways had already moved around the waterfront near Camp Butler and had either built shacks or taken over abandoned buildings along the river.[9]

The inundation of contrabands posed several problems for the Federal authorities. Even though the contrabands were a major drain on the Southern labor force, Ben Butler noted that:

> The negroes came pouring in day by day. I found work for them to do, classified them and made a list of them so their identity might be fully assured, and appointed a "commissioner of negro affairs" to take this business off my hands, for it was becoming onerous.[10]

Once in command, General Wool specified that a strict accounting be made of all work accomplished by contrabands and issued orders proscribing the use of contrabands as servants by officers. Many took jobs in the various military departments to assist with tasks ranging from distribution of food to manual labor. In November 1861, 352 were employed in the Quartermaster Department, 20 by the Commissary, 41 with the Engineers, 18 in Ordinance, 18 by the Medical Department, and 453 as general laborers. Rates of pay were established, clothing was distributed and food was provided to these former slaves. A value of $5,526.22 for clothing and $834.80 for shoes was issued in a 10-month period. Medical services and housing were also provided to contrabands employed by the U. S. Army. "Two large, commodious buildings" were erected at Newport News Point for the contrabands supporting Union troops at Camp Butler. Many of the ex-slaves sought other means to make a living. Enlistment in the U. S. Navy was opened to blacks by Secretary of the Navy Gideon Wells and Flag Officer Louis Goldsborough actively recruited contrabands. Thus, numerous former bondsmen found berths on ships such as the U.S.S. *Minnesota*. This was a popular move as black sailors would receive a $10 monthly wage. Others became even more inventive oystering and growing crops for sale to Union troops. An informal market was established outside of Camp Butler. Every morning after reveille, blacks would appear from the nearby countryside to sell all sorts of produce, fish and fowl.[11]

Some problems did arise in the U. S. Army's relationship with contrabands. Several soldiers tried to purchase food from the contraband markets and then refused to pay their debt. This practice was stopped when contrabands began operating only on a barter or cash-and-carry system. The U. S. Army also found it necessary to provide food and clothing to the young, infirm and other contrabands otherwise unable to provide for themselves. At Camp Butler, a superintendent of contrabands, one Sergeant Smith, endeavored to profit from his position by shortening the rations given to these blacks or refusing to provide meals to some individuals. Smith was removed from his position and court-martialled.[12]

A policy was developed whereby housing and food would only be provided to those employed by the U. S. Army. Consequently, contraband communities were established outside of the Union camps. The largest, known as Slabtown or the Grand Contraband Camp, was erected atop the ruins of Hampton. It was the very circumstance that Magruder wished to stop when he had ordered the town's destruction. Nonetheless, communities began to emerge, fostered by the arrival of the American Missionary Association. The AMA was an association of "abolitionists and church people" who believed that the need for providing education to former slaves "seemed like a call from on high." The AMA's first representative, the Reverend Lewis C.

Lockwood, arrived on the Peninsula on September 3, 1861, and was quickly followed by other ministers and educators. Lockwood reported that the contrabands had "a great thirst for knowledge . . . parents and children are delighted with the idea of learning to read."[13] Several schools were soon established, which included blacks as teachers. John Oliver, a black AMA worker, established and taught in two schools near Camp Butler. Other schools were established at Fort Monroe, Camp Butler and in the Chesapeake Female College. Even ex-President John Tyler's home near Hampton was taken over for use as an AMA school. Local black educator Mary S. Peake moved her pre-war school into more spacious quarters at the Chesapeake Female College. Peake continued to operate her school until she died of tuberculosis in the spring of 1862.[14]

Efforts to educate, care for and utilize the thriving contraband community consumed much energy, but Wool's primary concern since becoming Commander of the Union Department of Virginia was to improve his defensive capabilities. Wool was virtually surrounded by Confederates. Only the water link to points north, secured by the U. S. Navy, gave Wool the capability not only to maintain the Union presence on the lower Peninsula, but to flourish as the only symbol of the Union in Virginia. Fort Monroe continued to be strengthened and by September 1861, 103 guns and 17 mortars were mounted in the fort. Fort Calhoun's armament was also upgraded with seven 8-inch Columbiads and two rifled 42-pounders.[15]

Wool still needed more men, as he wrote on October 6, 1861: "We want more regiments. I only ask that you will give me sufficient number of troops to defend this place. The enemy have been re-enforcing their troops."[16] Confederate pressure had indeed been increasing all across the quasi-no man's-land. Numerous skirmishes took place between Camp Butler and Young's Mill. On October 12, twelve Federals were captured near Newport News Point. One Southern attempt to ambush a Federal foraging party near New Market Creek Bridge only resulted in the Confederates shooting at each other. Additional skirmishes occurred on November 11 and 12, contesting control of this bridge. By the onset of winter there was little to be found to forage for in the no man's land as both sides had left behind a path of destruction. Farms had been pillaged and barns burned; the lush countryside had become a desolate scene.[17]

The Confederate Navy, with its minimal resources, also endeavored to contest Federal control of Hampton Roads. The Teaser, Yorktown, and Patrick Henry ventured out on several occasions (August 31, September 13, and December 2) to shell Newport News Point. These excursions caused little damage to Camp Butler.[18] The gunboat, C.S.S. *Northampton*, made an unexpected raid into Hampton Roads on December 29, 1861. The Northampton was able to capture the schooner *Sherwood*, which was being towed by the *Express* from Newport News Point to Fort Monroe. The Confederates were able to take the *Sherwood* into Norfolk despite being pursued by several Union gunboats. These forays, while providing the Confederates with some sense of success, were unable to disrupt Union shipping or the Camp Butler toehold commanding the James River.[19]

Even though many Confederate soldiers shared cavalryman William Corson's disappointment that "the Yankees never come out from their camp far enough to give us the benefit of a little brush,"[20] Magruder was quite content to concentrate on his fortifications. Even though his "Army of the Peninsula" had grown to almost 9,500 men, thereby outnumbering the Federals at Fort Monroe and Camp Butler, "Prince John" constantly feared, from late summer onwards, that Federal troops would march against his incomplete works. When the Unionists reinforced Newport News Point in September, he moved 2,000 troops under the command of Lieutenant Colonel Henry Forno of the Fifth Louisiana Infantry to Warwick Court House to support the Young's Mill position, using Captain H. H. Curtis of the Warwick Beauregards to assist with troop dispositions.[21]

Since Big Bethel, Magruder had kept his primary focus on strengthening his defenses. He constantly entreated Richmond with requests for more troops, artillery, and slaves to work on his series of earthworks he proposed to build across the Peninsula. He eventually would establish three defensive lines. His forward line of defense began at Young's Mill on Deep Creek, crossed the Peninsula to Harwood's Mill and Howard's Bridge on the Poquoson River, and followed that river to Ship's Point on the York River. Magruder's second line began at Mulberry Island on the James River and followed the Warwick River to within one and a half miles of Yorktown. Yorktown was fortified with a series of redoubts, some of which were built atop the British works remaining from the 1781 siege. This line was complemented by fortifications on the east side of the York River (which was less than a half mile wide at this point) at Gloucester Point and across the James to a work on Burwell's Bay known as Fort Boykin and at Harden's Bluff directly across the river from Mulberry Island Point. Prince John's final defensive position on the Peninsula was developed a few miles below Williamsburg along the line first proposed by Colonel Benjamin S. Ewell. This line comprised a series of fourteen redoubts, complete with supporting redans and rifle pits, between College and Queen's creeks, with its center anchored by Fort Magruder (Redoubt #6) astride the Williamsburg Road.[22]

Magruder decided to make the Warwick River - Yorktown position his primary defensive line on the Peninsula. Officers under his command generally concurred with this decision. Colonel Hill Carter, concerned about his loss of artillery for use on Mulberry Island, wrote from Jamestown, "I can only hope that Yorktown and Mulberry Island will be made impregnable, else the Peninsula will be in danger, and perhaps Virginia overrun."[23] Prince John focused all of his furious and apparently inexhaustible energy into building the Peninsula fortifications. Magruder mobilized every resource available, including as many as 600 slaves per day[24] and the soldiers from his 9,500-man command, to construct these fortifications as vigorously as possible. Men were detached to build gun carriages for 32-pound Columbiads at Macy's Sawmill on the Warwick River and soldiers who were pre-war overseers, such as James P. Hopkins of the 32nd Virginia, were "detailed to superintend the working on the batteries along the Warwick River."[25]

The Confederate command immediately recognized that the Peninsula's James River flank was extremely vulnerable. Unless the Southrons were able to close the river to movement by the Federal fleet, Union gunboats could simply steam up river, thereby by-passing the Southern defenses. Magruder noted this problem and advised Richmond on July 9, 1861, that:

> The work contemplated on Mulberry Island, if that point is geographically situated as represented, could be of greatest importance in defending this place and Richmond. If the enemy was forced by such a work to march up the Peninsula, there are several lines which would at once be fortified where he would meet with very rough treatment or be repulsed. I think he would be entirely defeated. At present, and without this work, these lines can easily be turned and landing made above them on James River. If it be decided to fortify at Mulberry Island, no time should be lost . . .[26]

Robert E. Lee appointed Captain George N. Hollins, C.S.N., to command the James River defenses and advised Magruder "the construction of the battery at Day's Point and the projected batteries at Mulberry Point, and the one opposite will . . . diminish the danger of an attempt upon Williamsburg."[27]

Magruder was not quite satisfied as he was concerned that any water battery on Mulberry Island would not defend the position against a land attack made possible by an amphibious assault. He advised Richmond:

> Whilst I was extremely glad to hear that works are to be erected on Mulberry Island and opposite, as they will be obstacles to the enemy in any attempt to ascend the river, yet that any work erected on

this side of the river could be carried by the enemy, either by storm or by siege on the land side, and then that their ships could pass up. Mulberry Island (so-called) is not an island, but a peninsula, and therefore any work on it, however strong, can be taken . . . The work at Mulberry Island is very important and ought at once to be built . . . The spot where the work is to be erected — and that is the proper spot — is cut off from the mainland by an impassable marsh, but this marsh is very near where the work is to be, and the ground on the land side of the marsh commands the work. From this side at a distance of half a mile the enemy could erect batteries of heavy guns and perhaps make our work untenable; at all events much time would be required to make it secure against a land attack.[28]

On August 14, 1861 work had begun on the Mulberry Island Point water battery under the direction of naval officers. Designed for six cannon, the battery mounted only four, and Magruder continued to fear that it would be flanked "if the enemy can land at the mouth of the Warwick River."[29]

The Confederate Navy attempted to limit the Federal riverine access. On August 26, Lieutenant Catesby ap. Roger Jones was ordered to take six canal boats filled with granite and sand and sink them in the Swash Channel off Mulberry Island. Magruder wanted more done to block the channels and requested that barges also be sunk at the entrance to the Warwick River.[30]

The organization of Stringham's fleet in Hampton Roads in preparation for its movement against Hatteras Inlet alarmed Magruder and prompted him to alert his troops to an impending Union attack up the James River. He ordered the 14th Virginia to march to Land's End at the southern tip of Mulberry Island and to erect fortifications that would command the entrance to the Warwick River. Magruder exhorted the men to "defend your position to the utmost" and added, "also report whether you have sufficient spades to make the work."³¹

Additional reports of Union gunboats operating off Newport News Point made Magruder believe that the Federals had "the intention of going up the James River."³² Magruder, unsure of the enemy's purpose, advised Colonel Hodges of the 14th Virginia to "immediately take position with his whole force near the work at Mulberry Point, near Crawford's House, to defend it and prevent a landing so far as it may be in your power." A cavalry picket was left at Land's End to watch for any enemy attempt to steam up the Warwick River and reinforcements from Jamestown, Major J. M. Patton's command containing the Greensville Guard and the Charles City Southern Guards, were added to the covering force on Mulberry Island.³³

Even though the anticipated Union attack never materialized Magruder continued to fret about his James River flank believing that "Everything must be got and kept in perfect readiness at Mulberry Island." Prince John lamented that the defenses that had been erected were plagued by a lack of troops and artillery. He pestered Richmond with requests for support noting that the newly constructed water batteries on Mulberry Island would be "of no avail unless the embankments which I have caused to be thrown up on the shores there can be furnished with heavy guns."³⁴ Two 42- pounder cannonades were eventually provided for the Land's End battery and the Confederate navy agreed to station the C.S.S. *Patrick Henry* off Mulberry Island to assist in the defense. A telegraph line was installed connecting Mulberry Island Point with Lee Hall, Yorktown and Williamsburg to keep Magruder in touch with his weak flank.³⁵

Despite ordering his command on October 3, 1861, to be "hutted for the winter"³⁶ in preparation for the cold season, Magruder kept units on alert, continually cancelling furloughs and moving troops from one position to another to counter Northern troop dispositions. The C. S. Navy finally fulfilled Magruder's request and on October 17 sunk rock- and sand-filled canal boats at the mouth of the Warwick River to block its entrance.[37] Magruder was still disheartened by his exposed flank and pressed Richmond for more heavy artillery, writing:

> It is a matter of great moment that the defenses at ... Mulberry Point should be as strong as possible. The work at Mulberry Point can contain two more guns ... The river is better commanded at that point than at any other below Jamestown; and if it can be rendered safe there, troops as well as field guns could be used below.[38]

Magruder even sought to trade cannon from the gunboat C.S.S. *Teaser*. His request to obtain these guns helps to detail the Confederate positions on the lower Peninsula:

> The lowest fort on James River, on the left bank, is Mulberry Island Point; opposite is Harden's Bluff fort, both strong on the water fronts. By a glance at the map it will be seen that if the enemy can land at the mouth of Warwick River, he can march to Mulberry Island Point and take the fort there in the rear. The troops on my line from the mouth of Deep Creek, which is the same as that of Warwick River, to Harwood's Mill, at the head of Poquoson River, cannot go to the succor of Mulberry Island Point without making a march of some 20 miles around the head of Warwick River; besides, the right flank of my own line is below Warwick River. That flank must be secured and the fort at Mulberry Island Point, both in full sight of the enemy at Newport News, now at least 8,000 strong. I have therefore caused one regiment (500 strong) to take post at Land's End, on the right, at the mouth of Warwick River, and have thrown up an entrenchment there, but these guns of the *Teaser* are necessary for the armament of this entrenchment. I have caused rifle-pits to be made to protect the men, and sunk canal boats across the mouth of the river.[39]

Magruder's fears were only increased when a hurricane devastated the sea level Mulberry Island Point battery later in October. Prince John lamented this calamity, reporting:

> The work is in sight of the enemy. Negroes have deserted from it and informed the enemy of the situation. They will attack it, I presume, as soon as they can make preparations, and, if they carry it, as they probably will, in its present state, a great disaster may happen.[40]

The C.S.S. *Patrick Henry* and the C.S.S. *Jamestown* were assigned to guard the James River off Mulberry Island Point to block any Union advance while work began anew on the fortifications.[41]

Almost six months had now passed since the Battle of Big Bethel. Battle lines had been drawn, but were still incomplete. The commanders on the lower Peninsula were both concerned that the enemy could capture their exposed positions and, accordingly, constantly requested that their government provide them with more men and armaments. Each used the theme that their positions were critical to the success of their nation's war effort. Magruder and Wool recognized the Peninsula's strategic importance: as a springboard for attack and as an avenue of defense. They were both determined to use their minimal resources to secure control of Hampton Roads and the Peninsula. The next six months would witness the eyes of America focused on the Peninsula.

Chapter 7

The Gathering Storm

Besides the skirmishes, endless alerts, various details and earthwork construction, Confederate soldiers serving on the Peninsula spent a fairly good life between Hampton's burning and the arrival of the 1862 campaign season. Southrons probably never ate better anywhere or at any other time during the war. Cavalryman William Corson confirms this abundance in a letter to his future wife:

> Our camp teems with market wagons every morning that bring vegetables, butter, milk, eggs, chickens, shoats, watermelons, and most anything that can be had at the Richmond market. There is the finest crop of sweet potatoes raised here that I ever saw grow anywhere. Our boys have feasted on fine fish and watermelons until it is difficult to find sale for them . . . Oystering will soon commence and then we will feast indeed. Taking all things into consideration I think this is the most delightful country I ever saw and but for the chills I would rather live here than any place I know. The streams here furnish the finest fish in the world and teem with waterfowl in the fall and winter. The growing crop of corn, where it is worked, is excellent and if it can be saved will feed the army here a long time.[1]

Soldiers obviously lived in a land of plenty and even took time to discourse the flavor of local oysters. A friendly competition ensued to prove whether or not the Warwick River variety was superior to those from the York River.

The local citizens welcomed the soldiers as best they could; food and hospitality were shared without a second thought. Maria Curtis, wife of Captain H. H. Curtis of the Warwick Beauregards, befriended the soldiers camped on her farm, Endview, and across the Yorktown Road at Lebanon Church. Her home eventually became a Confederate hospital and her caring for these men prompted the Mecklenburg Grays to present Mrs. Curtis with a silver loving cup in January 1862 as a tribute to her kindness.[2]

All was not perfect, though, as many soldiers complained of nights when "musketeers (mosquitoes) swarmed around in myriads." Corson commented that his cavalry unit was forced to move its camp on several occasions due to flies. Sickness of all types affected the soldiers greatly; the Warwick Beauregards' first recorded death was Private William H. Smith, who succumbed to typhoid fever on July 24, 1861. Another soldier lamented that the only thing that they had in abundance "other than rain and mud was sickness."[3] The 15th North Carolina Regiment, numbering about 1,100 officers and men, was assigned to the Peninsula in late June 1861. The regiment was assigned to the construction of earthworks, however, by August over eighty percent of the men were stricken with fever. The entire regiment was re-assigned to a healthier location since the men, who were originally from the piedmont section of North Carolina, were not use to the Tidewater climate. Almost fifteen percent of the 15th died from sickness that summer.[4]

Despite the diseases that raged through the camps, the Confederates were able to build comfortable winter quarters nestled amongst their fortifications as William White of the Richmond Howitzers wrote from Mulberry Island:

> We have comfortable log cabins, built by our own men, with glass windows, plank floors, kitchen attached, etc. . . . Time does not hang very heavily on my hands, for I am now drilling a company of infantry . . . Then we get up an occasional game of ball or chess, or an old hair hunt . . . Fortunately we have managed to scrape up quite a goodly number of books, and being in close communication with Richmond, we hear from our friends daily.[5]

These comforts aside, the soldiers remained constantly aware of the battles that would surely come in the spring as White noted:

> Soon the spring campaign will open and then farewell to the quiet pleasures of "Rebel Hall" . . . No more winters during the war will be spent as comfortably and carelessly as this. Soon it will be a struggle for life, and God only knows how it will all end. My health has but little improved, but I had rather die in the army than live out.[6]

Magruder spent the entire winter focused on expanding his defensive perimeters and worried that the Federals would attack before his preparations were complete. Another alert was raised by Magruder in late January following news of the Federal fleet's rendezvous in Hampton Roads to transport Burnside's command to Roanoke Island. He ordered the troops at Land's End that "if vessels were seen coming up the James River, a gun was to be fired from Land's End and repeated every five minutes."[7]

The alert was just another false alarm; however, Magruder redoubled his efforts strengthening the fortifications on Mulberry Island as well as along the Warwick River. Prince John reported to Richmond in late February that the Mulberry Island Point Battery would be made impregnable by building a covering work a half mile away on high ground. Built around the Crafford family farmhouse, it was designed to protect the water battery from land attack. Fort Crafford would become the largest earthen fortification in the Warwick Line, covering almost eight acres. The pentagon-shaped fort had an 8-foot high outer wall, a dry moat and an inner wall almost twenty feet high. Armed with eight heavy cannon with emplacements for eight smaller pieces, Magruder called Fort Crafford "very strong" and considered it capable of withstanding a month-long siege.[8]

Additional earthworks were constructed crossing Mulberry Island about a mile below the Mulberry Island Point Battery.

Stretching from the Warwick River to the James River, it was intended to support Fort Crafford and was referred to as the Miner's Farm Line. Artillerist William White was positioned in this new defensive line and described the fortifications in his diary:

> Mulberry Island is the nearest water-battery on the north side of the James River to Newport News, and mounts seven or eight heavy guns. It is supported by the Day's Point battery on the south side of the James, mounting seventeen guns. Magruder, as soon as we reached this place, sent us six hundred negroes to throw up heavy fortifications. Our position here is quite a strong one; our left flank is the Warwick River, on our right is a deep marsh and the heavy battery at Mulberry Island; on our front is a broad, open field, our guns commanding it.[9]

Prince John's defensive perimeter looked rather impressive by early March. On Mulberry Island alone Magruder had constructed the water-battery on Mulberry Island Point, a one-gun battery on the Warwick River, a water-battery and trenches at Land's End, and entrenchments along Brick House Creek and Miners' Farm and Fort Crafford.[10]

If there was a glaring weakness, it was the troop strength of the Army of the Peninsula. Magruder's command had been reinforced to 13,000 men, but on March 4, 1862, he was ordered to detach 5,000 men to Suffolk.[11] The Confederate government knew that the Federals were planning an offensive in Tidewater Virginia, however, Davis and Lee were unsure exactly where the attack might land. Norfolk appeared to be the likely target, especially since Burnside's campaign in coastal North Carolina was moving northward toward the Chesapeake and Albemarle and the Great Dismal Swamp canals. With Fort Monroe as a base and the U. S. Navy's ability to control the waterways, the Confederacy's control of Southeastern Virginia seemed in great jeopardy.

The Union war machine was finally stirring on almost every front in early 1862. The Federal successes in Tennessee and along the Mississippi had the Confederacy in dire straits. Lincoln was anxious to deliver the coup de grace and ready to strike a blow against Richmond that might well win the war. The Army of the Potomac had been poised outside of Washington ready to march since late 1861, however, its commander hesitated to order the army into action. Therefore, Lincoln's goal in early 1862 was to goad Major General George Brinton McClellan to launch a campaign to capture the Confederate capital.

George McClellan had arrived in Washington in August 1861 following the Bull Run debacle. Named the commander of the Army of the Potomac, he quickly set about reorganizing the army into a well-trained and cohesive fighting force. McClellan was just thirty-four years old and totally confident in his ability to achieve great success. He believed that he had been called upon to save the nation.[12]

McClellan was born in Philadelphia, Pennsylvania on December 3, 1826. The son of a prominent doctor, McClellan attended local preparatory schools and the University of Pennsylvania until 1842 when he entered West Point. He graduated in 1846, at the age of nineteen, second in his class. McClellan was appointed 2nd Lieutenant in the Corps of Engineers and served with Winfield Scott's army during its advance on Mexico City. His gallant service and capability to construct bridges and roads earned him two brevets. Following the Mexican War, McClellan worked on the construction of Fort Delaware, the Red River expedition transcontinental railway surveys, and as an instructor at West Point. He translated and adapted a French manual on bayonet drill and was a member of the board of officers sent to Europe to study European armies during the Crimean War. This experience enabled him to develop the "McClellan saddle" which remained in use by the U. S. Army until its cavalry units were disbanded in the 20th Century.[13]

McClellan resigned his commission in 1857 and became the chief engineer of the Illinois Central Railroad. In 1860 he moved to Cincinnati, Ohio as president of the Ohio & Mississippi Railroad. When the Civil War erupted McClellan was named major general of Ohio Volunteers by Governor William Dennison. Little Mac, as he was nicknamed, was then made Major General, Regular Army and given command of the Department of the Ohio on May 3, 1861.[14]

When several pro-Union western counties of Virginia seceded from the state to rejoin the Union, McClellan organized a force of almost 20,000 men and moved into that mountainous region. A small force of Confederates (numbering 4,500), commanded by Brigadier General Robert S. Garnett attempted to block McClellan's advance. On July 11 McClellan sent Brigadier General William S. Rosecrans' brigade up the slopes of Rich Mountain during a heavy rain. Rich Mountain was captured and the surviving Confederates fell back in disarray only to be defeated once again at Carrick's Ford on July 13. McClellan won instant fame for his troop's victory which secured West Virginia for the Union and control of the important Baltimore & Ohio Railroad.[15]

George McClellan was the first Northern hero of the war. Following Irwin McDowell's repulse at Manassas, he immediately set himself to the task of rebuilding the demoralized army. The Army of the Potomac quickly grew in size and confidence under McClellan's guidance. The general, now also styled the Young Napoleon, became the idol of his men. He could be seen riding through the streets of Washington on his horse Daniel Webster (Devil Dan) rushing from camp to conference to camp displaying a dash and soldierly presence that impressed soldier and civilian alike.[16] McClellan was full of confidence and believed himself to be "the power of the land."[17]

The Young Napoleon reached the apex of military power when Lincoln named him on November 1, 1861 to replace the aged and infirmed Winfield Scott as commander-in-chief of the Federal armies. Lincoln worried that he had perhaps placed too heavy a responsibility on the young soldier's shoulders, but McClellan merely replied, "I can do it all."[18]

Pressure, however, was beginning to mount for McClellan to take some action against the nearby Confederate army at Manassas Junction. The Union capital was virtually blockaded by Confederate batteries on the lower Potomac. It was an embarrassment to the Union and the Radical Republicans howled that McClellan must do something about it. Whispers were heard stating that McClellan, a Democrat who had made no effort to disguise his politics or his dislike of the anti-slavery movement, was in league with the secessionists. Lincoln, frustrated by McClellan's continual delays, ordered the Army of the Potomac in January to march against the enemy no later than February 22, 1862.[19]

McClellan demurred, stating that he was in the process of finalizing a grand strategic plan to capture Richmond and end the war. Known as the Urbanna Plan, McClellan proposed to move his entire army to Annapolis, Maryland, and then down the Chesapeake Bay to the Rappahannock River. The landing at Urbanna, McClellan explained, would threaten the Confederate lines of supply and communication as well as interposing the Union army between General Joseph E. Johnston's army near Manassas and the Confederate capital. Richmond was less than 50 miles from Urbanna and McClellan believed his army could swiftly move on to capture the Confederate capital.[20]

While McClellan put forth that the Urbanna Plan would avoid the costly casualties that would surely come from a direct march through Northern Virginia to Richmond, Lincoln and Secretary of War Edwin Stanton were skeptical about the plan, especially since it would leave Washington virtually unprotected. Nonetheless, Lincoln agreed to the plan, provided McClellan would leave 40,000 men to defend the capital. Little Mac reluctantly accepted this condition and began planning his campaign.[21]

Simultaneous with McClellan's presentation of his grand plan to by-pass the main Confederate army by way of Urbanna, that army's commander, General Joseph E. Johnston, was concerned about his advanced position near Manassas. Johnston had almost 45,000 men, but feared that his army would either be flanked or attacked by McClellan's much larger force. On February 20, Johnston met with President Jefferson Davis and advised him that his army must retreat to the Rappahannock River in the early spring. Davis, beset by Federal advances at virtually every front, could only accept Johnston's decision.[22]

During this period of crisis as the Confederacy awaited the impending Union attack in Virginia that was sure to come in the spring, Magruder continued his defensive preparations. Prince John had already assured Jefferson Davis that "I have taken not only the best but the only way of successfully defending this Peninsula with the means at my disposal, and this defense will be successful." He added that he would do his utmost "to prepare for the emergency of a landing in this Peninsula or on the Rappahannock River, which I now think more probable, or for an attack on James River."[23] In any event, Magruder was prepared to do his duty.

On March 7, 1862, McClellan held a council of his general officers to finalize the Urbanna Plan. He sought a vote of confidence for the concept and his commanders voted 8 to 4 in favor of the plan. The next day, March 8, McClellan and his commanders reviewed the Urbanna Plan with Lincoln. Lincoln, once again agreed to the concept, provided that the Confederate batteries on the Potomac would be captured, sufficient troops would be left behind to defend Washington, and that the campaign would begin in ten days.[24] McClellan accepted all of these conditions, however, events in Manassas and in Hampton Roads would quickly change the strategic picture.

Chapter 8

"Give 'Em A Broadsides Boys, As She Goes"

Since Norfolk's capture by local Confederates, the Federals at Fort Monroe and Camp Butler had been hearing rumors that the Southerners were building a huge ironclad at Gosport Navy Yard. Several spies and pro-Union yard workers had been keeping the Federal command informed of this ironclad's progress. Concerns about the Confederate ship reached as far as the White House, but Assistant Navy Secretary Gustavus V. Fox had assured Lincoln that "you need not give yourself any trouble whatever about that vessel"[1] during a cabinet meeting in February 1862.

The U. S. Navy in Hampton Roads was equally confident as Captain John Marston, commander of the U.S.S. *Roanoke*, commented, "I am anxiously expecting her and believe I am ready."[2] The U. S. Navy had reasons to be confident. After all, the Federals maintained an apparent superior force between Old Point Comfort and Newport News Point. Hampton Roads was the main station of the North Atlantic Blockading Squadron. The fleet was commanded by Captain Louis M. Goldsborough. Goldsborough had replaced Silas H. Stringham in September 1861 and had served in the U. S. Navy since becoming a midshipman at the age of seven. Now fifty-six years old, he was a huge man with a powerful temper. Goldsborough had turned the Hampton Roads blockading force into a strong complement of warships. At the fleet's heart were the two sister steam screw frigates U.S.S. *Minnesota* and U.S.S. *Roanoke*. Each carried an impressive broadside. The *Minnesota's* battery consisted of one 10-inch and twenty-eight 9-inch Dahlgren smoothbores, fourteen 8-inch guns, two 24-pounders, and two 12-pounders. She was Goldsborough's flagship. The station also included two sailing vessels: the 50-gun U.S.S. *Congress* and the 24-gun sloop-of-war U.S.S. *Cumberland*. The *Cumberland* featured perhaps the most powerful armament. Formerly a 44-gun frigate, she had been "razed" down to a sloop and armed with a compliment mounting twenty-two 9-inch smoothbores, one 10-inch smoothbore and a powerful 70-pounder rifle. The fleet was supported by the steamer *Cambridge*, the storeship *Brandywine*, three coal ships, a hospital ship, five tugboats, a side-wheel steamer and a sailing bark. It was an impressive force, yet, there were significant weaknesses. The *Roanoke's* engines were virtually unusable, and all the vessels were under-manned. More importantly, there were no ironclads assigned to the Union fleet.[3]

Across Hampton Roads the Confederates seemed hemmed in behind the batteries at Sewell's Point and Craney Island defending the entrance to the Elizabeth River. Yet up the river a virtual miracle was taking place. The capture of Gosport Navy Yard in April 1861 had been a godsend for the Confederacy. It had been the U. S. Navy's largest navy yard and its evacuation was bungled by the yard's commander Commodore C. S. McCauley. The Federals had mounted an effort to destroy the yard and save various ships before the Confederates could seize it, but the job was badly done. The dry dock was not destroyed, foundries were unharmed and over 1,200 cannon were left behind.[4] A Richmond newspaper reported two days after Gosport's capture that "we have material enough to build a Navy of iron-plated ships."[5]

Perhaps one of the most important items left behind during the yard's destruction and evacuation was the U.S.S. *Merrimack*. Launched in 1855 and commissioned on February 20, 1856, the *Merrimack* was the world's first fire steam powered, propeller-driven frigate. Two hundred seventy-five feet long, with a displacement of 3,211 tons, she carried 40 heavy cannon and was considered "a magnificent specimen of naval architecture." After a cruise to Europe, the *Merrimack* returned to Boston for an engine overhaul in 1857. The *Merrimack* was recommissioned into service six months later and sailed to the Pacific where she became the flagship of the Pacific squadron. Yet, her engines were still unsatisfactory and the *Merrimack* returned to her home port of Norfolk on February 16, 1860.[6] She was then placed in ordinary for repairs where the *Merrimack* remained until the secession crisis reached Virginia. An effort was made by Engineer-in-Chief of the Navy B. F. Isherwood to make the vessel able to move under its own steam. However Commodore McCauley refused to permit the *Merrimack* to leave Norfolk fearing that it would incite the local populace to attack the yard. Secessionists then sunk boats to block the Elizabeth River channel and on April 20 the *Merrimack* was scuttled by the retreating Federals. As the officers and men charged with the yard's destruction pulled away from Gosport on the U.S.S. *Pawnee* their unfortunate work seemed complete.[7]

Gosport quickly became the major shipyard in the Confederacy. Even before the Southerners could begin the job of repairing the damage, Confederate Secretary of the Navy Stephen R. Mallory announced:

> I regard the possession of an iron-armored ship as a matter of the first necessity. Such a vessel at this time could traverse the entire coast of the United States, prevent all blockades, and encounter, with a fair prospect of success, their entire Navy.
>
> If to cope with them upon the sea we follow their example and build wooden ships, we shall have to construct several at one time; for one or two ships would fall an easy prey to her comparatively numerous steam frigates. But inequality of numbers may be compensated by invulnerability; and thus not only does economy but naval success dictate the wisdom and expediency of fighting with iron against wood, without regard to first cost.[8]

Mallory, a former U. S. Senator from Florida and chairman of the Committee on Naval Affairs,[9] sought Lieutenant John Mercer Brooke, an 1847 Annapolis graduate, to identify the feasibility of a Confederate ironclad construction program. Brooke produced a functional design of a shallow draft vessel featuring an iron casemate situated midway between bow and stern with its sides sloping upward at a 45 degree angle. All of the machinery would be protected below the waterline. The design appeared to meet the Confederacy's needs, and Mallory decided to test the concept by using the hulk of the *Merrimack*. Mallory advised the Confederate Congress that it would cost $450,000 to rebuild the *Merrimack* as a frigate whereas only $172,523 would be required to transform her into an ironclad.[11]

Even before the Confederate Congress had appropriated the necessary money, work had already begun on the *Merrimack*. Three weeks after she had been declared as hulk "consumed to a mere hull"[12] by Lieutenant Wise who had actually applied the torch that burned the ship, the *Merrimack* had been raised and placed in dry dock. On July 11 work had begun cutting away the burnt timber down to the berth deck.

If Mallory had made any mistakes with his shipbuilding program it was the arrangements he made to supervise the *Merrimack's* conversion into an ironclad. Captain French Forrest, a " blusterer of the real old-tar school" who had served in the U. S. Navy for over 40 years, was yard commandant. While he maintained only administrative control, he did not approve of the ironclad project.[13] Yet, the real conflict would be between Brooke, who was charged with supervising the *Merrimack's* armament and armor plating, and Naval Constructor John L. Porter, a Portsmouth native who had previously supervised several ship construction projects for the U. S. Navy, and was charged with the actual construction and Chief Engineer William P. Williamson who would oversee overhaul of the machinery. This divided responsibility, no one individual being in overall command of the project, would cause problems, especially between Brooke and Porter. Both individuals would claim the *Merrimack* to be their design.[14] Eventually, Lieutenant Catesby ap Roger Jones would be assigned as executive officer of the ironclad in November 1861 to expedite construction and to ready the ship for active service. This early appointment (Jones had actually served on the *Merrimack* before the war) was made to lessen the friction between Brooke and Porter.[15]

Work proceeded on the *Merrimack's* conversion; however, numerous other problems would arise. A decision was made to utilize the old engines of the *Merrimack* because the South did not have the capacity to build new ones in a timely manner.[16] Tredegar Iron Works in Richmond was contracted to produce the iron plate for the *Merrimack's* shield. The armor plating was only designed to be one- inch thick. Tests by Brooke and Jones on Jamestown Island prompted Brooke to change the design to two-inch iron plates. This forced Tredegar to re-tool its plate rolling capacity, causing other delays.[17] Even when the plates were completed there was a transportation problem getting the iron from Richmond to Gosport Navy Yard. The only solution found to expedite shipment was to route some of the plates to Weldon, North Carolina, and then transfer them to the Seaboard and Roanoke Rail Road for transport to Norfolk.[18]

The *Merrimack's* transformation into an ironclad was a remarkable test of Confederate ingenuity and resources. Even though some questioned whether or not the *Merrimack* would float following her conversion, the vessel was launched on February 17, 1862, and recommissioned as the C.S.S. *Virginia*.[19] Although far from finished, she appeared to be a powerful vessel. Over 268 feet in length, her casemate was 178 feet long at the base and sloped upward at a 36 degree angle. The casemate was constructed of four inches of oak laid horizontally, eight inches of pine laid vertically and twelve inches of pine laid horizontally. It was bolted together and then sheathed with two-inch thick two-by-six iron plates laid horizontally. A second course of similar iron plate covered the first layer vertically. The casemate's roof was grated with two-inch iron bars supporting rafters consisting of yellow pine and white oak. Three hatchways were constructed to provide access to the fourteen-foot-wide deck. At the front of the casemate was a twelve-inch-thick iron conical pilothouse. The main deck extended a little over twenty-nine feet in front of the casemate and fifty-five feet behind it. The deck, designed to be almost awash with the sea, was covered with one inch of iron. An additional course of one-inch iron plate extended three feet from the deck to a depth of three feet around the vessel.[20]

The *Virginia* was armed with a battery developed by Brooke. Six 9-inch Dahlgren smoothbores and two 6.4-inch Brooke rifles completed the broadside battery. At each end of the casemate three gun ports were pierced for the two 7-inch Brooke rifles which served as pivot guns. A six-foot long, 1,500-pound cast iron ram, bolted two feet under water, completed the *Virginia's* weaponry.

The *Virginia* may have appeared fearsome, but there were numerous defects. The ram was improperly mounted by Porter who had not really approved of its use. One flange securing the ram was cracked during its mounting. Nothing was done to correct the problem. Porter had also made significant miscalculations concerning the ship's displacement. The decks were not under water as planned and a slight swell could expose the thinly armored hull below the waterline. Lieutenant Jones was shocked by this situation commenting, "We are least protected where we most need it. The constructor should have put on six inches where we now have one." Ballast was added and with 150 tons of coal the vessel settled allowing the water to reach above the eaves.[21]

There were other significant problems. With her 268-foot length and a draught of 22 feet,[22] the *Virginia* proved to be difficult to maneuver. The two salvaged 600-horsepower engines of the old *Merrimack* struggled to propel the *Virginia*. Lieutenant John Taylor Wood later commented, "From the start we saw that she was slow, not over five knots . . .She steered so badly that, with her great length it took from thirty to forty minutes to turn . . .She was as unmanageable as a water-logged vessel."[23]

Nevertheless, the *Virginia* was the hope of the Confederate Navy and a supreme effort was underway to send her into combat. While final preparations were underway as the ironclad rode at its moorings the *Virginia's* crew was being organized. Even though Catesby Jones had played an important role in the ironclad's conversion and had "the undue expectations" of receiving the command,[24] Mallory selected Franklin Buchanan to command all of the James River defenses. This avoided the time-honored seniority system as the *Virginia* was placed under Buchanan's jurisdiction and was named his flagship.[25]

Buchanan was an excellent choice for this command. A Marylander and grandson of a signer of the Declaration of Independence, he had served in the U. S. Navy since he was appointed a midshipman in 1815. Franklin Buchanan had served as the first superintendent of the United States Naval Academy at Annapolis, commanded the sloop *Germantown* during the Mexican War and commanded the U.S.S. *Susquehanna* during Matthew C. Perry's cruise to Japan. When the war broke out he was in command of the Washington Navy Yard and resigned his commission following the April 19 Baltimore riots. A Unionist by conviction, when he realized that Maryland would not secede, Buchanan strove for reinstatement, but Gideon Wells refused his request. Buchanan was immediately named a Captain in the Confederate Navy and assigned to the Office of Orders and Detail. On February 24, 1862, he was detached to get the *Virginia* ready for combat.[26]

Great things were expected of both Buchanan and the *Virginia*. Mallory's orders to Buchanan included his hopes for the vessel use. "The *Virginia* is a novelty in naval construction, is untried and her power unknown . . . Her powers as a ram are regarded as very formidable, and it is hoped that you may be able to test them." He also suggested that the ironclad should be steamed to New York or up the Potomac to Washington. Such a bold move could surely bring victory to the Confederates.[27]

Buchanan spent the last days of February and early March preparing the ironclad for combat. Gunpowder was in short supply and the crew had been recently recruited from Magruder's and Huger's commands. Buchanan lamented the delays. On March 2 he wrote John Bankhead Magruder:

> She is by no means ready for service, she requires eighteen thousand two hundred pounds of powder, howitzers are not fitted and mounted on the upper

deck to repel boats and boarders and none of the port shutters are fitted on the ship. Much of the powder has now arrived, and other matters shall not detain us.[28]

Two days later, however, Buchanan reported to Mallory that the ironclad was ready for service.

Buchanan was indeed ready for action, but bad weather forced a delay until March 8. Yet many Confederates were still unsure of the vessel's capabilities as the ironclad steamed away from its dock at Gosport Navy Yard around 11 a.m. Both sides of the river bank were "thronged with people," wrote the *Virginia's* surgeon Dinwiddie B. Phillips, "most of them, perhaps, attracted by our novel appearance, and desirous of witnessing our movements through the water."[29] Midshipman Hardin B. Littlepage remembered one man shouting "Go on with your old metallic coffin! She will never amount to anything else!"[30]

Most of the officers and crew, as well as the workmen who were still on board completing final adjustments, all believed the trip down river was just a trial run, but Flag Officer Franklin Buchanan had other thoughts.[31] "Old Buck" had been assigned to the *Virginia* because of his aggressive nature and he planned to test the vessel in actual combat with the enemy. Buchanan had corresponded with Magruder in late February to develop a joint Army-Navy operation against Newport News Point. He envisioned that such an attack could dislodge the Union hold on Hampton Roads. Even though Prince John had initially agreed to this plan, he backed off as time neared for execution stating that "the roads were too impassable for artillery."[32] He further lamented:

> The enemy is very heavily reinforced both at Newport News and Fort Monroe with infantry and six batteries of light artillery . . . It would have been glorious if you could have run into these as they were being landed from a Baltimore boat and a commercial transport.[33]

Magruder confided to Richmond that "no one ship can produce such an impression upon the troops at Newport News as to cause them to evacuate the fort." Prince John believed that "no important advantages can be obtained by the *Merrimac* further than to demonstrate her power, which, as she is liable to be injured by a chance shot at this critical time, had better be reserved to defeat the enemy's serious efforts against Norfolk and James River. He also recommended that "the *Merrimac* be stationed a little above Newport News, to prevent the gunboats coming up the swash channel leading to the Warwick River and turning the right flank of his line of defense."[34] Buchanan was undaunted by the joint operation's cancellation or the thought that his ironclad be used as a floating battery. Old Buck was determined to strike directly at the enemy's fleet.

The *Virginia* moved slowly down the Elizabeth River and was eventually joined by the two gunboats, C.S.S. *Raleigh* and C.S.S. *Beaufort*. The *Beaufort* took a towline from the *Virginia* to assist steering the ironclad into deeper water. The *Virginia* neared Craney Island and members of the crew could now look across Hampton Roads and see the Union vessels at anchor off Newport News Point. Around this time Buchanan stepped onto the gun deck and reportedly informed the crew:

> Sailors in a few minutes you will have the long-expected opportunity to show your devotion to your country and our cause. Remember that you are about to strike for your country and your homes, your wives and your children. The Confederacy expects every man to do his duty, beat to quarters![35]

By 1:30 p.m. the *Virginia* had entered Hampton Roads, dropped the towline and steamed toward the Union vessels.

March 8 "was a fine mild day, such as is common in southern Virginia during the early Spring," one Union officer wrote, "and everyone on board our ship was enjoying the weather . . ." The peaceful scene was broken when it was announced "that thing is a-commin at last sir."[36] Sight of "the roof of a very big barn belching forth smoke as from a chimney on fire"[37] remembered the tugboat *Zouave's* Acting Master Henry Reaney, put the entire Union fleet into action. The Federals had been expecting the ironclad for some time and Goldsborough had positioned the *Congress* and *Cumberland* off Newport News Point to engage the Confederate ironclads, giving time for the other Union warships to join in the action. Goldsborough hoped to catch the *Virginia* in a crossfire with his big frigates like the *Minnesota* and block her retreat. "Nothing, I think," he wrote Gideon Wells, "but very close work can possibly be of service in accomplishing the destruction of the *Merrimack* and even of that a great deal may be necessary." However, Goldsborough was in North Carolina on March 8 and the Federal response to the *Virginia* was left in the hands of Captain John Marston of the U.S.S. *Roanoke*.[38]

As the Union ships "Beat to Quarters," Brigadier General John Mansfield telegraphed Major General Wool at Fort Monroe advising him that, "The *Merrimack* is being towed down by two steamers past Cranby [sic] Island towards Sewell's Point. So reported to me from the *Cumberland*." Shortly thereafter he reported again, "The *Merrimack* is close at hand."[39] The *Congress* and *Cumberland* now cleared for action. The tugboat *Zouave*, stationed to support these vessels moved towards the *Virginia* and fired the first shot of the day from its thirty-pound Parrott rifle. The U.S.S. *Roanoke*, U.S.S. *Minnesota* and U.S.S. *St. Lawrence* began their preparations to move toward Newport News Point.[40]

It took the *Virginia* over an hour to steam across Hampton Roads. Buchanan's ship was joined enroute by other vessels of his James River Squadron including the C.S.S. *Patrick Henry*, C.S.S. *Jamestown* and the C.S.S. *Teaser*. Buchanan had already made his decision how to attack the awaiting Federal fleet. His first target was the U.S.S. *Cumberland*. He had reviewed this matter with the Chief Engineer H. Ashton Ramsay earlier that day and had informed Ramsey:

I am going to ram the *Cumberland*, I'm told she has the new rifled guns, the only ones in their whole fleet we have cause to fear. The moment we are out in the Roads I'm going to make right for her and ram her.[41]

As the *Virginia* began her run at the *Cumberland*, the Union ships and shore batteries began shelling the ironclad with little effect. The *Beaufort* was the first Confederate vessel to fire a round and the *Virginia* opened fire around 2:00 pm as she passed the *Congress*. The *Congress'* shot had no effect, whereas, the *Virginia's* broadside dismounted a gun on the *Congress* and started two fires.[42] The range was 1,500 yards, but Buchanan methodically passed the frigate and moved toward the *Cumberland*. The two ships exchanged fire. The shot "had no effect on her," as Thomas O. Selfridge recounted, "but glanced off like pebble stones."[43] The *Virginia's* seven-inch Brooke gun sent shot through the *Cumberland's* hull, one of which decimated a entire sixteen-man gun crew. Buchanan now gave the order for Chief Engineer Ramsay to reverse the engines as the ironclad rammed in the *Cumberland's* starboard side creating a hole, according to Lieutenant John Taylor Wood, "wide enough to drive in a horse and cart."[44] Catesby Jones remembered that "the noise of crashing timbers was heard above the din of battle."[45] The *Cumberland* was mortally wounded, the ramming made only worse by a shot from the *Virginia's* bow rifle which killed ten men. The *Cumberland* immediately began to sink to starboard thus trapping the *Virginia's* ram within her. The *Virginia's* engines struggled to free her from being pulled under the waves with the *Cumberland.* The ironclad survived only because her ram broke off under the strain of the *Cumberland's* weight.[46]

The *Virginia* backed clear and continued to pour shot and shell into the *Cumberland*. Both ships were now engulfed in gun smoke. The *Virginia's* sloped sides, coated with grease to help deflect shot, began to crackle and pop from the heat. Midshipman Hardin B. Littlepage recalled that the ironclad seemed to by "frying from one end to the other." Littlepage later recounted one excited exchange between two crew members: "Jack, don't this smell like hell?" "It certainly does, and I think that we'll all be there in a few minutes."[47] It was indeed hell on the *Cumberland*. Master Moses S. Stuyvesant remembered it as "a scene of carnage and destruction never to be recalled without horror."[48] Yet, the stricken vessel refused to surrender. "Solid broadsides in quick succession were sent into the *Merrimac* at a distance of not more than one hundred yards,"[49] Thomas Selfridge recounted after the fight. Even though most of the *Cumberland's* shot bounced harmlessly off the ironclad, the *Virginia* suffered most of its damage during this phase of the engagement. Her starboard cutter was shot away, the muzzles of two guns were broken, several iron plates were loosened (but not penetrated), and her smokestack was riddled with shot.[50] About 3:15 p.m. the *Cumberland* lurched forward and sank with all her flags flying as Executive Officer (and acting commander) Lieutenant George U. Morris called to his crew, "Give them a Broadside boys, as she goes."[51]

Having destroyed the *Cumberland*, Buchanan now turned his ironclad toward the *Congress*. The Union vessel had tried to escape the *Virginia* with the help of the *Zouave*, but had only managed to run around with her bow facing Newport News Point thus leaving just her stern guns available to return fire. While the *Virginia* completed her long, awkward turn, the gunboats *Beaufort* and *Raleigh* had kept the *Congress* at bay. The shallow draft only allowed the *Virginia* to approach within a hundred yards. During the next hour the Confederate ironclad pounded the *Congress*. With her commander, Lieutenant Joseph B. Smith, killed and her two stern guns disabled, the *Congress* stuck her colors and surrendered.[52]

Buchanan ordered the *Raleigh* and *Beaufort* to finalize the final surrender, remove the wounded and burn the ship. Each of the gunboats moved alongside the *Congress*, the *Beaufort* closest to shore. Lieutenant William Parker , commander of the *Beaufort*, went on board the *Congress* to accept its surrender and commented, "My God, this is terrible. I wish this war was over."[53]

The removal of the wounded sailors had just begun when the Federal troops on Newport News Point opened fire on the Confederates. General Mansfield had witnessed the entire fight and had reported to Wool late that afternoon:

> We want powder by the barrel. We want blankets sent up tonight for crews of the *Cumberland* and *Congress*. The *Merrimack* has it all her own way this side of Signal Point and will probably burn the *Congress* now aground with white flag flying and our sailors are swimming ashore.[54]

The *Congress* may have surrendered, but Mansfield certainly had not and he was determined to strike back at the Confederates. Mansfield ordered detachments from the 20th Indiana and 1st New York Mounted Rifles with three rifled cannon down to the beach to open fire on the Confederate gunboats. As his men continued to remove wounded from the *Congress* Parker shouted, "Make haste, those scoundrels on the shore are firing at me now." The *Beaufort*, suffering more than ten casualties, backed away from the *Congress* with thirty prisoners on board.[55]

Buchanan was enraged by the Beaufort's seemingly uncalled for retreat. He then sent Lieutenant R. D. Minor with eight volunteers in the *Virginia's* one remaining cutter, supported by the C.S.S. *Teaser* under the command of Lieutenant William A. Webb, to destroy the *Congress*. As Minor later recounted, when he drew near the *Congress*:

> The soldiers on shore opened on me . . . and very soon two of my men and myself were knocked down. I was only down a second or two, and, steering my crippled boat for the *Teazer* . . . then I was taken to the *Virginia,* where it had already been reported that they were firing upon me, and the flag officer, seeing it, deliberately backed our dear old craft up close astern of the *Congress* and poured gun after gun, hot shot and incendiary shells into her.[56]

Buchanan's battle blood was now boiling. Lieutenant John R. Eggleston heard the commander yell, "Destroy that —— ship! She's firing on our white flag!"[57] Buchanan then climbed on top of the *Virginia* to gain a better view of the action and was soon seriously wounded when a minie ball went into his thigh. He was carried below and ordered Jones to "Plug hot shot into her and don't leave her until she's afire."[58]

Catesby Jones now assumed command of the *Virginia* and continued firing on the *Congress* until she was ablaze. "Dearly did they pay," wrote Eggleston, "for their unparalleled treachery."[59] Yet there was more work for the Confederate ironclad to accomplish in Hampton Roads as the sun began to set. The Union fleet had tried to respond to the *Virginia's* foray, but the *Minnesota, Roanoke* and *St. Lawrence* had all run around moving from Old Point Comfort toward Newport News Point. Two of the Confederate gunboats, *Jamestown* and *Patrick Henry*, had been shelling the *Minnesota* as the Union vessel tried to refloat. The *Patrick Henry* dropped out of action when a shot from the *Minnesota* damaged her engine. Jones turned the *Virginia* against the stranded frigate, but could only approach to within a mile of the *Minnesota* because of her draft. After ineffectively shelling the *Minnesota* for a few minutes, Jones ordered the *Virginia* to Sewell's Point as their was some danger of the ironclad running aground herself because the tide had ebbed, and it had grown "so dark that we could not see to point the guns with accuracy."[60]

"It was a great victory," Lieutenant Minor later wrote as he confirmed the *Virginia's* deadly impact on the Federal fleet.[61] The Union losses were staggering: two major ships sunk, the *Minnesota* and *Zouave* damaged and over 280 casualties versus 27 Confederate dead and wounded.[62] The *Virginia* had suffered some damage, but Jones was determined to finish destroying the Union fleet on the morrow.

Chapter 9

Battle of the Ironclads

Lincoln viewed the March 8 events as the greatest Union calamity since Bull Run.[1] Secretary of War Edwin W. Stanton became "almost frantic," according to Gideon Welles' observations, stating that "McClellan's mistaken purpose to advance by the Peninsula must be abandoned." Stanton feared, as Welles noted, that the *Merrimack* would soon "come up the Potomac and disperse Congress, destroy the Capitol and public buildings . . ."[2] Little did the Northern leaders realize that the *Virginia* was considered by Buchanan so unseaworthy that it could not leave Hampton Roads.[3]

As Union leaders feared for the worse, the U.S.S. *Monitor* entered Hampton Roads aglow from the flames consuming the *Congress*. Whereas the *Virginia* was "an ingenious adaption of materials at hand and a tribute to her builder's skill at improvision, the Monitor was a completely new concept of naval design created by Swedish inventor John Ericsson. Yet, it almost was not built.

The U. S. Navy had initiated its ironclad program in August 1861. Secretary of the Navy Gideon Welles established an ironclad board consisting of Commodore Joseph Smith, Commodore Hiram Paulding and Captain Charles H. Davis to review designs and to select one to three prototype vessels for construction. It was only by chance that Ericsson's concept was even reviewed by the board as the temperamental engineer was not highly revered in naval circles because of the U.S.S. *Princeton* fiasco.[4] Cornelius Bushnell's *Galena* design was selected, but the board questioned the vessel's seaworthiness and Bushnell sought counsel. Cornelius Delamater, a leading New York iron founder, advised Bushnell to seek out Ericsson for advice. During this meeting Ericsson showed Bushnell his floating battery design that had been offered to France during the Crimean War. Bushnell recognized the brilliance of the concept and offered to promote this novel design before the ironclad board.[5]

Bushnell reviewed the design with Gideon Welles, who wrote in his diary that the ironclad was "extraordinary and valuable." However, the ironclad board was not as impressed, ridiculing it as another of "Ericsson's follies." Captain Davis told Bushnell to "Take the little boat home and worship it as it would not be idolatry, because it was in the image of nothing in the heaven above or on the earth beneath or in the waters under the earth."[6]

Yet Lincoln was impressed by Ericsson's model, commenting, "All I have to say is what the girl said when she stuck her foot into the stocking. It strikes me there's something in it."[7] Ericsson himself travelled to Washington to meet with the board to thoroughly explain his ironclad concept. He won the entire board's agreement. "He thrilled every person present in your room," Bushnell later recounted to Welles, "with his vivid description of what the little boat would be and what she could do." Ericsson concluded his presentation with the comment, "Gentlemen, after what I have said, I consider it to be your duty to the country to give me an order to build the vessel before I leave this room."[8]

The board did just that and on October 4, 1861, a contract was given to Ericsson and his partners Bushnell, John Griswold and John Winslow to build at a cost of $275,000 an:

> "Iron-Clad Shot-Proof Steam Battery of iron and wood combined, with the length to be one hundred and seventy-nine feet, extreme breadth forty-one feet and a depth of five feet or deeper . . . The party of the first agrees to furnish masts, spars, sails and rigging of sufficient dimensions to drive the vessel at a rate of six knots per hour in a fair breeze and will also furnish a condenser for making fresh water for the boilers on the most approved plan . . . Shall have proper accommodations for her stores of all

kinds, including provisions for 199 persons for ninety days, and shall have a speed of eight knots per hour under steam for twelve consecutive hours, and carry fuel for her engines for eight days consumption at that speed.

Should the vessel fail in performance for speed, sea service, failure of the turret or safety of the vessel, the men of the party of the first part hereby bind themselves, their heirs . . . to refund to the United States the amount of money advanced to them on said vessel.

The contract was signed and Ericsson went immediately to work on his ironclad.[9]

The ironclad's keel was laid at Continental Iron Works, Greenpoint, Long Island, New York, on October 25, 1861. Several subcontractors worked on the project. Rennsselaer Works fabricated the iron bar and rivets for the main deck. Albany Iron Works, Holdane and Company (New York) and H. Abbott and Company (Baltimore) produced the iron plate. Delamater Works built the vessel's engines, while the curved iron plates for the turret were made by Abbott and Company, and the turret was assembled by Novelty Iron Works in New York. Since the turret was too heavy to transport, it was disassembled and then rebuilt at Continental Iron Works.[10]

By January 1862 the ironclad was beginning to take shape and Lieutenant John Lorimer Worden was selected as its commander. Worden had served in the U. S. Navy since 1834 and had been a prisoner of the Confederates after a secret mission to Fort Pickens, in Pensacola Bay, Florida.[11] Recently exchanged, Worden accepted the command and advised Commodore Smith of the ironclad board, "After a hasty examination of her," he was, "induced to believe that she may prove a success. At all events, I am quite willing to be an agent in testing her capabilities."[12]

Flag Officer
Franklin Buchanan
Mariners' Museum

Lieutenant
Catesby ap Roger Jones
Mariners' Museum

Lieutenant Commander
John Lorimer Worden
Mariners' Museum

Lieutenant
Samuel Dana Greene
Mariners' Museum

The U. S. Navy also searched for a proper name for the vessel. Ericsson was asked for a suggestion, to which he replied:

> In accordance with your request, I now submit for your approbation a name for the floating battery at Green Point. The impregnable and aggressive nature of this structure will admonish the leaders of the Southern Rebellion that the batteries on the banks of their rivers will no longer present barriers to the entrance of the Union forces.
>
> The iron-clad intruder will thus prove a severe monitor to those leaders. But there are other leaders who will also be startled and admonished by the booming of the guns from the impregnable iron turret. "Downing Street" will hardly view with indifference this last "Yankee notion," this monitor. To the Lords of the Admiralty the new craft will be a monitor suggesting doubts as to the propriety of those four steel-clad frigates . . . On these and many similar grounds I propose to name the new battery *Monitor*.[13]

Welles could only agree with Ericsson's logic.

The *Monitor* was launched on January 30, 1862. Since it was an experimental vessel there were several problems; none of which, however, were beyond solution. It was an engineering marvel, containing several patents. The ironclad's most impressive feature was its steam powered rotating circular turret mounting two 11-inch Dahlgrens. The turret was constructed of eight layers of nested one-inch thick, curved rolled plates bolted together every six inches with the nuts facing inward so that it could be easily repaired if loosened during battle. The gun ports were equipped with shutters and the armor plate protecting this section of the turret was laid in nine courses. The turret had an interior diameter of twenty feet and a height of nine feet with a sliding hatch on the roof. This was the main access to the vessel.

Two small steam engines turned the turret on a series of three-inch wheels.[14]

Overall, the *Monitor* was 173 feet in length, weighed 776 tons and had a beam of forty-one and a half feet. The ironclad's draft was eleven feet with a freeboard of less than one foot. It was virtually awash with the sea. The hull was sheathed with one inch of iron and the deck was covered with four and a half inches of armor plate. All of the ship's machinery, magazine and quarters were positioned below the waterline. A pilothouse was the only other main feature protruding from the deck other than the turret. It was a rectangular box of iron, standing three feet above the deck and made of 9-nine-by-twelve inch iron bars bolted at the corners. An one-half inch observation slit was included below the upper tier of iron bars. The anchor well was located forward of the pilothouse.[15]

It had taken a little over one hundred days to complete the ironclad and the U. S. Navy was ready for it to see service. When the *Monitor* was launched Assistant Navy Secretary Fox had written Ericsson, "I congratulate you and trust she will be a success. Hurry her for sea, as the *Merrimack* is nearly ready at Norfolk and we wish to send her there."[16] Gideon Welles had hoped to get the *Monitor* to Hampton Roads while the *Virginia* was still under construction. He believed the Union vessel could have easily steamed up the Elizabeth River and destroyed the Confederate ironclad as it sat in dry dock.[17]

The *Monitor* was commissioned on February 25, 1862. Lieutenant Worden assembled a hand-picked crew which would eventually number sixteen officers and forty-nine men. Many were amazed by the ironclad as Acting Assistant Paymaster William F. Keeler wrote to his wife, "I shall not attempt a description of it now, but you may rest assured your better half will be in no more danger from rebel compliments than if he was seated with you at home. There isn't even danger enough to give us any glory."[18] Others were unsure of the *Monitor's* abilities. Master Louis N. Stodder noted that "she was rather a hasty job, was the *Monitor.*[19]

Quartermaster Peter Truscott added, "She was a little bit the strangest craft I had ever seen."[20] Seaman David R. Ellis made perhaps the most telling remark about the *Monitor* as it readied to leave New York commenting, "She had not been pronounced seaworthy, and no one could safely judge of her fighting qualities."[21]

The *Monitor* had already begun her sea trials on February 19 and additional minor defects were discovered which required correction. Major problems, however, were found with the steering system. Ericsson and U.S.N. Chief Engineer Captain Alban C. Stimers, who had supervised the *Monitor's* construction and had been assigned to stay with the ship to judge its effectiveness in action, endeavored to solve the malfunction. It was finally corrected on the evening of March 5 and the *Monitor* was now judged ready. Commander David Dixon Porter, one of the officers sent by the Navy Department to judge the *Monitor*, proclaimed the ironclad "a perfect success, and capable of defeating anything that then floated."[22] Worden had already received his sailing orders from Commodore Hiram Paulding commander of the New York Navy Yard: "When the weather permits you will proceed with the *Monitor* under your command to Hampton Roads and on your arrival report to the senior officer there . . . wishing you a safe passage."[23]

On the afternoon of March 6, 1862, the U.S.S. *Monitor* left New York under tow by the steam tug *Seth Low*, accompanied by the steamers *Sachem* and *Camtuck*. The weather was fine as the ironclad began its voyage; by the next morning, however, a gale had worked up the coast and, as Captain Stimers noted, "the sea commenced to wash right across the deck."[24] The turret, which had been specially prepared before leaving New York to prevent leaks, failed to stop water from entering the vessel. The water gushed through the turret "like a waterfall." Executive Officer Lieutenant Samuel Dana Greene wrote that the angry sea "would strike the pilot-house and go over the turret in beautiful curves, and it came through the narrow eye-holes in the pilot-house with such force as to knock the helmsman completely around from the wheel." Water soon began to come down the smokestack and wet the belts which operated the blowers circulating air through the vessel. The coal fires went out creating fumes that overcame the engineers and firemen. They were saved only by being taken to the top of the turret to be revitalized with the fresh air. The boiler fires were extinguished, and the engines stopped, which, in turn, stopped the steam-powered pumps. Greene later wrote that "the water continued to pour through the hawse-hole, and over and down the smoke-stacks and blower-pipes, in such quantities that there was imminent danger that the ship would flounder."[25]

Worden was seasick, and Green set about saving the ship. It was rapidly filling with water. The hand pumps were tried, but they were not powerful enough to pull the water out through the turret hatch. Greene organized a bucket line to bail out the water. It did little to combat the rising water. Acting Assistant Paymaster Keeler wrote later about the floundering vessel that "things for a time looked pretty blue, as though we might have to 'give up the ship.' " The *Monitor's* flag was flying the ship's flag upside down indicating distress, but only when Greene was able to hail the *Seth Low* and order her to tow the *Monitor* toward the shore and calmer water. Captain Stimers and others were soon able to restart the engines and steam pumps. The *Monitor* appeared saved.[26]

The ship and crew passed through a calm evening. Greene had just laid down in his bunk at around 3:00 a.m. March 8, when:

> I was startled by the most infernal noise I ever heard in my life . . . We were just passing a shoal and the sea suddenly became very rough . . . It came up with tremendous force through our anchor well and forced air through our hawse-pipe where the chain comes, and there the water would come through in a perfect stream, clear to our berth deck, over the ward-room table.[27]

The waves were once again crashing over the *Monitor's* decks and there was danger that the blower system would once again fail.

Greene "began to think that the *Monitor* would never see daylight" as the wheel ropes jumped off the steering wheel and the ship began to sheer stressing the tow line with the *Seth Low*. Fortunately, the steering problem was fixed and the ironclad was able to ride out the storm until daylight. Then the *Seth Low* noticed the *Monitor's* distress signal and towed her into calmer water near the shore. Somehow the *Monitor* had survived two close calls with the angry sea. Lieutenant Greene wrote later about the stormy trip from New York, "I think I lived 10 good years."[28]

Late afternoon on March 8, the *Monitor* finally rounded Cape Henry. As the ship steamed toward Fort Monroe the crew heard sounds of distant cannon fire and cleared the ship for action. When the *Monitor* entered Hampton Roads, Keeler noted:

> The shelling seemed to let up. All manner of ships, sail and steam, were running out of Hampton Roads, leaving like a covey of frightened quails and their lights danced over the water in all directions. A huge glow glimmered red and yellow in the Roads, fire leaping high in the air around what appeared to be burning masts and spars.[29]

The *Monitor*, as ordered, anchored near the U.S.S. *Roanoke* amidst all of the chaos left in the wake of the *Virginia's* attack. Worden reported to Captain John Marston, acting commander of the Union naval forces in Hampton Roads. Marston had received a telegraph from Gideon Wells instructing him to immediately send the *Monitor* up the Potomac to defend Washington against the Confederate ironclad. He realized that the best defense for the Capitol was in Hampton Roads and he order the *Monitor* to anchor near where the *Minnesota* was aground and to protect that ship from the *Virginia*.[30]

Worden found a pilot, Master Samuel Howard of the bark *Amanda*, who volunteered to serve on the *Monitor* and moved next to the *Minnesota*. Greene then went on board the *Minnesota* and conferred with her commander Captain Gershon Van Brunt. Van Brunt expected to float his ship at the next high tide and required no assistance.[31]

The crew members of the *Minnesota* had a different attitude. The frigate's chief engineer Thomas Rae remembered that when he shouted down to the engine room that "The *Monitor* is alongside," the crew "gave a cheer that might have been heard in Richmond."[32] Greene told Van Brunt that the *Monitor* would do everything it could to protect the *Minnesota*. As he returned to the *Monitor* "the *Congress* blew up, and certainly a grander sight never was seen, but it went right to the marrow of our bones." Worden and Greene remained on the deck of the ironclad waiting for the enemy vessel's return.[33]

When morning came the *Minnesota* was still aground and the *Virginia* was making preparations to finish its job of destroying the Union fleet. The seriously wounded Buchanan and Lieutenant Minor were finally convinced to leave the ironclad. Chief Surgeon Dinwiddie Phillips supervised this task and as he returned to the *Virginia* he surveyed the ship's damage from the previous day's action. He counted ninety-eight indentations in the iron from enemy shot and noted that the smokestack was so riddled that it "would have permitted a flock of crows to fly through it without inconvenience."[34]

Catesby Jones got the *Virginia* underway from its mooring near Sewell's Point around 6:00 am on March 9 accompanied by the *Patrick Henry, Jamestown,* and *Teaser*. Due to heavy fog, the small fleet was delayed entering Hampton Roads until nearly 8:00 am. Jones saw that the *Minnesota* was still aground as the *Virginia* closed within range. At 8:30 am a shot was sent through the frigate's rigging. The *Monitor* now moved out away from the *Minnesota*. The Confederates were amazed by this sight. Lieutenant Hunter Davidson thought at first that "the *Minnesota's* crew are leaving her on a raft." Lieutenant James H. Rochelle of the *Patrick Henry* noted "such a craft as the eyes of a seaman never looked upon before — an immense shingle floating in the water, with a gigantic cheese box rising from its center; no sails, no wheels, no smokestack, no guns. What could it be?" Jones instantly recognized it as Ericsson's iron battery.[35]

The *Monitor* headed straight for the *Virginia*. Worden knew that his ironclad was the only thing that could save the *Minnesota*. Van Brunt had made it very clear that he intended to destroy his still grounded ship if threatened by the *Virginia*. For the next four hours the two ironclads pounded each other mercilessly with shot and shell. The battle was mostly fought at a range of less than one hundred yards. Worden hoped that by firing his heavy shot, 168-pound spherical projectiles using 15 pounds of powder, from his 11-inch smoothbore Dahlgrens, such pounding would loosen or break the *Virginia's* iron plates. In turn, the *Virginia* was at a disadvantage. She had only explosive shells, hot shot and canister specifically, to use against wooden vessels. Chief Engineer Ramsay wrote later that, "If we had known we were to meet her, we would have at least been supplied with solid shot for our rifled guns."[36] Thus, Jones' strategy was first to concentrate on the *Minnesota* and if necessary to try to ram or board the *Monitor*.

The *Monitor* opened fire at 8:45 am and continued to block the *Virginia's* path toward the *Minnesota*. The two ironclads soon began circling each other, continually firing salvos for the next two hours. The *Monitor's* small size and quickness frustrated the Southerners who tried to fire at the *Monitor's* gun ports but the turret revolved too quickly. Lieutenant Eggleston complained that "we never got sight of her guns except when they were about to fire into us." Eggleston was later chided during the battle by Catesby Jones for not firing his gun at the Union ironclad. He retorted to the *Virginia's* commander that, "It is quite a waste of ammunition to fire at her. Our powder is precious, sir, and I find I can do the *Monitor* as much damage by snapping my finger at her every five minutes."[37]

The *Monitor's* turret truly amazed the Confederates, yet the Federal shot continued to bounce off the sloped, iron sides of the *Virginia*. The scene of the *Virginia* was likened to a page from Dante's Inferno as Chief Engineer Ashton Ramsay later wrote:

> On our gun deck, all was bustle, smoke, grimy figures and stern commands, while down in the engine and boiler rooms the 16 furnaces were belching out fire and smoke and the firemen standing in front of them, like so many gladiators, tugged away with devil's claw and slice-bar, inducing by their exertions more and more intense combustion and heat. The noise of the cracking, roaring fires, escaping steam, and the loud and labored pulsations of the engines, together with the roar of battle above and the thud and vibrations of the huge masses of iron which were hurled against us, produced a scene and sound to be compared only with the poet's picture of the lower regions.[38]

All was not perfect on board the *Monitor* despite her many technological advantages. The turret crew felt tremendous relief when the *Virginia's* first shots failed to penetrate the iron sides. The scene in the turret was similar to that on the *Virginia,* as Assistant Paymaster William Keeler later wrote:

> The sounds of the conflict were terrible. The rapid fire of our guns amid the clouds of smoke, the howling of the *Minnesota's* shells, which were firing broadsides just over our heads (two of her shots struck us), mingled with the crash of solid shot against our sides (not from the *Virginia*) and the bursting of shells all around us. Two men had been sent down from the turret, knocked senseless by balls striking outside the turret while they happened to be in contact with the inside wall of the turret.[39]

And there were other problems on board the Federal ironclad: The turret did not perform precisely as designed. The port stoppers proved to be almost too heavy to operate and only one gun could be fired at a time. Lieutenant Dana Greene, in command of the turret, eventually decided to leave both ports open. This became a necessity so to enhance the gun crews' vision since the communication system between the pilothouse and turret failed to perform. Lieutenant Keeler was used as a runner to convey orders from Worden to Greene. The turret's rotating mechanism also malfunctioned due to water damage incurred while the *Monitor* was almost overcome by the sea enroute to Hampton Roads. The turret, because of rust that had quickly formed, could not be stopped with any precision, making it virtually impossible to make well aimed shots. Eventually, the guns were discharged "on the fly" as the turret turned past the target. Another flaw was discovered: the turret could not fire at the Confederate vessel when facing the bow because the pilothouse was in the way.[40]

After almost two hours of combat Worden ordered the *Monitor* out of action to replenish ammunition in the turret. Jones took immediate advantage of the lull and moved the *Virginia* toward the *Minnesota*. The Confederate ironclad, leaking at its bow due to the loss of its ram the day before, now ran aground and was unable to deflect its guns to defend itself. The *Virginia* was in serious danger. The *Monitor* approached and, according to Engineer Ramsay, the Union vessel:

> Began to sound every chink in our armor — everyone but that which was actually vulnerable, had she known it. The coal consumption of the two day's fight had lightened our prow until our unprotected submerged deck was almost awash. The armor on our sides below the waterline had been extended but about three feet, owing to our hasty departure before the work was finished. Lightened as we were, these exposed portions rendered us no longer an ironclad, and the *Monitor*

might have pierced us between wind and water had she depressed her gun.[41]

Somehow Ramsay was able to increase the weak engines' steam enough to drag the *Virginia* off the shoal. Jones, frustrated by his ship's ineffectual fire against the Federal ironclad, decided to ram the *Monitor*. The *Virginia* steamed straight at the *Monitor*, yet the more nimble Northern vessel was able to veer away right before the Southern ship struck. The *Monitor* was hit with a glancing blow which, according to Lieutenant Keeler, the "heavy jar nearly throwing us from our feet." The Confederates thought they had seriously damaged the *Monitor,* thinking that they had made the Union ironclad "reel beneath our terrible blow." Jones' order, however, to reverse the engines just before impact had lessened the blow and had caused no damage to the *Monitor.* In fact, the *Virginia* suffered the worse damage. The ramming caused another leak in the ship's bow.[42]

The *Monitor's* evasive action enabled Jones to once again maneuver toward the *Minnesota.* Several shots were sent against the stranded frigate, one of which struck the tug *Dragon.* The *Dragon's* boiler burst and the tug, which had been alongside the *Minnesota* to tow that vessel to safety, sunk.[43]

Worden was able to steer his ship between the Confederate ironclad and the Union frigate. He now decided to ram the *Virginia*, seeking to strike the larger ironclad's propeller to disable her. The *Monitor* missed her target because of a malfunctioning steering system and as the Union ship passed the stern of the *Virginia*, Lieutenant John Taylor Wood fired his seven-inch Brooke pivot gun at the *Monitor's* pilothouse. The shell struck the observation slit as Worden was peering out. The explosion created "a flash of light and a cloud of smoke" which blinded Worden. The *Monitor* veered off onto the shoal as Worden was taken below for treatment.[44]

The *Monitor* appeared out of action as minutes ticked by while Executive Officer Dana Greene made his way from the turret to the pilothouse. The *Minnesota's* commander, Captain Gershon Van Brunt, feared for the worse and began making preparations to scuttle his ship. Jones considered renewing the attack against the *Minnesota*, but the receding tide prompted him to order the *Virginia* back to Sewell's Point. As the *Virginia* steamed away, Greene had finally taken over command in the *Monitor's* pilothouse. Greene, however, did not pursue the Confederate vessel as his orders were merely to protect the *Minnesota*.

A Union soldier, Asher Williams, summed up the dramatic events when he wrote from Camp Butler:

> We had a lively time here three weeks ago. The rebel steamer *Merrimac* with five other gunboats attacked this place. They succeeded in destroying two men of war stationed here and then commenced shelling the camp, nearly all their shells went over the camp doing us no damage. They left us then to seek another of our vessels, but concluded to wait until morning as the *Minnesota* (our vessel) had run aground. Next morning, the *Merrimac* was seen steaming towards the *Minnesota* to annihilate her as she had done the others but how woefully they were mistaken for during the night a box of iron called the *Monitor* had arrived and gave the rebels more than they bargained for after five hours the rebels gave it up. We are momentarily expecting her again. Another rebel gunboat comes down the river every day to see if we are still alive. They will find us ready as soon as they get ready.[45]

Neither ship had been seriously damaged during the four-hour battle and both claimed victory. The *Monitor* had indeed won a tactical victory as the Union ironclad had stopped the *Virginia* from destroying the *Minnesota*. However, the strategic victor was the *Virginia* as its mere existence enabled the Confederates to control Hampton Roads and the entrance to the

James River thereby defending the water approach to Norfolk and Richmond. The Federals feared that the *Virginia* would try to steam out of Hampton Roads and realized that the *Monitor* was the only weapon in her path. Accordingly, Secretary of the Navy Gideon Welles ordered that "the *Monitor* be not too much exposed, and that in no event shall any attempt be made to proceed with her unattended to Norfolk."[46] The Confederate Naval Secretary, Mallory, wanted the *Virginia* to strike against Northern cities. Buchanan wrote Mallory while recovering from his wounds:

> The *Virginia* is yet an experiment, and by no means invulnerable as has already been proven in her conflict on the 8 and 9 . . . The *Virginia* may probably succeed in passing Old Point Comfort and the Rip Raps . '. . she has then to be tested in a seaway . . . Should encounter a gale, or a very heavy swell, I think it more than probable she would founder.[47]

The two ironclads were destined never to fight each other again, even though both sides concocted schemes for capturing their enemy's vessel. The *Virginia* appeared in Hampton Roads again on April 11, having been repaired and fitted with a new ram. Her new commander was the former U. S. Navy forty-eight-year veteran and hero Flag Officer Josiah N. Tattnal. Tattnal hoped to draw the *Monitor* up into Hampton Roads to use his gun boats to board and capture the Union vessel. In turn, the Federal navy had created its own plan of tempting the *Virginia* into the Chesapeake Bay where the Confederate ironclad could be rammed and captured. Although a show of force was repeated several times during the following weeks, neither ship was willing to commit itself to battle.[48]

Chapter 10

Drums Along the Warwick

The events of March 8 and 9 left an indelible mark on the strategic balance of the Peninsula. Even though the first engagement between ironclad vessels broke off in a draw, the check given to the *Virginia* by the *Monitor* relieved the Federals' fears of a broken blockade with Northern cities attacked. The battle, however, had even more immediate implications than being a major turning point in naval warfare, as the undefeated *Virginia* blocked the entrance to James River and closed this approach to Richmond to the Federals. The mere existence of the *Virginia* would have a powerful influence on the campaign that was soon to begin on the Peninsula.

Simultaneously with the Confederate naval victory on March 8, Joe Johnston had abandoned his fortifications around Manassas and retreated to the Rappahannock River.[1] This completely upset McClellan's plans as a Union landing at Urbanna would no longer achieve the same strategic results. The Army of the Potomac made a brave march forward on March 10 and ventured into the Confederate defenses only to discover logs mounted as "Quaker Guns." Once again McClellan suffered an embarrassment, and Lincoln's confidence in his commander-in-chief eroded even further. The next day the President relieved McClellan as commander-in-chief of the Federal armies, but since his troops had finally taken the field, Lincoln retained Little Mac as commander of the Army of the Potomac. Lincoln believed that McClellan held too much responsibility and wanted the general to focus on the Army of the Potomac's drive against Richmond. The President assumed the role of commander-in-chief. McClellan, in turn, was greatly insulted by the political machinations "persecuting a man behind his back," but, nevertheless, mollified by his continuance as Army of the Potomac Commander.[2]

McClellan was committed to an amphibious operation and decided to proceed with his secondary concept: an advance against Richmond by way of the Peninsula. He believed that by using "Fort Monroe as a base" the Army of the Potomac could march against Richmond "with complete security, altho' with less celebrity and brilliancy of results, up the Peninsula."[3] While his corps commanders all agreed to a new concept, there were serious concerns about the Confederate ironclad. The Army of the Potomac's Chief Engineer Brigadier General John G. Barnard believed that the *Virginia* "paralyzes the movement of this army by whatever route is adopted."[4] McClellan sought to allay these fears by contacting General Wool and Assistant Navy Secretary Gustavus Fox to obtain their opinions from Hampton Roads. Fox replied that: "The *Monitor* is more than a match for the *Merrimack*, but she might be disabled in the next encounter . . . The *Monitor* may, and I think will, destroy the *Merrimack* in the next fight; but this is hope, not certainty . . ."[5] Wool concurred with this opinion. He had already received orders on March 9 from McClellan to hold Fort Monroe "at all hazard" against the Confederate ironclad. Wool began work to block the *Virginia's* access into the Chesapeake Bay by mounting a fifteen-inch Rodman gun, nicknamed the "Lincoln Gun," next to the twelve-inch "Union Gun" on the beach in front of the Old Point Lighthouse. Wool was sure that the *Monitor*, supported by these two powerful guns, would effectively close the mouth of Hampton Roads to any sortie by the *Virginia*.[6] Even though the *Virginia* still blocked the James River to his use, McClellan believed that with naval support he could open the York River by overrunning the Confederate positions at Yorktown and Gloucester Point, then on to West Point and Richmond. McClellan advised Lincoln on March 13 that he intended " . . . to take the field immediately upon arriving at Fort Monroe . . . by rapid movements to drive before me, or capture the enemy on the peninsula, open the James River, and push on to Richmond before he could be materially reinforced from other portions of his territory . . ."[7]

Endeavoring to fulfill President Lincoln's March 8 order that McClellan begin his campaign within ten days, on March 17 the Army of the Potomac began its grand movement to the Peninsula. In less than three weeks, 389 vessels delivered to Fort Monroe and Camp Butler 121,500 men, 14,592 animals, 1,224 vehicles, 44 artillery batteries "and the enormous quantity of equipage . . . required for an army of such magnitude."[8] McClellan announced to his men as they prepared to leave their camps around Washington: "The moment for action has arrived, and I know that I can trust in you to save our country . . . I will bring you face to face with the rebels . . . where I know you wish to be, — on the decisive battlefield."[9]

Waiting for this massive force was John Bankhead Magruder's 13,000 strong Army of the Peninsula. Magruder had been aware of the steady build-up of Union troops on the Peninsula since "the glorious achievement of the Confederate states war-steamer *Virginia*."[10] In fact, he had anticipated this circumstance when he reported to Richmond a day after the March 9 engagement that: "Finding, as I anticipated that the naval attack produced no effect upon the fort except to increase its garrison, I contended myself with occupying the most advanced posts, Bethel and Young's Mill where the troops are now."[11] Magruder, nonetheless, kept his soldiers at work improving every aspect of his Peninsula defenses. Lieutenant Robert Miller of the 2nd Louisiana wrote that:

> General Magruder has caused all of the roads to be blockaded between our lines and Newport News, so that it is next thing to an impossibility for anyone to get along much less an army. The state of inactivity we have been in has been very harassing to us but we have spent it profitably and our Reg. has done more work than any two others on the Peninsula.[12]

Confederate engineers also sought ways to enhance Magruder's river flanks. Even though the *Virginia's* mere existence blocked the James River to the Union, "ironclad fever" had spread throughout the command and engineers identified the best method to defend land batteries against the possible advance of the *Monitor* or any other Federal ironclads. Alfred Rives, Acting Chief of the Engineer Bureau, reported:

> The recent conflict at Newport News shows conclusively that water-batteries, especially those near deep water, cannot injure materially properly constructed iron-clad vessels, nor contend with them . . . The only point on the Peninsula where I think casemates of value is Mulberry Island Point. The enemy cannot approach that point nearer than about half a mile, and properly constructed casemates may resist their fire at that distance.[13]

Confederate engineers set forth quickly rebuilding the defenses on Mulberry Island. Mulberry Island Point Battery had five 42-pounders mounted and fourteen casemates were under construction. Bomb-proofs were added to Fort Crafford. Robert E. Lee, now serving as Jefferson Davis' Military Advisor, urged the work forward as Rives wrote to Captain John J. Clarke, the engineer in charge of battery construction at Mulberry Island Point:

> It seems almost needless to urge upon you the vigorous prosecution of the works at Mulberry Point, but I do so at the suggestion of General Lee, who thinks it a matter of paramount importance. I received to-day a telegram from General Magruder to the effect that he had directed you to place the 42 and 68 pounders in barbette in the work surrounding Crafford's house. In this, from the lights before me, I should think the general probably right. The work on the point can then be prosecuted untrammeled by guns in position.
>
> I send you to-day 1,000 sand bags, and you will receive with this letter the first installment of bolts for the casemate battery. I have been trying in vain, so far, to procure wrought-iron protection for the

> embrasures, but think that I have succeeded to-day in making a plan and procuring flat-bar railroad iron from the Richmond and Danville Railroad Company which will be perfectly satisfactory. A tracing will be sent to you to-morrow. I shall write a note this evening to Colonel Gorgas requesting him to send you immediately a 6.4 inch rifle gun, 64-pounder, columbiad pattern, with barbette carriage pintle-block, which is here on hand complete. One casemate carriage will be finished this week and five the next, if promises may be relied on.
>
> General Lee is particularly desirous that all your unmounted guns should be mounted immediately, and in the present state of affairs I do not think you can do better than to mount them all in the covering works around Crafford's house. Of that, however, you will probably be the best judge.[14]

By Mid-March it became obvious that the Federals intended to march up the Peninsula toward Richmond rather than attempt, as the Confederates had supposed, an attack against Norfolk. Wool's command now numbered over 13,000 troops, and on March 14 Magruder reported that the Federals were becoming aggressive pressuring the Confederate pickets on the Warwick Road. Prince John was anxious, and on March 10 he warned Richmond:

> The enemy again drove in the pickets to-day on the Warwick road after exchanging fire. He appears to be operating with a considerable advance guard, supported by heavier bodies, between it and Newport News, so that it is difficult to cut off the advance troops without entangling my handful of men with very superior numbers lying in wait . . . So, if the enemy persevere, I shall be compelled in a very short time to withdraw the regiments which are now in front of the second line, viz, from Yorktown to Mulberry Island.[15]

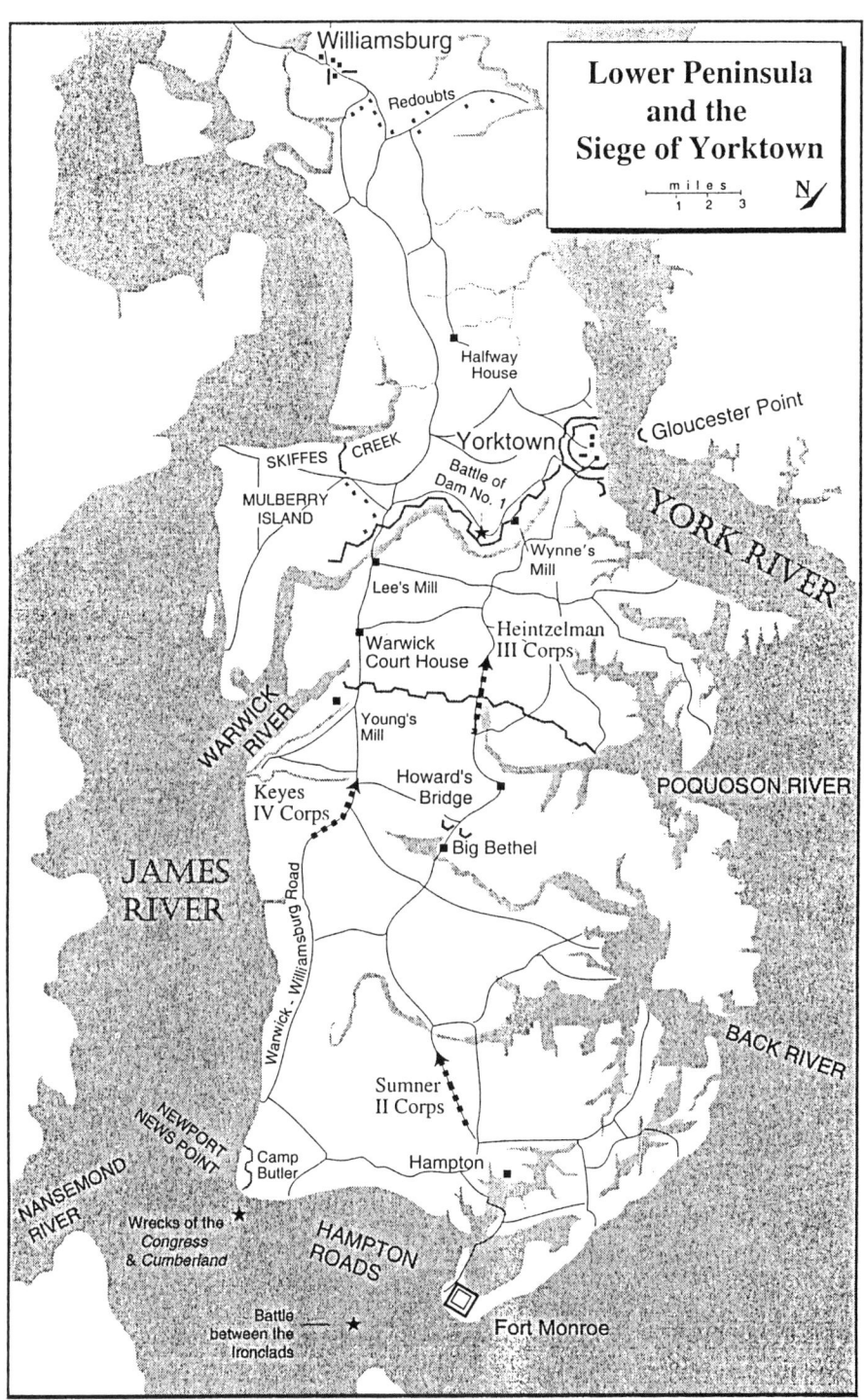

The Army of the Peninsula was now beginning to receive a trickle of reinforcements, however, the additional troops and supplies did not mollify Magruder's belief that his army was in an evergrowing tenuous situation. He once again advised Richmond:

> I have prepared as my real line of defense positions at Harwood's and Young's Mills . . . In my opinion, this advance line . . . might have been held by 20,000 troops . . . Finding my forces too weak to attempt defense of this line, I was compelled to prepare to receive the enemy on a second line, on Warwick River. Keeping then only small bodies of troops at Harwood's and Young's Mills.[16]

Robert E. Lee agreed with Magruder's assessment and advised him:

> A defensive line between Yorktown and Mulberry Island by damming and defending the Warwick River promises the happiest results. I would therefore recommend to you, should you concur in this opinion, to apply as great a force on the work as possible. With your left flank resting on the York River and your right defended by the batteries on James River, with the aid of the *Virginia* and other steamers, I think you may defy the advance of the enemy of the Peninsula, supported as this line would be by your second system of defenses.[17]

Lee later added that the Warwick Line "can be best held as long as your flanks are not turned by the passage of the enemy up either river. If you abandon that line, I know no better position you could assume on the Peninsula."[18]

Magruder complied with Lee's directive, but continued to fret about the growing Union presence. He bombarded Richmond constantly with letters and telegrams for more men and artillery to the extent that Lee chided him for his repetitive requests. Prince

John believed he had little hope of holding Yorktown against the Federal onslaught. His defenses mounted eighty-five heavy guns and fifty-five field pieces, but he had insufficient manpower to hold both his river defenses and the twelve mile line between Mulberry Island and Yorktown. He advised Lee that, "I have made arrangements to fight with my small force, but without the slightest hope of success."[19] While he admitted doubt to Richmond, Prince John did not reveal his fears to his own troops. He issued a patriotic call to repel "the ruthless tyrants," advising his Army of the Peninsula that "these frowning battlements on the heights of York are turned in this second war of liberty against the enemies of our country."[20] On March 28, 1862, Magruder once again wrote his troops: "The enemy is at length advancing. We shall fight him on the line of the Warwick River."[21]

The Army of the Peninsula had made its final arrangements for defending this avenue to Richmond by April 1, 1862. Magruder later reported his defenses to be:

> The Warwick Line, upon which we rested, may be briefly described as follows: Warwick River rises . . . about a mile and a half to the right of Yorktown. Yorktown and Redoubts Nos. 4 and 5, united by long curtains and flanked by rifled pits from the left of the line until . . . it reaches the Warwick River . . . a sluggish and boggy stream, 20 or 30 yards wide . . . running through a dense wood fringed by swamps. Along this river are five dams — one at Wynn's Mill, one at Lee's Mill, and three constructed by myself. The effect of these dams is to back up to the water along the course of the river, so that for nearly three-fourths of its distance its passage is impracticable for either artillery or infantry. Each of these dams is protected by artillery and extensive earthworks for infantry . . .[22]

A majority of Magruder's slender force, now numbering 11,000 men, was positioned along the Warwick. His troop dispositions left 6,000 men holding the garrisons at Gloucester Point, Yorktown and Mulberry Island. The balance of the line was defended by 5,000 men. Troops were, however, arriving from Richmond as reinforcements even before McClellan began his advance. The 9th Alabama arrived at Lebanon Church after a boat trip down from Richmond to King's Wharf. The march to the Warwick Line was difficult as Edmund Dewitt Patterson recounted that it was "a march that beggars description. The night was so dark that it was impossible to see anything . . . The mud and water was literally knee deep . . . Some men fell in mudholes and had to be dragged out . . . ."[23]

Magruder maintained a small advance force at Howard's Bridge and Young's Mill. The Union troops were already making strong reconnaissance up the Peninsula to "ascertain the position and strength of the enemy."[24]

Even though the reconnaissance of Brigadier General William F. "Baldy" Smith's division "gained information that the enemy held Young's Mill in strong force," it was actually only held by two regiments commanded by Brigadier General Lafayette McLaws. Magruder was just beginning his ruse of strength and it was working. "I wish Young's Mill held to the last without fighting for it," Prince John commented, as "I am maneuvering to give the enemy the idea we are in great force."[25]

George McClellan arrived on the Peninsula on April 2, 1862 happy to be free of "that sink of inequity" Washington.[26] His demotion from commander-in-chief to just that of the Army of the Potomac made him now determined to achieve success. Despite the advice of his Chief Engineer John G. Barnard to move against Norfolk first,[27] McClellan decided to march against Yorktown and Gloucester Point and then establish his base at West Point for his attack on Richmond.

McClellan tried to enlist the cooperation of Commodore Louis M. Goldsborough's fleet to quicken the capture of Confederate York River defenses, but the Federal fleet was too

Major General
George B. McClellan
Library of Congress

Brigadier General
Erasmus Darwin Keyes
USAMHI

Brigadier General
Winfield Scott Hancock
National Archives

Brigadier General
Lafayette McLaws
Museum of the Confederacy

occupied with the *Virginia* to mount an expedition against the Gloucester Point batteries. Without naval participation, McClellan still believed he could take Yorktown through a brief siege.[28]

Since the James River was declared by the naval authorities closed to the operations of their vessels by the combined influence of the enemy's batteries on its banks and the Confederate Steamers *Virginia, Yorktown, Jamestown*, and *Teaser*, McClellan resolved to flank the Confederates out of their positions at Yorktown thereby opening the James River with a Southern retreat. McClellan's information, provided by Allan Pinkerton and Major General John E. Wool, indicated that Magruder's force of 15,000 to 20,000 men was at Yorktown, with his right flank unsecured. The Federal commander thought he could interpose his troops across the Confederate line of retreat, trapping "Prince John" at Yorktown like Washington had cornered Cornwallis. Maps provided by General Wool indicated good roads and no water barriers, so McClellan seemed confident of a quick victory on the lower Peninsula. Brigadier General Samuel P. Heintzelman's Third Corps, followed by elements of Brigadier General Edwin Vose Sumner's Second Corps, was to march on the Hampton - York Road through Big Bethel directly to Yorktown so to hold Magruder in his defenses. McClellan believed that Heintzelman's advance would flank the Confederates out of their Young's Mill strong point. The path would then be clear for Brigadier General Erasmus Darwin Keyes' IV Corps to march up the Warwick Road through Warwick Court House to the Half-Way House northwest of Yorktown thereby cutting the Confederate line of retreat.[29]

The Union army began its march on April 4, 1862. Keyes' IV Corps left Newport News Point with Brigadier General Baldy Smith's division, supported by the 5th U. S. Cavalry, in the advance. The Federals brushed aside Confederate pickets at Water's Creek and prepared to encounter the Southern "strong works and . . . force at Young's Mill." When Smith's division reached the mill "the enemy retreated at our approach," Keyes reported, "firing only a few shots."[30] The IV Corps had reached its goal for the first day's march without any bloodshed. Keyes' troops were amazed at the extensive Confederate works at Young's Mill as Private Wilbur Fisk of the 2nd Vermont recalled that "We drove the enemy from a position they had fortified and that night occupied the place ourselves. The rebels left quite a village of huts or barracks, and from appearances, they had enjoyed much more comfortable quarters during the winter than we had ourselves."[31] The IV Corps commander was happy that the Confederates had not made a more resolute stand at Young's Mill, as Keyes reported to General McClellan that, "The enemy's works at Young's Mill are so strong, that with 5,000 men he might have stopped my two divisions there a week . . ."[32] The Confederate works at Young's Mill were very extensive, as Lieutenant Charles Harvey Brewster of the 10th Massachusetts Volunteers wrote:

> The road went down in a sort of ravine, and right across from the dam on one side to the bank on the other was a line of logs about 4 inches in diameter and firmly planted in the ground close together and at about 10 feet height cut off and sharpened to a point. Where the road went through there was a strong gate, right behind this a high bank, crowned by a fort with embrasures for two guns. There every knoll was crowned by a breastwork for rifle men and stretching away as far as we could see were breastworks with embrasures for cannon, and behind these were the Barracks, enough to contain 4 or 5,000 soldiers.[33]

It was the same story at Big Bethel on the York-Hampton Road. Heintzelman's III Corps had taken the lead from Hampton marching toward Yorktown. The troops had expected a strong defense at the scene of the Union defeat the year before, but instead of a "line of fire run along their breastworks . . . Not a sound came from them and not a man could we see," recounted Private Oliver W. Norton of the 83rd Pennsylvania Infantry. "We came up to the front and our color guard leaped the ditch and planted the flag of the Eighty-third on the fortifications so long disgraced by the rebel rag. Great Bethel was ours and not a man hurt."[34]

Magruder's first defensive line impressed all the Federal soldiers, yet they were vacant. Consequently, the Union army had made good progress on April 4, and from Young's Mill, Keyes expected to be able to reach the Half-Way House on the morrow.

The IV Corps began its march at 6:00 a.m. on April 5. Smith's division once again led the march. At 7:00 a.m., it began to rain, "pouring in torrents, rendering the roads well-nigh impassable," which slowed the troops' progress. Then, around 11:00 a.m., the march was stopped by a large force of Confederates occupying a strong position at the Lee's Mill crossing of the Warwick River. Neither Lee's Mill, the Warwick River's course across the Peninsula, or the Confederate fortifications were noted on the maps available to the Union command. The Federals were shocked by the "very serious resistance they encountered at Lee's Mill. Flames appeared on all sides," reported Baldy Smith as his men approached the river. He was forced to advise Keyes that "we shall not be able to reach the Half-Way House on the Yorktown - Williamsburg Road today . . ."[35]

The crossing at Lee's Mill was held by approximately 1,800 Confederates, including Colonel Alfred Cumming's 10th Georgia and several batteries, under the overall command of Brigadier General Lafayette McLaws. Lee's Mill was considered a "naturally strong position" by Magruder's Chief of Artillery Colonel H. C. Cabell. All the approaches to this mill dam crossing were covered by redoubts constructed along the mill pond or overlooking the Warwick as it "follows a tortuous course through salt marshes . . . from which the land rises up boldly to a height of 30 or 40 feet." Redoubts dotted the frontlines at Lee's Mill, which were manned by several batteries including local artillerists serving in Captain Joseph B. Cosnahan's company of the 1st Peninsula Artillery.[36] Manning one of Cosnahan's guns at Lee's Mill was former

Warwick County Clerk of the Court 1st Lieutenant William B. Jones. Jones' cannon fire helped to repulse the initial Union assault. Agitated by continued Federal counterbattery fire, Jones returned fire so hot that the Northern battery quickly retreated out of range. His spirited leadership at Lee's Mill reportedly earned him the nickname of "Hell Cat Billy" and promotion to Colonel Cabell's adjutant.[37]

Faced by such determined resistance that magnified the strength of the Confederate defenses, Keyes realized that his flanking movement to trap Magruder at Yorktown was stymied. He wrote McClellan from his headquarters at Warwick Court House that, "Magruder is in a strongly fortified position behind the Warwick River, the fords to which have been destroyed by dams, and the approaches to which are through dense forests, swamps and marshes. No part of this line as discovered can be taken without an enormous waste of life."[38]

Federal Chief Engineer Brigadier General John G. Barnard concurred with Keyes' assessment and remarked that "the line is certainly one of the most extensive known to modern times." Lee's Mill, noted McClellan, was "incapable of being carried by assault."[39] The brief engagement at Lee's Mill cost the Confederates ten casualties, but it had far reaching implications. Halted before the unexpected array of enemy entrenchment, McClellan resolved to deploy the 103 heavy guns he had brought to the Peninsula and lay siege to Magruder's defenses.

McClellan's hesitation at the Warwick River set the stage for a carefully organized Confederate ruse. Magruder began shuttling his soldiers to and fro to create the illusion of many troops arriving on his line and moving into positions of great strength. Private Edmund Dewitt Patterson of the 9th Alabama wrote that he and his fellow Confederate soldiers "have been traveling most of the day . . . with no other view than to show ourselves to the enemy, at as many different points of the line as possible."[40] Magruder earned the title of the "Master of Ruses and Strategy" for his make-believe show of strength, constantly as Corporal J. W. Minnish wrote, "Bringing in regiments from less exposed positions on the line, marched them in a circle, as it were, all day emerging from the woods on one part of the line, into the wood below, then on a "Double quick" behind the hill and woods to appear again as fresh troops arriving."[41] "It was a wonderful thing," recorded diarist Mary Chesnut, "how he played his ten thousand before McClellan like fireflies and utterly deluded him . . ."[42]

Despite outnumbering Magruder almost four to one, McClellan soon became convinced that he faced more than 100,000 Confederates. McClellan just could not rationalize that any smaller force would dare defend such a 12-mile front. April 5 was simply a bad day for McClellan. Not only were his plans for a rapid movement past Yorktown ruined by the unexpected Confederate defenses at Lee's Mill, but also by Lincoln's decision not to release Irwin McDowell's I Corps to his use in a flanking movement against the Southern batteries at Gloucester on the York River. The U. S. Navy, too, refused to attempt any offensive action in either the James or York rivers because of the C.S.S. *Virginia*. Since neither the Navy nor Lincoln would provide him with the support necessary to assault Gloucester Point thereby uncovering the Confederate defenses, McClellan believed he had no other alternative but siege warfare.[43]

April 6 was a day of reconnaissance. Thaddeus Lowe's balloon, "Intrepid," made its first appearance over the Confederate lines. Many Federal officers wanted to know what was behind Magruder's brave front of frowning forts. Union field artillery was brought into position and opened fire on the enemy's position at Lee's Mill, then limbered and moved to another nearby field to repeat the action. Confederate counter-fire often forced the Federals to find cover, which would prompt loud cheers from the Southerners.[44] Infantry units skirmished up and down the line simply to draw a response, "while engineers and scouts observed and reported," Lieutenant Edgar N. Newcomb of the 19th Massachusetts wrote his sister.[45] Private Patrick Lyons of the 2nd Rhode Island recorded in his diary that "all the action was only to gain the feel of the enemy and find out what force they had here, not to bring on an engagement."[46] Baldy Smith, however, believed the line to be weaker than what met the eye. He ordered Brigadier General Winfield Scott Hancock to investigate the Warwick between Lee's Mill and Dam No. 1. As Hancock began to initiate his reconnaissance in force, McClellan ordered that no advances were to be made against the enemy until engineers had thoroughly studied the Confederate line. The attack, which Smith believed was a sure success, was called off.[47] McClellan decided to ignore this possible avenue of attack almost simultaneously with his receipt of Lincoln's telegram urging him to "break the enemies' lines from York-town to Warwick River at once. They will probably use time, as advantageously as you can."[48] "Little Mac" paid little attention to Lincoln's advice, writing his wife, "I was much tempted to reply that he had better come and do it himself."[49] McClellan was committed to a siege and determined to avoid "the faults of the Allies at Sebastopol and quietly preparing the way for a great success."[50]

Chapter 11

Burnt Chimneys

Magruder was amazed by the Union response to his bold, yet weak, defensive line and once again became a hero of the Southland. "The assuming and maintaining the line by Magruder, with his small force in the face of such overwhelming odds," wrote Brigadier General Jubal A. Early, "was one of the boldest exploits ever performed by a military commander . . ."[1] Prince John, however, soon realized why McClellan hesitated to attack. He wrote Richmond that McClellan, "to my utter surprise . . . permitted day after day to elapse without an assault. In a few days the object of his delay was apparent. In every direction; in front of our lines; the intervening woods, and along the open fields, earthworks began to appear . . ."[2]

Once his engineers conducted their surveys of the Confederate defenses, McClellan decided to concentrate his siege engineering on Yorktown. His plan was to assault the Confederate works in the vicinity of the historic town once his heavy artillery had breached them. "Little Mac" laid out fifteen batteries for the heavy 8- and 13-inch seacoast mortars and enormous 100- and 200-pounder Parrott guns as well as 20- and 30-pounder Parrott and 4.5 inch Rodman siege rifles he had brought to the Peninsula.[3] His men were now put to work under constant fire from the Confederate lines building the roads, rifle pits, and gun emplacements necessary to eventually pound the Confederates into submission. Thomas B. Leaver of New Hampshire wrote that, "It seems the fight has to be won partially through the implements of peace, the shovel, axe and pick."[4] Other soldiers commented about the difficult work noting the unusual sight of thousands of men at work in the darkness, "like a train of busy ants . . . shoveling away with now and then a shell bursting near," as Gilbert Thompson recorded in his diary.[5]

Across the Warwick River from Mulberry Island, Brigadier

General John J. Peck had his men busy constructing rifle pits and batteries. Their work, however, was often disrupted by "the enemy's vessels," Peck noted, as the Southern gunboats "could control the navigation and reach our lines with heavy guns." Peck requested heavy artillery, "a small number (say two) of 8-inch howitzers and two 8-inch mortars," to contest Confederate control of the mouth of the Warwick. He asked McClellan, "Would not possession of the island enable the commanding general to control in a considerable degree the James River in case the Navy fails to do the work?" McClellan replied to Peck's superior, General Keyes, with the terse comment, "I think more heavy artillery necessary to make much impression on Mulberry Island than General Peck specifies." The Union commander seemed willing to ignore opportunities along the Warwick and focused on the completion of his siege lines.[6]

Observing all the immense labor by their Northern counterparts, Confederate soldiers expected an assault at any time. Surgeon James Montgomery Holloway of the 18th Mississippi wondered, "Why they do not attack us is strange for they have a heavy force and every day's delay only gives us the opportunity to strengthen our defenses."[7] Magruder countered as "His men and a considerable body of Negro laborers had been and were still engaged in strengthening the works by working night and day, " Jubal Early later wrote, "so that their energies were taxed to the utmost limit."[8] Yet, Prince John carried off his charade of a powerful army and buoyed his troops' morale in the grand fashion that only he could exhibit. "When Magruder's cavalcade at a full gallop inspected the thin lines of the Warwick, it was a sight for men and gods," Moxley Sorrel wrote. "Of commanding form and loving display, he had assembled a numerous staff, all, like himself, in the most showy uniforms."[9] Magruder was indeed the very heart and soul of the thin, brave front along the Warwick River.

Magruder even became so bold as to launch sorties across the Warwick against the Union pickets. Cadmus Wilcox on April 11 sent out a strike force from Wynne's Mill that drove the enemy skirmishers back from the river's edge into their entrenchment.[10]

The Confederates at Dam No. 1 would often cross the river at night to establish picket posts on the Union side of the dam. Confederate W. H. Andrews remembered wading through the cold water along the dam on the evening of April 15 and reaching close enough to the Union pickets "to hear them whisper." After spending the night in the mud on the river bank, Andrews recrossed the river just before dawn. When he and his compatriots reached the Confederate earthworks and apparent safety, "the alarm was given." Andrews recounted:

> The soldiers to a man, sprung to their feet. Their guns flashed over the works, and for the time being, I thought that I was a dead man. But just in time to save us, someone spoke. The guns were withdrawn from over the works and we ascended safe, but badly scared. It certainly was a close call, and one I don't wish to go through with again.[11]

The Confederate Navy continued to harass McClellan and disrupt his desire to move up the York River towards Richmond. On the morning of April 11 the *Virginia* once again steamed into Hampton Roads accompanied by several gunboats. The Federal fleet scattered out of the harbor into the Chesapeake Bay while Fort Wool fired two shots at the *Virginia*, both of which fell short. The *Virginia* then moved into the center of the roadstead, occasionally trading fire with the Union forces. The Federals, unfortunately for them, focused all their attention on the Confederate ironclad which enabled the *Jamestown* and *Raleigh* to slip across Hampton Roads to Newport News Point. There the two Southern steamers were able to capture three Union transports. The Confederate fleet, confident that its show of force had let the Union command realize that Hampton Roads was under its control, steamed back to Craney Island by late afternoon.[12]

The Army of the Potomac seemed destined to have to

force its way through the Confederate fortifications without naval support. The army was indeed ready to try. The Northern divisional commanders and their soldiers all sought an opportunity to break the siege and assault what they considered to be a weak Confederate line along the Warwick. The Federals finally did launch one attack on April 16 at Dam No. 1, the midpoint of Magruder's line. This failed Union assault, also referred to as Burnt Chimneys or incorrectly called Lee's Mill, was a baptism of fire for many soldiers, like Vermonter Private Wilbur Fisk, who would remember it as a short, vicious fight along "a creek with a wide dam, which drank the blood of many of our men."[13]

      Union and Confederate troops had been facing each other across the Warwick at Dam No. 1 since the siege's beginning. The dam was one of three built by Magruder to turn the sluggish stream into a defensive asset. It was located between two pre-war tide mills, Lee's Mill and Wynne's Mill. According to Sergeant W. H. Andrews of the 1st Georgia Regulars, the dam had turned the meandering Warwick from twelve to fifteen feet in width to seventy-five or one hundred yards across. The position had been strengthened by a front line of rifle pits near the river's edge backed by two lines of deeper trenches. The first line contained several strong redoubts for artillery and the second was for the protection of unengaged infantry. The entire position mounted three guns. The dam itself, built at Garrow's Ford, was defended by a one-gun redoubt "occupied by a 12-pounder Napoleon double charged with canister," Sergeant Andrews recorded.[14] This gun was under the command of Captain Jordan. Two other guns, a brass 6-pounder commanded by Lieutenant Alexander Franklin Pope and a brass 12-pounder howitzer commanded by Lieutenant Edward Lumpkin from the Troup Artillery, were positioned in earthworks behind and to the right of the dam. Trees were felled to facilitate Confederate field of fire. The limbs had been thrown into the Warwick River as obstacles to make any attempted river crossing that much more difficult. Unfortunately, the redoubts had been poorly designed, thus the two supporting guns of the Troup Artillery were positioned too low to effectively shell the Union positions across the river.[15]

The Union and Confederate artillery at Dam No. 1 would often exchange salvos. Private Henry Berkley of the Hanover Artillery who was stationed in one of the redoubts defending the dam noted that each day his battery would commence "firing occasionally at the Yanks . . ."[16] Sergeant Andrews remembered a Federal shell bursting nearby while he and two fellow soldiers were resting against stumps behind the frontline at Dam No. 1. All three were hit with shrapnel; Andrews was wounded slightly in his knee, but his two friends were killed instantly. Andrews would never forget Private Boyle and the contrast between his dead countenance and the ambrotype of a smiling young woman in his pocket. "But such is life and such is war," Andrews reflected.[17]

Dam No. 1 was a dangerous, exposed position which the Confederates continued to strengthen despite the intermittent rifle and artillery fire. "There are about a thousand and one Negroes at work fortifying this place," wrote Private Edmund Dewitt Patterson when holding the rifle pits along the shore. "The Yanks are in plain view, and make us quite careful about having our heads exposed above the breastworks."[18] Some Federal soldiers observed the black slaves working on the Confederate fortifications and believed the Southerners were organizing them into regiments. Lieutenant Charles Harvey Brewster thought "that lots of the enemy's Pickets are negroes probably the chivalry do not like to expose themselves to such dangerous business."[19]

Many Union officers believed the Confederate line could be broken at several weak points along the Warwick River, but McClellan was determined to wait until all his heavy artillery was in place before bombarding Yorktown and only then launching a concerted assault. The outnumbered Southern soldiers' expected attack finally came on April 16. Since the siege's first day, Baldy Smith had wanted to attack the Confederate line, but McClellan had rejected the thought of any such move, telegraphing Lincoln on April 7: "The Warwick River grows worse the more you look at it."[20] On April 15 McClellan reviewed Smith's position at Garrow's Field across from Dam No. 1. The place had been named by the Vermont troops holding the position as Burnt Chimneys for the three stark chimneys that defined the site as the only remaining remnant of the Garrow family farm.[21] The house, Merry Oaks, had been burned by the Confederates (although many Southerners incorrectly blamed the Federals) just before the Union troops approached the Warwick River. The Garrow family had already suffered an even greater loss a few months before when John Toomer Garrow, a private in the Warwick Beauregards, had contracted "camp fever" at Wynne's Mill and died in November 1861.[22] Merry Oaks' charred remnants appeared to be, according to Confederate artillerist Henry Berkley, as "a useless . . . destruction of private property . . . but such is war."[23]

McClellan, having observed the continued Confederate defensive preparations, decided to allow Smith's troops to move against the Confederate works at Dam No. 1. He wanted Smith to disrupt the Confederate efforts to strengthen their earthworks, silence their batteries and gain control of the dam. As McClellan left Garrow's Field the evening before the attack, he rode among his troops telling them, "Goodnight my lads; we will find out what is in front of us and then go at them."[24]

Smith received confirmation of McClellan's intentions at dawn and immediately Brigadier General W. T. H. Brooks' Vermont Brigade began to deploy toward the river. About 8:00 a.m. on the 16th, under cover of artillery fire provided by Captain Thaddeus P. Mott's 3rd New York Battery, Colonel Brad N. Hyde's 3rd Vermont and Colonel Edwin H. Stoughton's 4th Vermont moved through the woods on both sides of the dam. All six companies of the 3rd Vermont and Companies B and G of the 4th Vermont deployed as skirmishers on the river's edge.

The Confederates were taken somewhat by the "fire of shell upon us," Colonel Levy of the 2nd Louisiana later reported.[25] The six guns of Mott's Battery dueled with the three Confederate guns positioned near the dam. Confederate rifle fire slackened, but their artillery counterfire proved effective. The first shell fired by the Confederates disabled one of Mott's guns, killing three gunners and wounding several more.[26] The 12-pounder in the redoubt defending the dam had been disabled and replaced by a 6-pounder from the Troup Artillery under the command of Lieutenant Pope. The old artillerist, Magruder praised Lieutenant Pope's handling of his gun which "was served with the greatest accuracy and effect and by the coolness and skill with which it was handled the greatest odds against us were almost completely counter balanced."[27] Yet, the Union cannon fire soon began to have a telling effect on their Confederate counterparts. After three hours of artillery and rifle fire, the Southerners appeared to have abandoned their one-gun battery.[28]

Now Smith began a personal reconnaissance of the Confederate positions. The Union artillery fire and Vermont skirmishers were successful in halting work on the Southern entrenchments and had silenced their battery, achieving McClellan's initial goal for this action. Smith reported "that the gun in the angle of the upper work had been replaced by a wooden gun, and that scarcely anybody showed above the parapet, the skirmishers from the 4th Vermont doing good execution."[29] Lieutenant E. M. Noyes, aide to General Brooks, then crossed the waist-deep river below the dam and approached within fifty yards of the Confederate works undiscovered.[30] The Federals realized that the Southern position at Dam No. 1 was extremely weak and could perhaps be carried with an assault.

McClellan arrived on the scene at noon, accompanied by his royal French aides, the Prince de Joinville and the Comte de Paris. Upon hearing Noyes' report and grasping the possibility of carrying the Confederate works thereby splitting the Warwick Line in two, he ordered Baldy Smith to bring up his entire division. McClellan qualified the command by advising Smith to avoid a general engagement if serious resistance was encountered.[31]

Smith reinforced his position with Captain Romeryn B. Ayres' Battery F, 5th U. S. Artillery, and Captain Charles C. Wheeler's Battery E, 1st New York, and planned to use units from the 3rd Vermont Regiment to test the Confederate positions across the river. If the Vermonters were successful in driving the enemy out of their rifle pits, they were to cheer and wave a white handkerchief and more troops would be sent across the Warwick. Smith also ordered the rest of his division, two brigades under the command of Winfield Scott Hancock and John W. Davidson, to be ready to exploit any success achieved by the Vermonters.

Following an apparently effective Federal cannonade, Smith sent four companies of the 3rd Vermont across the river to capture the Confederate rifle pits below the dam. These men were under the command of Captain Fernando C. Harrington. They crossed the Warwick under heavy fire and captured the enemy's position along the water's edge. It had been a difficult passage. The Vermonters had to carry their muskets and cartridge boxes over their heads while contending with a muddy, root-filled river bottom and trees felled by the Southrons to serve as obstacles. Eventually, most of the 192 men who entered the shoulder-deep water — the wounded being dragged by coat, collar or arm — made it to the other side and gave a great cheer as they chased the Southerners out of their entrenchments.[32]

Surprised by the Vermonter's bold rush and confused by an unauthorized order, the 15th North Carolina fell back in a panic that one Vermonter, Erastus Buck, thought made them "look like a flock of sheep."[33] It was the North Carolinians' first day in the trenches at Dam No. 1, having just returned to Magruder's command after brief duty near Goldsboro, North Carolina, and it was their first engagement. The Carolinians fell back behind a redoubt where the 15th's commander, Lieutenant Colonel William McKinney, tried to rally and reform his men. McKinney was killed instantly by a ball through the forehead as he readied his men for a counterattack.[34] The 15th then huddled behind a redoubt and the entire Confederate line at Dam No. 1 was in disarray.

The Green Mountain Boys, however, were also in a dangerous position. Most of their ammunition was wet and useless. Expected reinforcements never materialized. Captain

Captain Alonzo Hutchinson
3rd Vermont
Vermont Historical Society

Private William Scott
3rd Vermont
Vermont Historical Society

Musician Julian Scott
3rd Vermont
Vermont Historical Society

Captain Samuel E. Pingree
3rd Vermont
Vermont Historical Society

Alonzo Hutchinson, who had been entrusted with Brooks' handkerchief to give the signal for reinforcements, lay mortally wounded on the banks of the Warwick. At this moment, Baldy Smith had taken his second fall from his horse and was somewhat senseless. Leadership among the Vermonters had fallen on the shoulders of Captain Samuel E. Pingree of Company F, as Harrington seemed to have faded away from action. Pingree, however, was seriously wounded, his thumb shot off and bleeding profusely from a wound in his hip.[35]

Meanwhile, the Confederate lines were stirring like a hornet's nest. Brigadier General Howell Cobb, a former governor of Georgia and commander of Cobb's Legion, reinforced the 15th North Carolina with the 7th, 8th, 11th, and 16th Georgia Regiments and the 2nd Louisiana. Cobb reorganized the Confederate troops, "riding in among the men," according to Lafayette McLaws, and "they recognized his voice and his person, and promptly retook their positions."[36] The 7th Georgia led the Confederate counterattack amidst "the greatest applause and hollering,"[37] Georgian Eli Pinson Landers recounted to his mother after the battle. The Vermonters, however, were slow to give up their toe hold on the Confederate side of the Warwick despite the mounting pressure from Cobb's troops and regiments commanded by Colonel George Thomas "Tige" Anderson.. An order was given to retreat back across the river and was organized by Lieutenant Robert D. Whittemore of Company E since Pingree was faint from loss of blood. Some soldiers did not hear the command and were slow to respond. Others, like Erastus Buck, felt that "a retreat was almost sure destruction" and attempted "to make the last and desperate charge."[38] These few men could not stem the Confederate tide. All the Vermonters now reluctantly withdrew across the Warwick. Regaining their rifle pits, the resurgent Rebels continued their fire and, according to Lieutenant Buck, made the water "boil with their bullets."[39]

The Union troops had held the Confederate trenches for almost forty minutes and suffered a majority of their casualties while recrossing the "fatal stream." Musician Julian Scott

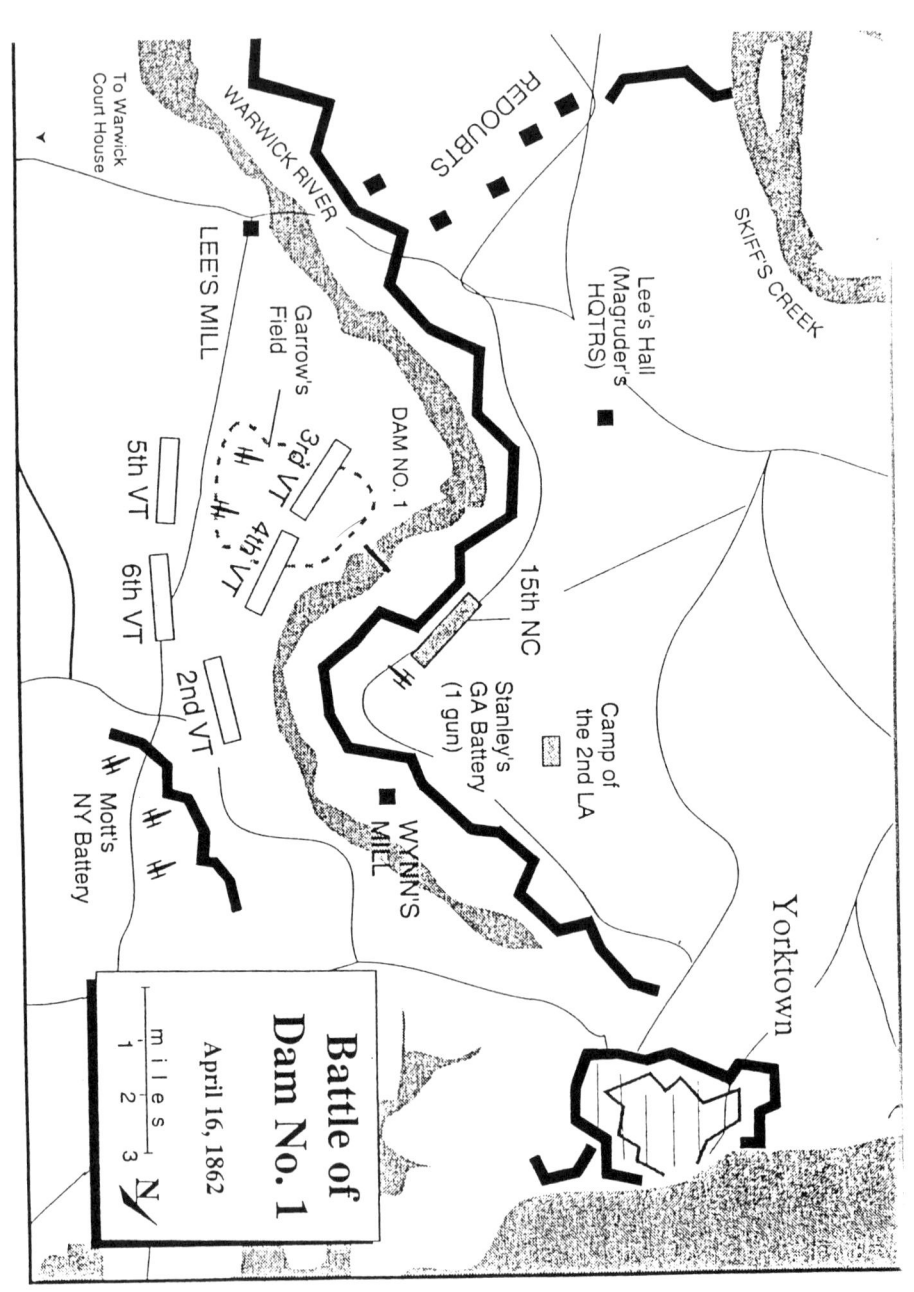

described the gunfire to a New York Tribune reporter as being "just like sap-boiling, in the stream, the bullets fell so thick."[40] it had been a vicious little fight, as Private Landers of Cobb's Legion described "the Truth" about the Confederate counter-attack:

> We did not have time to organize our regiment. We all run in and shot when we had the chance and never formed no line. If a man could get behind a tree it was alright. Some of the boys never fired a gun. Some lay behind logs as close to the ground as young rabbits till the battle was over. One or two of our company run back to camp but as for my part I thought I would stay till the fun was over . . . It did not frighten me as bad as I expected it would but I tell you when the bullets would whistle around my head I felt sort of ticklish.[41]

Brigadier General Lafayette McLaws quickly brought his entire division into the vicinity of Dam No. 1 to halt any possible breakthrough. Baldy Smith, now back on his horse and apparently lucid, decided to try the Confederate lines once again with another piecemeal attack. At 5:00 p.m., following a Federal cannonade from twenty-two guns, Smith sent units from Stoughton's 4th Vermont to cross above the dam to capture the one-gun battery and troops from Lord's 6th Vermont below the dam to recapture the Confederate rifle pits. Neither attack was successful due to heavy fire from the Confederate entrenchments.[42] By dark, the Battle of Dam No. 1 was over, with 165 Federal and 145 Confederate casualties.

The attack against Dam No. 1, the weakest section of the Confederate defenses, failed because the Federals were unwilling to rapidly commit additional troops to support the Vermonter's initial assault. General Smith reflected after the battle that among the men of the 3rd Vermont who crossed the river, there were "more individual acts of heroism performed than he had ever heard of."[43] The Confederates even referred to the Vermonters as "brave rascals." Two Medals of Honor would be awarded for gallantry on April 16. Captain Samuel E. Pingree, later governor of Vermont, received his in 1891 for bravery during the engagement. The other was presented to Julian Scott in February 1865. The sixteen-year old Scott crossed the river at least two times following the first assault saving "no less than nine of his comrades." One of these men was the mortally wounded Private William Scott. Scott was known as the "sleeping sentinel" and had been pardoned by President Lincoln in late 1861 from a firing squad. His reprieve had led him to say, "I will show President Lincoln that I am not afraid to die for my country."[44] Scott fulfilled his pledge at Dam No. 1. The battle was the Vermont Brigade's first engagement and the Vermonters' conduct was "worthy of veterans," McClellan later noted in his report about the engagement. Corporal George Q. French wrote his friends at home about the battle: "The 3rd Vermont has won a name, but Oh! at what a cost."[45]

There were also numerous recriminations after the battle as many thought, like Corporal French, that "a glorious victory might have been gained."[46] Harrington was accused of not providing effective leadership (some soldiers said that he never crossed the Warwick) and was later discharged by "special order of the War Department" on July 23, 1862. The blame for the failure to break Magruder's line at Dam No. 1 fell on Baldy Smith, who some accused of being drunk on the battlefield. His two falls off his horse did not strengthen his case, but he was later exonerated.[47] Others blamed no one but simply declared the attack a "Dam failure."[48] Smith concluded that the attack was not pressed because of McClellan's orders not to bring on a major engagement, stating "Thus a fair opportunity to break the Warwick line was missed . . ."[49]

Chapter 12

Siege

Confederate artillerist Corporal J. W. Minnish called the Union attack at Dam No. 1 simply "ten days too late."[1] McClellan, however, wrote Secretary of War Edwin Stanton that his army had made good progress on April 16 along the Warwick, to which Stanton replied: "Good for the first lick! Hurrah for Smith and the one-gun battery. Let us have Yorktown with Magruder and his gang before the first May and the job will be over."[2]

McClellan had no intention of pressing forward despite Stanton's urging and quickly dismissed the engagement from his mind. He reinforced the York River with the ironclad USS *Galena* and concentrated on building emplacements for his heavy guns and parallel trenches necessary for his grand bombardment that would force the Confederate evacuation of the Warwick - Yorktown Line.

The siege was to last another two weeks. While McClellan worked on his preparations, General Joseph E. Johnston continued reinforcing Magruder's army. He finally came to the Peninsula in the second week of April to take command of the combined force which would eventually number 56,000 men. Even though he lauded Magruder's "delaying tactics,"[3] he was dismayed by what he found on the Peninsula. After he inspected Magruder's defenses on April 12, Johnston returned to Richmond and advised President Davis that he could not hold the Warwick - Yorktown Line. "Labor enough has been expended here to make a very strong position," the commanding general wrote, "but it has been wretchedly misapplied by the young engineer officers. No one but McClellan could have hesitated to attack. The fight for Yorktown must be one of artillery, in which we cannot win. The result is certain; the time only doubtful."[4]

Robert E. Lee and Secretary of War George W. Randolph

(who had fought at Big Bethel) counseled that the Warwick - Yorktown Line should be held as long as possible because a retreat from the Peninsula would mean the loss of Norfolk. With Norfolk gone, the C.S.S. *Virginia* would be without a port, and her crew would have to destroy her, thereby opening the James River to the Federal Navy. Davis ordered Johnston to hold the line on the Peninsula.[5] Johnston believed the capital should be defended on the outskirts of Richmond and never intended to totally comply with President Davis' command to hold the Warwick - Yorktown Line. He later wrote, "The belief that events on the Peninsula would soon compel the Confederate government to adopt my method of opposing the Federal army, reconciled me somewhat to the necessity of obeying the President's order."[6]

The siege dragged on despite Johnston's protestations and with it the soldiers suffered from exposure and enemy fire. Lieutenant Robert H. Miller of the Concordia Rifles wrote his mother from Wynne's Mill that he and his men "have dug Rifle pits and are compelled to eat-sleep and stand in them from day to night and from night to day."[7] The soldiers continually complained about standing or sitting in trenches "with water up to our knees," as Sergeant W. H. Andrews of the 1st Georgia Regulars remembered of his service at Dam No. 1.[8] A member of the Richmond Howitzers, Richard Channing Price, thought he had "gotten along very well without my boots, though I should have liked to have them in this wet weather."[9] "During the month of April," Jubal Early later wrote, "there was much cold, rainy weather, and our troops suffered greatly, as they were without tents or other shelter."[10] Private Patterson could only agree when he wrote in his diary that there was "rain and mud in abundance, and the only articles, except sickness that we have a sufficiency of . . . "[11]

"In addition to all this," Jubal Early commented later about the soldiers' living conditions along the Warwick, "their rations were very limited and consisted of the plainest and roughest food . . . All this told terribly on the health of the men, and there was little or no hospital accommodations in the rear."[12] James B. Griffin of Hampton's Legion agreed with Early's assessment as he wrote his wife: "The living here is pretty tight. We get nothing but bread and meat, and occasionally coffee — Mostly Sassafras Tea. Butter and milk is unknown."[13] Food, or the lack thereof, was a problem for both armies. McClellan's army required tons of supplies each day which caused the Union soldiers to forage the countryside to augment their meager Army rations. Pennsylvanian Oliver W. Norton justified such appropriations because any food found on a local farm "is nothing else but secesh, and when Uncle Sam can't furnish food, I see nothing wrong in requiring it of our enemies."[14] Lieutenant Charles Brewster of the 10th Massachusetts wrote his mother, "The inhabitants here have fled leaving everything and the woods are full of cattle, horses and hogs. Our boys have been bringing in quarters of beef all day long. They build up a fire, hang up the beef on a stake and soon are revelling in roast beef, or beef steaks, or Pork or mutton."[15] Such feasts were savored by the soldiers and not uncommon. Often the soldiers sought refuge in a good meal once they were relieved from the frontline duty. Alabamian Edmund Dewitt Patterson wrote:

> Our mess were gathered around a camp kettle filled with "peasoup" up in one of the cabins that had been built by the 2nd Fla. for winter quarters — each with a spoon, and all eating out of the kettle and enjoying it hugely — when all at once a shell burst over our house, and we thought perhaps that there was going to be a general attack, but heard nothing more for about half a minute. Then a shell came through our little cabin, cutting a log out of each side of it, passing over our heads, and ruining our soup with mud and splinters. It was just as well that it did for we all lost our appetites . . . [16]

The food and weather may have been generally miserable, but the soldiers had an even greater fear of the daily and intermittent, yet constant, rifle and cannon fire. "There is more or less skirmishing every day between the Pickets," South Carolinian James Griffin wrote. "Occasionally a man is struck but not often."[17]

It was still dangerous work as Sergeant Andrews noted that "it was worth a man's life to show his head above the works."[18] New Jersey Private Alfred Bellard observed one soldier "more venturesome than the rest, mounted the magazine [sic] of the fort in plain sight of the rebels. In a moment the shells were flying around lively."[19] "Many a poor Yankee has fallen in view of us," wrote Confederate Robert E. Lewis with glee at Lee's Mill. "How the devils squall when they are shot and how strange it may seem I rejoiced at it. The whiz of shells and bullets sound as natural as the bark of a dog."[20] One night members of Birney's Zouaves were on picket duty at Lee's Mill when unit members watched a Confederate officer swinging a lantern walk down to the river. When Private John McGraw prepared to shoot him, another soldier, Williams Albertson, grasped his rifle saying, "Don't fire, Jack; it looks like murder to shoot him."[21]

The Union army deployed companies from Berdan's Sharpshooters at various locations up and down the twelve-mile line. These sharpshooters, according to Private Bellard, "were always on the look out for game, and woe to the rebel who put himself in their way."[22] "These sharpshooters are the greatest terror to the enemy," wrote Charles Brewster, "and well they may be for no sooner does one of them Rebels show himself then plunk goes a bullet into his body, and he is done from secession for this world."[23] At Garrow's Chimneys (Dam No. 1) George Armstrong Custer wrote that he supervised the construction of a rifle pit for Berdan's men that was close enough to the Confederate lines that "the voices of the enemy could be distinctly heard while engaged in ordinary conversation" and from which the "sharpshooters took particular delight . . . as it afforded them a fine opportunity to exercise their peculiar accomplishment."[24] Either hidden in rifle pits or concealed in tree top positions, the sharpshooters added a fierceness to the siege, as Confederate artillerist Major Robert Stiles wrote: "The Federal sharpshooters were as audacious and deadly as I ever saw them." Stiles considered them "a fearful thing. The regular sharpshooter often seems to me little better than a human tiger lying in wait for blood."[25]

It was difficult for the Confederates to respond to this Union marksmanship as Jubal Early commented, "Our whole armament for the infantry consisted of smooth-bore muskets, and our artillery ammunition was too scarce to permit its use in a contest with sharpshooters." The lines were so close and the rifle fire so deadly at Dam No. 1 and Wynne's Mill that "it had been necessary to cut zig-zag trenches, or bayous, to enable the men to pass into and from the works with as little exposure as possible," Early added.[26] "It was as much as a man's life was worth to even peep over the top of the parapet," Corporal J. W. Minnish remembered when he visited the Confederate trenches at Dam No. 1 after the April 16 engagement. Minnish witnessed the skill of Northern marksmen when one soldier placed his hat on a stick and held it above the parapet for a brief moment and then withdrew it. Upon examination, Minnish found "the crown neatly perforated by an enemy's bullet." Southerns struck back as Minnish watched "Big Bill Griffith" from the 1st Kentucky slowly take aim at puffs of smoke from a tall pine tree. Soon the Union sharpshooter "tumbled down into the dam with a loud splash. That ended that."[27]

The siege also had its informal truces between the opposing forces witnessing varying levels of bantering and some relief from the shot and shell. Sergeant George B. Noyes of the 11th Maine Volunteers was amazed that the Lee's Mill area was such "a place of desecration and desolation," but also advised his father that "On the opposite side of the river we can observe the rebel batteries. The Johnnies on picket are quite friendly. We lay down our arms, meet between the lines, and hold conversation, etc., for a few minutes, then return respectfully to our lines."[28] James Rush Holmes of the 61st Pennsylvania wrote his aunt, "As they have only a large swamp between them they can talk as well as if in a room together, they throwing up Bull Run to our boys and we Fort Donaldson and other places."[29] Such lapses of aggression were usually temporary, yet they reinforced the ironic futility of this war between the states. "It is not odd to think," Brigadier General Philip Kearny wrote his wife, "that Magruder, one of my best friends, is one of the chief men here. This is a most unnatural war."[30] Besides these thoughts,

General
Joseph E. Johnston
Museum of the Confederacy

Brigadier General
Howell Cobb
University of Georgia

Brigadier General
Jubal A. Early
Museum of the Confederacy

Brigadier General
Gabriel J. Rains
USAMHI

and briefly formed friendships, most of the soldiers simply wished the siege to end, as Lieutenant Robert Miller expressed to his mother: "The April sunshine changed to rain, and the heavens have been weeping bitter bitter cold tears ever since perhaps for the prospect of blasted human happiness that is so soon to follow."[31]

The siege's monotony was occasionally broken by the sight of balloons floating over the lines. Professor T. S. C. Lowe moved his balloon, "Intrepid," to Yorktown. Flights became a familiar sight with Fitz-John Porter taking several trips above the lines. During one of his flights, the balloon's moorings slipped and Porter drifted over the Confederate works but fortunate winds blew him back for a safe landing behind Union lines. Despite this mishap, Porter's engineers used the "Intrepid" for observation and mapmaking duties. A second balloon camp for the "Constitution" was established at Warwick Court House on April 10.[32] George Armstrong Custer enjoyed the dubious honor of making several ascents in this balloon to observe the Confederate defenses between Lee's Mill and Dam No. 1.[33] The Confederates responded not only with artillery (cannons elevated by E. Porter Alexander to serve as anti-aircraft guns) but also with their own balloon. It was a roughly made hot air device, rather than Lowe's gas type, commanded by Captain John Randolph Bryan of Magruder's staff. Several flights were made from Lee Hall, Wynne's Mill, and Yorktown to observe the Federal siege preparations. An errant flight caused by a broken tether rope ended the Southron flying experiment.[34] Another form of amusement and interest for Federal troops was the deployment of "coffee mill guns" at Warwick Court House. The Agar Gun was invented by Wilson Agar and was a hopper-fed weapon fired by turning a hand crank.[35] Several of these rapid-fire guns were assigned to the 56th New York Volunteers and were brought into service below Lee's Mill. While stationed near the court house, Private Patrick Lyons of the 2nd Rhode Island witnessed an Agar Gun "go to the front; this kind of gun is capable of being fired very rapidly which gives it the name of the Corn Sheller and is very destructive against a body of infantry."[36] The Confederates took no notice of this new weapon. Other than instilling some confidence in the Federal troops, neither these rapid-fire guns nor balloons had any impact on the siege.

Johnston returned to the Peninsula following his day-long conference with President Davis on April 17. He brought with him G. W. Smith's and James Longstreet's divisions which would bring the army's total strength on the Peninsula to 56,000. It was almost half the number of McClellan's army. Johnston reorganized the command structure giving D. H. Hill command of the Yorktown - Gloucester defenses, Longstreet the Confederate center, and Magruder the right wing from Dam No. 1 to Mulberry Island. G. W. Smith's troops were held in reserve below Williamsburg near the Half-Way House. This reorganization resulted in Magruder's virtual demotion from commander of the Army of the Peninsula to a divisional commander. Three other generals now outranked him on the Peninsula. This was particularly irksome to Prince John, as many had thought that he might be given command of all the Confederate troops now coming to the Peninsula. No longer the lead actor, Magruder began to sulk in his headquarters at Lee Hall, criticizing the design and armament of the very defenses he had developed.[37]

Even before his demotion to right wing commander, Magruder had begun the reorganization of his James River flank. It now became one of his primary concerns. On April 14 he had ordered his troops to abandon the Miner's Farm Line on Mulberry Island and built several new redoubts between Skiffes Creek and Lee's Mill to defend access to the Mulberry Island Road. This action provided Prince John with additional troops to fill the Warwick Line trenches between Lee's Mill and Dam No. 1, however, it left Fort Crafford and the Water Battery on Mulberry Island Point open to attack by a possible Union crossing of the Warwick River. Magruder had decided "to leave the Fort to its fate,"[38] yet the defense of Mulberry Island still troubled him. Even though the Virginia denied the Federal navy access to the mouth of the James River, Magruder requested that gunboats be assigned off Mulberry Island as they would be of "immense importance to prevent the enemy from crossing the Warwick and operating on James River." By April 21, the *Jamestown, Teaser, Raleigh, Patrick Henry* and *Beaufort* were stationed off Mulberry Island and occasionally shelled the Union lines.[39] Magruder's troop dispositions reported to Johnston on April 24:

> My forces now occupy, in a strictly defensive attitude, the Warwick Line, with the exception that that portion of the Warwick River intervening between Lee's Mill and Miner's Farm, which was originally within our lines, has been abandoned as against any serious demonstration of the enemy . . . the abandonment of the lower portion of the line on Warwick River, influenced doubtless in this determination by a belief in the strength and formidable character of the works at Mulberry Island Point, sufficient in this belief with the aid of the *Virginia*, to maintain itself alone and unsupported except on the water side by our steamers against any efforts of the enemy.[40]

The entire Confederate army was also going through the throes of unit reorganization due to the passage of the Conscription Act on the same day as the Dam No. 1 engagement. One of Robert E. Lee's reasons for pressing Johnston to hold the line on the Peninsula was to give the army time to complete this transformation from one-year volunteers to soldiers serving for the War's duration. Conscription was not popular with the troops. Private Jesse Reid of the 4th South Carolina who camped behind the lines in Warwick County, noted that the troops talked of nothing but the Conscription Bill and he was not alone in opposition. In one letter to his family, Reid acknowledged that Conscription would "do away with all the patriotism we have."[41] James Griffin believed that "this is quite an unfortunate time for all these changes, inasmuch as we are in sight of the Enemy, and may be attacked at any moment."[42] The local regiment, 32nd Virginia, held its reorganization while in the trenches. New officers were selected for the Warwick Beauregards (Co. H) as well as other companies. The men were rather dissatisfied and when the army retreated towards Richmond, many soldiers, like Privates David and Edward Hopkins of York County, simply deserted.[43]

When the siege entered its fourth week Joe Johnston started thinking of retreating. On April 29, Johnston once again advised Richmond that because of McClellan's overwhelming strength in heavy artillery, he could not hold the Peninsula. His divisional commanders generally agreed with this opinion. D. H. Hill believed that the Confederates could only withstand a two-day bombardment, but Johnston felt otherwise, stating "about two hours."[44] While Johnston planned his evacuation Lee endeavored to prompt the *Virginia* to attack the Federal vessels threatening Yorktown. Tattnal simply would not risk his ironclad, citing that his ship was too unseaworthy to steam past Fortress Monroe and then have to face the entire Union fleet. The Union had by now added two more ironclads, U.S.S. *Galena* and the iron-hulled Naugatuck, to the U.S.S. *Monitor*. Tattnal advised both Lee and Mallory that the *Virginia* would be handled "with proper prudence" to halt any Union move towards Norfolk or up the James River.[45]

Meanwhile, McClellan was making his final preparations for his grand bombardment which he expected to unleash on May 5. Brigadier General William B. Franklin's division, which had been on board transports since its arrival in the York River on April 22, was disembarked at Wormley Creek on May 2 to give greater force to the eventual infantry assault against the Confederate line. McClellan had given up hope of running these troops pass the York River batteries with the *Galena* prior to his bombardment.[46] The U. S. Navy simply refused to move up the river until the Confederate batteries on both sides of the river were disabled. McClellan, nonetheless, expected the Southern forces to try to hold their Peninsula defenses. He was confident of his eventual victory as he advised Lincoln, "I see the way clear to success and hope to make it brilliant, although with but little loss of life."[47]

But the drama was not to end as McClellan expected. Johnston ordered the withdrawal of his army on May 2, but poor staff work, weather and roads delayed the retreat. The order had not taken many Confederates by surprise, as James Griffin wrote his wife on April 28, " I don't think this is the place for us to fight . . . I wouldn't be surprised if our army falls back from here . . ."[48] Others, however, were disheartened by the prospects of abandoning the Peninsula, particularly Magruder. Prince John spent his last hours on the Peninsula ill in bed, dismayed by his May 2 orders to move his troops towards Richmond, as one of his staff, Hugh Thomas Douglas, recounted:

> I shall never forget the morning that General Magruder, lying on his sick bed worn out by the arduous duties of three weeks, a strain enough to have killed any ordinary man, summoned me to his room and directed me to prepare for the move. The tears coursed down the old man's cheeks and rising on one arm with dramatic effect, he pointed to his little army, and said "Sic transit gloria, Peninsula."[49]

On the evening of May 3, the Confederates unleashed a tremendous bombardment to cover their retreat toward Williamsburg. By morning, the trenches were empty.[50]

The Federal command was caught off balance by this unexpected Confederate withdrawal. The Union soldiers were, however, jubilant that the siege was now over. Soldiers raced to win everlasting glory by placing their unit's colors first atop the Confederate earthworks. Edward Wilson of Birney's Zouaves achieved this honor when he affixed the Stars and Stripes on the crest of the Lee's Mill battlements.[51] As the soldiers entered the Confederate positions they were shocked to discover the torpedoes left behind to retard their advance. Developed by Brigadier General Gabriel J. Rains, these land mines were actually 8- or 10-inch Columbiad shells buried a few inches under the soil and set with primers so that they exploded when stepped on or moved. It was the first use of this controversial weapon during the Civil War and these buried shells injured scores of Union soldiers.[52] At Lee's Mill Private Albert Berry of the 23rd Pennsylvania was able to save the life of a Sergeant Caldwell when Caldwell stepped on a torpedo, triggering its fuse. Berry acted quickly to empty his canteen on it thereby putting it out.[53] McClellan was shocked by this barbaric weapon and since the torpedoes were delaying the advance of his troops, he "ordered that they should be discovered and removed by the Confederate prisoners."[54]

Despite the torpedoes, the Union soldiers were amazed by the abandoned extensive works, military stores, camps and huge siege guns left behind by the Confederates. Lieutenant Edgar N. Newcomb of the 19th Massachusetts found perhaps the most telling memento left behind by the Confederates written on an abandoned tent: "He that fights and runs away, will live to fight another day. May 3."[55]

The four-week siege had long lasting implications. McClellan's initial hesitation in front of Magruder's defenses gave the Confederacy time to mobilize its forces for its defense of Richmond. Even though McClellan did not take advantage of breaking the Confederate lines on several occasions early in the siege (notably on April 16 at the Battle of Dam No. 1), it is the presence of the C.S.S. Virginia that enabled the siege to last as long as it did. The Federal navy believed that it could not support an attack against the York River batteries, an action that could have broken the siege by flanking the Confederate defenses, because it had to protect McClellan's army from the Virginia. The Union command had no knowledge of the Virginia's numerous weaknesses nor the fact that the Confederate batteries defending the James River were not as strong or well positioned as those on the York. The Federal navy simply did not act resolutely in support of McClellan. Denied the use of the James River, and concerned about casualties, McClellan felt he had no alternative but to besiege the imposing Confederate works. Although often criticized for his retreat from the Peninsula, Joseph Johnston was right that his defenses could not withstand McClellan's planned bombardment. While he saved his army from possible destruction, Johnston's hurried retreat would have a telling impact on the Confederate control of Hampton Roads.

Chapter 13

Occupation and Surrender

Some months afterwards John Bankhead Magruder wrote his report detailing his army's defense of the Peninsula:

> From April 4 to May 3 this army served almost without relief in the trenches. It rained almost incessantly; the trenches were filled with water. The weather was exceedingly cold; no fires could be allowed; the artillery and infantry of the enemy played upon our men almost continuously day and night; the army had neither coffee, sugar, nor hard bread, but subsisted on flour and salt meat, and that in reduced quantities and yet no murmurs were heard.[1]

It may have been a heroic stand, against insurmountable odds, but as the Confederate troops marched along the muddy roads to Williamsburg they left behind forevermore the Peninsula now in the hands of the "Yankee invader."

Abraham Lincoln was disenchanted with McClellan's progress up the Peninsula and decided to go to Fort Monroe so to prompt greater action. Lincoln arrived at Old Point Comfort the evening of May 6, accompanied by Secretary of War Edwin Stanton and Secretary of Treasury Salmon Chase. His goal was to meet with McClellan at Yorktown as well as to urge forward the long contemplated movement against Norfolk. Since the Confederate army was now in retreat towards Richmond, Lincoln immediately met with both Major General John Wool and Flag Officer Louis N. Goldsborough to plan how to end the *Virginia's* control of Hampton Roads.[2] The President recognized that this could only be achieved through the capture of Norfolk, thus he ordered Goldsborough to send his fleet to attack the Sewell's Point batteries the next day.

Around noon on May 8 the Union fleet, led by the *Monitor* and *Naugatuck*, began shelling Sewell's Point. Lincoln went to Fort Wool to observe the attack. Fort Wool's Sawyer and James rifles also joined in the bombardment until from behind Craney Island appeared the C.S.S. *Virginia*. The Confederate ironclad immediately steamed toward Sewell's Point, and the Federal ships retreated to the protection of Fort Monroe.[3]

The President was frustrated by this turn of events and ordered Wool to land his troops at Ocean View on the Chesapeake Bay and then march toward Norfolk. Under the cover of a naval bombardment, the Union troops landed at Ocean View on May 9 and began their march to town. The Confederates evacuated Norfolk, Portsmouth and the Gosport Navy Yard as the Union approached.[4]

Norfolk had been an endangered Confederate city as soon as Johnston's men pulled out of their trenches along the Warwick River. Major General Benjamin Huger had realized his isolated position; however, as Huger's men left for Petersburg, they failed to notify the *Virginia* of their evacuation. On May 10, Flag Officer Tattnal realized that the Sewell's Point batteries were empty of Confederate troops and he was left with just a few alternatives: attack the Union fleet, stay in Hampton Roads until forced to surrender because of lack of supplies, destroy his ship or retreat up the James River to Richmond. The move to Richmond appeared to be the best option, but there were problems. The *Virginia* drew 22 feet of water, but the channel up the James to Richmond was 18 feet according to the Confederate pilots. Tattnal had the *Virginia* lightened to the required draft by throwing overboard all of the coal and ballast. The ironclad met the pilot's requirements, but its unprotected hull was out of the water. When the pilots then informed Tattnal that due to contrary winds, the *Virginia* still took too much water to enter the channel, he resolved that the ship must be destroyed. The *Virginia* was then run aground off Craney Island and around 4:30 a.m. on the morning of May 11 the vessel was destroyed by her crew.[5] Chief Engineer Ashton Ramsay reflected, "Still unconquered, we hauled down our drooping colors . . . and with mingled pride and grief gave her to the flames."[6]

Hampton Roads and the Peninsula were now firmly under Union control and would remain so for the war's duration. Fort Monroe, Camp Harrison and Camp Butler would, however, continue to serve as a base of operations.

McClellan's constant requests for more troops as he moved closer to Richmond prompted Lincoln to make a command change at Fort Monroe. Major General John E. Wool was re-assigned as commander of the Union Eastern Military Department.[7] McClellan then assumed command of the Department of Virginia and the troops on the lower Peninsula were now directly commanded by Major General John A. Dix. Dix had served as an artillery captain on Fort Monroe during the 1820s as well as being President James Buchanan's Secretary of the Treasury. He had been commissioned a major general of volunteers in June 1861, and he now found himself in command of a department whose primary purpose was to shuttle troops to and from various battle fronts.[8]

Some activity did shake the doldrums out of this army of occupation. When the IV Corps was transferred from the Army of the Potomac to Newport News, the Confederacy quickly responded against this supposed threat against Richmond by sending Lieutenant General James Longstreet with Hood's and Pickett's divisions to besiege Suffolk in late April 1863. The siege never threatened Union control of Hampton Roads, and the Confederate troops were soon recalled to the Army of Northern Virginia.[9]

Dix was promoted to command of the Department of the East on July 18, 1863, and Major General John G. Foster assumed command of the newly created Department of Virginia and North Carolina. The Peninsula was placed in the department's District of Eastern Virginia. In November 1863, Major General Benjamin F. Butler replaced Foster as commander of the

Major General
John E. Wool
USAMHI

Commander
John Newland Maffitt
Mariners' Museum

Lieutenant
Hunter Davidson
City of Hampton

Lieutenant
J. Pembroke Jones
City of Hampton

department. The troops in Butler's command were then reorganized and reinforced under General U. S. Grant's directive into two corps: X Corps under Major General Q. A. Gilmore and XVIII Corps under Major General W. F. "Baldy" Smith. The newly minted Army of the James, commanded by Ben Butler, soon left the Peninsula for its failed Bermuda Hundred Campaign. Few troops were left on the Peninsula as Grant used all resources available to strangle the Confederate army around Petersburg and Richmond. Fort Monroe would serve one more time as a base for a major amphibious operation: the December 1864 expedition against Fort Fisher outside of Wilmington, North Carolina. Butler's expedition ended in a miserable failure and returned to Hampton Roads. Grant replaced Butler with Major General Alfred H. Terry, who finally captured Fort Fisher in January 1865. Terry then assumed command of the Department of Virginia, which included the Peninsula within its jurisdiction.[11]

The Confederacy never totally gave up hope of liberating the Peninsula, but the constant pressure on Richmond by the Federal army left it unable to make any concerted effort. As with the transformation of the steam frigate *Merrimack* into the ironclad *Virginia*, the South strove to use its limited resources to challenge Union naval superiority and occupation of Southern territory. The C.S.S. *Squib* is one such case and would bring the war back into Hampton Roads with a vengeance.

The C.S.S. *Squib*, also referred to as the Infanta, was a *David*-class steam-powered torpedo boat built in Richmond. Launched in 1864, the *Squib* was 46 feet in length with a six-foot, 3-inch beam and a three-foot, 6-inch draft. The boat had a one shaft condensing one-cylinder engine fired by one boiler and featured an eighteen-foot spar torpedo. The *Squib* was sheathed in boiler plate and had an iron cased 3 by 16 cockpit at the stern for its commander and helmsman. The crew was composed of six men.[12]

Lieutenant Hunter Davidson was the *Squib's* commander. Davidson attended the U. S. Naval Academy and served in the

U. S. Navy until resigning in April 1861. Initially assigned to the C.S.S. *Patrick Henry*, he served aboard the C.S.S. *Virginia* during its March 8 and 9, 1862, engagements against the Union fleet. Davidson was then assigned, because of his special aptitude, to the Torpedo Division of the Office of Ordnance and Hydrography. He eventually became head of the division when Commodore Matthew F. Maury went to England. Davidson used the converted tug C.S.S. *Torpedo* to conduct experiments with electric torpedoes. His success resulted in the sinking of the U.S.S. *Commodore Barney* and the U.S.S. *Commodore Jones* in the James River.[13]

Davidson had long believed that torpedoes, using percussion primers, could be used as an offensive weapon. Davidson supervised the construction of four vessels in Richmond for this service, one of which was the *Squib*, to counter Union control of the lower James River. After tests at the Rocketts Navy Yard, Davidson deemed the *Squib* and its spar torpedo ready for action in early April 1864.[14]

The *Squib* then slowly steamed, mostly at night to escape detection, "upward of a hundred miles outside our lines by river, patrolled by Federal gunboats," recounted Davidson, to a hiding place up the Pagan River. The *Minnesota*, perhaps because it was the Union frigate that escaped destruction by the C.S.S. *Virginia* on March 9, 1862, was selected as the prey in Hampton Roads.[15]

The North Atlantic Blockading Squadron flagship *Minnesota*, commanded by Captain H. H. Upsher, was quietly resting at anchor off Newport News Point during the dark hours of April 9, 1864. Officer of the deck, Ensign James Bartwistle, noticed that a vessel appeared off the *Minnesota's* port beam. When hailed, the answer came "*Roanoke.*" Ordered away or the boat would be fired upon, a further replay of "Aye, Sir, Aye" was made. The alarm was then sounded as the object rapidly approached the *Minnesota*. Before any further action could be taken, or the *Minnesota's* tender, the *Poppy* could respond, the unknown little steamer stuck the *Minnesota* "abaft the main chains" and a tremendous explosion followed. The *Squib* had struck with a vengeance.[16]

Davidson had steered his torpedo boat through the entire Union fleet to reach the *Minnesota*. The *Squib* approached the *Minnesota* perpendicularly so to avoid being swamped by the torpedo's explosion. The torpedo boat rammed the Union frigate and, within a second, the 53 pounds of powder contained in the torpedo exploded. The spar was "shattered to pieces" and, according to Davidson, "and the little steamer driven back forcibly." The engineer of the *Squib* had been ordered to stop the engine right before striking the enemy vessel and now, as the Confederate torpedo boat tried to reverse away and then steam forward, its single cylinder engine caught "on the center, and there we remained," wrote Davidson, " — it seemed to me about forty years — under the fire of the *Minnesota*."[17]

The torpedo's explosion had knocked many of the *Minnesota's* crew onto the deck, but the frigate was now alive to the threat and determined to sink the Confederate intruder. The *Minnesota's* marines began "peppering" the *Squib*, dead in the water fifty yards away, with musket fire as the frigate's gun crews prepared their cannon for action. The torpedo boat's engineer, Mr. Wright who Davidson called "one of the bravest and coolest men I ever knew,"[18] crawled forward into the dark and freed the engine. The *Squib* now sped toward the *Minnesota* and then veered off towards Norfolk, a move that Davidson thought would "throw his pursuers off the scent" under heavy fire. Davidson noted that the musket fire was so hot that "There was hardly a square foot on the little boat not marked by a bullet, and my hat and clothes were perforated . . ." The *Minnesota* was able to fire one of its 9-inch guns at the fleeing boat. The shot passed close under the *Squib*, lifting her stern out of the water. The shock lifted Davidson off his feet and hurled him against the small iron shield, breaking his thumb. Despite this heavy gunfire against his little vessel, Davidson was able to escape. After hiding out in a nearby creek, Davidson made another attack on the Union fleet on April

11. This time, however, the Federals were alert to the danger presented by the *Squib* and drove the torpedo boat off with cannon fire.[19]

The *Minnesota* was not seriously damaged. Davidson lamented that his torpedo had insufficient powder to do the work necessary to sink the Federal frigate. Confederate President Jefferson Davis was not impressed by the torpedo attack, asking later, "Humph, Why didn't he blow her up?" Nevertheless, Confederate Secretary of the Navy Stephen Mallory reported that the "cool, daring, professional skill and judgment exhibited by Lieutenant Davidson in this hazardous enterprise merit high commendation and confer honor upon a service of which he is a member." Davidson was promoted to the rank of Commander for his exploit with the C.S.S. *Squib*.[20]

The James River was the final stage of another naval drama, the sinking of the C.S.S. *Florida*, on November 28, 1864. The *Florida* was one of several vessels constructed in British shipyards for the Confederacy. Launched in 1862 as the *Oreto*, John Newland Maffitt took command of the ship in the Bahamas and led the re-christened *Florida* on a highly successful cruise during 1863. Maffitt originally joined the U. S. Navy in 1838, resigning in 1861. He had been a pre-war Warwick County resident, living between 1854 - 1857 in his home Carrieville overlooking the James River, while working on the Atlantic Coast survey charting the James River. Under Maffitt's eight-month command, the *Florida* and her satellites captured 47 Northern merchant ships. Sailing to Brest, France for overhaul, Maffitt became too ill to continue as the commerce raider's captain and was replaced by Lieutenant Charles N. Morris.[21]

Morris continued the *Florida's* career, capturing thirteen additional prizes until October 4, 1864, when this highly successful commerce raider was rammed and captured by the U.S.S. *Wachusett* in Bahia, Brazil. Despite this act being a violation of Brazilian neutrality, the *Wachusett* towed the *Florida* to Hampton Roads. When Brazil demanded the *Florida's* return, Rear Admiral

David Porter, commander of the North Atlantic Blockading Squadron, ordered "that Rebel vessel" sunk. On November 28, 1864, the *Florida* quietly sank off Newport News Point after a "collision" with another vessel.[22]

Even though it was quite apparent in late 1864 that the Confederacy was on its last legs, Union politician Francis P. Blair, Sr. convinced Lincoln that some effort should be made to obtain a mediated peace. After meeting with Blair, Jefferson Davis agreed to the proposal and sent Judge John A. Campbell, Senator Robert M. T. Hunter and Confederate Vice-President Alexander H. Stephens to confer with Lincoln. On February 3, 1865, the Confederate representatives met with Lincoln and Secretary of State William Seward aboard the steamer *River Queen* off Old Point Comfort. The Hampton Roads Peace Conference proved to be a total failure. Confederate demands for independence or the continuance were rejected by Lincoln and Seward. The war was destined to go on until its bloody end.[23]

A little more than two months after the conference's conclusion Lee would surrender at Appomattox. The victorious Union army now had thousands of Confederate troops to parole and return to their homes throughout the South. Since the Northern camps were already full with captured Confederates the Federal authorities decided to build a camp in Virginia. A site on Newport News Point, next to Camp Butler, was selected for this purpose. The Newport News POW Camp was quickly constructed in April 1865 and was described as being on a site of:

> Twenty-five acres, enclosed by a fence twelve feet high, inside of which is a railing twenty feet from the fence, which prisoners are not allowed to pass. Outside of the fence a gallery had been erected for the sentinels, from which they can observe who approached the railing and also any unusual disturbance among the prisoners.

Other facilities, including a hospital, were constructed.[24] The 122nd U.S. Colored Troops, Battery B, 2nd US Colored Light Artillery and the 1st U.S. Colored Cavalry were assigned to guard the camp. Colonel J. Ham Davidson commanded the camp.[25]

The use of black soldiers to guard the Confederates held in the Newport News POW Camp led to several unfortunate incidents. In late April two former Confederates were wounded by sentries (one accidentally) which increased the friction between the guards and prisoners. Racial tensions, compounded by fears of a prison escape, came to a deadly explosion on the evening of May 7, 1865. Approximately ten prisoners approached the guard, Private Harrison Woodson of the 122nd USCT, trying to sell him trinkets and taunting him about Lincoln's death. One ex-Confederate ignored Woodson's repeated commands to halt his steps onto the gallery, where prisoners were forbidden to go after dark. The sentry then tried to fire his musket, but it hand-fired and missed the prisoner. This shot alerted the officer of the guard to the escalating problem. The officer, a Lieutenant Harold, approached the scene and ordered the sentry while he was reloading his musket with double shot, "There is another man on the gallery now; why do you not use the bayonet on him?" Woodson leaped towards the prisoner, Private Benjamin Hurt, thrusting his bayonet into the prisoner's back. Hurt died immediately and fell into the privy. One prisoner said to Woodson, "You have killed him dead," to which the black soldier replied, "Yes, by God. They buried us alive at Fort Pillow."[26]

The Commissary-General of Prisoners ordered a court martial which indicated no wrong doing, but he also issued new regulations to avoid reoccurrence of similar incidents.[27] Union officials now realized the futility of imprisoning former Confederates until they were formally paroled and the Newport News POW Camp never reached its anticipated capacity. By July it was empty. The camp never held more than 3,490 prisoners, of which 168 died during captivity and 12 escaped. The authorities deactivated the camp in August 1865.[28]

One prisoner did remain incarcerated on the Peninsula, the former Confederate President Jefferson Davis. Davis was captured near Irwinville, Georgia, on May 10, 1865, and brought to Fort Monroe on board the steamer *William P. Clyde*. Casemate No. 2 was modified into a prison cell with iron bars fitted in the embrasure and archways enclosed with brick and heavy doors were installed. On May 22 Davis was taken to his cell by Major General Nelson A. Miles.

Davis was held captive under the strictest guard and regulations as he was charged with treason as well as being implicated in Lincoln's assassination. Limited food, and only a Bible for reading material, the former Confederate President was under constant watch by sentries. On May 23 Davis was shackled with iron "manacles and fitters" by order of Secretary of War Edwin Stanton. Davis resisted when the iron was placed upon his legs, but to no avail. It was not until May 28 that the shackles were removed thanks to the intercession of Post Surgeon Lieutenant Colonel John J. Craven. Craven was also able to improve the prisoner's confinement in many ways in an attempt to preserve Davis' declining health and eventually succeeded in having him moved to quarters in Carroll Hall. Eventually, Davis would be joined by his wife, Varina. He was allowed bail ($100,000) and was released on May 13, 1867.[29]

Most of the soldiers from the Peninsula had already found their way long before Davis' release. They had found their Peninsula homeland, however, utterly changed as W. H. T. Squires observed:

> Where broad acres of tobacco trembled, deep-green and golden, in years of peace and plenty, and stately rows of Indian corn lifted their fronds in martial array, thickets of weeds and underbrush had now unchallenged possession. Where once a modest cottage sheltered the farmer and his growing family, a ruined chimney, like a smoked skeleton, haunted the farm . . . Poverty,

wretchedness, hunger, death, and despair clutched the heart of the land.[30]

Several battles, a major campaign and three years of Union occupation had left the landscape scarred.

The passing armies had not been kind to the Peninsula. Magruder had practiced a scorched earth policy and the Union troops looted and destroyed many of the remaining farms and houses. The experience of Warwick County's Lebanon Church clearly documents the war's harsh impact upon the community. In 1861 the church was used by the Mecklenburg Cavalry as a commissary and following the Confederate retreat, Union troops used the building as a horse stable. The damage from troop usage was so extensive that services could not resume at Lebanon Church until the late 1860s.[31]

McClellan took steps while he was on the Peninsula to stop the pillaging and destruction of surrounding houses as Colonel Charles S. Wainwright of the New York Volunteers wrote:

> Whatever may be the crime of the inhabitants it is not right for individuals, whether officers or privates to judge and punish them . . . the inhabitants our fellow citizens though they are rebels. Our object is to put down the rebellion, not to widen the breach of estrangement, or to impoverish our own country.[32]

Despite these sentiments, looting continued and the nearby farmland laid bare. At Warwick Court House, the soldiers looted the county records and the little village itself, as Charles Harvey Brewster described the scene in a letter home:

> . . . We took up the line of march up the road past Warwick Court House, which is about half as big as our barn and built of brick. As we passed the open door we could see a safe broken open and any quantity of papers strewed about. The village

consists of a store, Tavern, Ct. House, Jail and one or two houses . . . There was an old house in the village, and in 15 minutes there was not a board left on it, neither roof floor nor anything. One of our boys received enough for himself and the three officers, and we made a floor and down we laid, and were soon fast asleep.33

The looting of documents by the passing Union soldiers was described by Asher Williams in a letter home:

About sunset we came to a halt in a wheat field at a place called Warwick C.H. . . . A brick building about the size of a Smoke House which was used as a kind of County Clerk's office, the records and documents of the county were kept there . . . Next is the court house a brick building about the size of a carriage house up our way. The court room is about the size of an office. There are two wings to the building and each have one smaller room in, that is now a kind of commissary. Next is another little smoke house with grated windows which was the jail. These buildings are all in a line. The C.H. is the largest of the whole group. Altogether they perhaps cover a quarter of an acre. The office was full of books and papers. Some very old ones that had been written long before the Revolution by King Georges officers. A guard was over them but I was lucky and got a handful of deeds and c. I have one written in 1669. I send you some of them. Shortly after I got mine a stop was put to taking any more.[34]

Union soldiers may have called the Peninsula "nothing more than a wild wilderness,"[35] while resident George Ben West lamented, "How changed everything was on our return."[36] The modern Peninsula was to grow out of the ashes of the Civil War. Everyone recognized its wonderful location, as Asher Williams noted, "surrounded by nothing but the river between us on three sides,"[37] which offered tremendous economic promise during the post-war era. Poet Joaquin Miller reflected upon this very theme when he visited Newport News Point, the Camp Butler earthworks still visible, when he wrote:

> The huge sea monster, the *Merrimac*
>   The mad sea monster, the *Monitor*
> You may sweep the sea, peer forward and back
>   But never a sign or a sound of war.
>   A vulture or two in the heavens blue;
> A sweet town-building, a boatman's call;
>   A far sea song of a pleasure crew;
> The sound of hammers. And that is all.
>
> And where are the monsters that tore the main?
> And where are the monsters that shook this shore?
>   The sea grew mad! And the shores hot flame!
>   The mad sea monsters they are no more.
> The palm, and the pine, and the sea sands brown
>   The far sea-songs of the pleasure crews;
>   The air-like balm in this building town —
>   And that is a picture of Newport News.[38]

Endnotes

Chapter 1
1. Charles Campbell, History of the Colony and Ancient Dominion of Virginia (Philadelphia, 1860) 75.
2. Lyon G. Tyler, (ed.), Narratives of Early Virginia, 1606-1625 (New York, 1966), 200.
3. Ibid., 202.
4. William Stith, History of the First Discovery and Settlement of Virginia (Williamsburg, 1747), 138.
5. Tyler, 223-224.
6. Robert Arthur and Richard P. Weinert, Jr., Defender of the Chesapeake: The Story of Fort Monroe (Shippensburg, PA, 1989), 5, 8.
7. Ibid., 8.
8. Rogers Dey Whichard, The History of Lower Tidewater Virginia (New York, 1959), 2: 195-196.
9. Journals of the House of Burgesses, (Richmond, 1905-1915), 42.
10. Arthur and Weinert, 14-17.
11. Virginia Gazette, 17 March 1781.
12. William Maxwell, ed., Virginia Historical Register and Literary Advisor (Richmond, 1973),4 : 25-28.
13. Lt. Col. Banistre Tarleton, History of the Campaign of 1780 and 1781 in the Southern Provinces of North America (London, 1787), 292.
14. Tarleton, 307.
15. Arthur and Weinert, 18.
16. H. W. Flourney, ed., Calendar of Virginia State Papers, 1808-1835 (Richmond: Superintendent of Public Printing, 1892; New York, 1968), 10: 206, 231.
17. V. C. Jones, "The Sack of Hampton, Virginia," American History Illustrated, 9: 36-44.
18. Arthur and Weinert, 23-33.
19. Ibid., 34, 39-40.
20. Ibid., 43-61.
21. James T. Stensvagg, ed., Hampton: From the Sea to the Stars, (Virginia Beach, 1985), 32.

Chapter 2
1. John V. Quarstein and Parke S. Rouse, Jr., Newport News: A Centennial History, 24-33.
2. "Vignettes of Yesterday: A Letter to the Pioneers," by George B. West in Alexander Crosby Brown, ed., Newport News' 325 Years: A Record of Progress of a Virginia Community (Newport News, 1946), 275.
3. George Benjamin West, When the Yankees Came (Richmond, 1977), 41.
4. "History of the Virginia Peninsula," unpublished, anonymous article in vertical file of Newport News Main Street Library's Virginiana Room.
5. The Farmer's Register, Vol. 3, No. 4, August 1835, 319.
6. Inscription on fly-leaf in Edward Jenner, An Inquiry Into the Cause of the Variolae Vaccinal- The Cow Pox (London, 1801).
7. William and Mary Quarterly, 1st Ser., 15 (July 1906), 52.
8. Ibid., 51.
9. "News From Warwick County," Tyler's Quarterly Historical and Genealogical Magazine 7 (1926): 68.
10. "Sale of Negroes," Virginia Gazette, 16 February 1854.
11. Ibid.
12. A Hornbook of Virginia History, Pub. No. 25 (Richmond, 1965), 84.
13. Quarstein and Rouse, 29.
14. Stensvaag, 97-98.
15. Ibid., 93-96.
16. Quarstein and Rouse, 29; Stensvaag, 67-84, and Arthur and Weinert, 84-85.
17. Joseph Martin, A New and Comprehensive Gazetteer of Virginia and the District of Columbia: Containing a Copious Collection (Charlottesville, 1835), 288.

18. Diary of Captain Edward Rush Young, M.D., unpublished manuscript, 32.
19. Quarstein and Rouse, 31-33.
20. Ibid.
21. West, When the Yankees Came, 3.

Chapter 3

1. Quarstein and Rouse, 45.
2. Virginius Dabney, Virginia: The New Dominion (Garden City, New York, 1971), 284-294.
3. War of the Rebellion: A Compilation of the Official Records of the Union and Confederate Armies (Washington, 1880-1901), 130 Vols. (hereinafter cited as OR), Series I, Vol. I, 119 and 353.
4. Francis B. Heitman, Historical Register and Dictionary of the United States Army (Washington, 1903), 374.
5. OR, Series I, Vol. II, 21-23.
6. OR, Series I, Vol. II, 612.
7. OR, Series I, Vol. II, 853-854.
8. OR, Series I, Vol. II, 788-789.
9. Les Jensen, 32nd Virginia Infantry (Lynchburg, Virginia, 1990), 3-11.
10. OR, Series I, Vol. II, 862-863.
11. Ibid.
12. Ibid., 641-642, 643, 648-651.
13. Mark Mayo Boatner, III, The Civil War Dictionary (New York, 1959), 109.
14. OR, Series I, Vol. II, 640-641.
15. Arthur and Weinert, 100.
16. Robert Seager, II, and Tyler too, A Biography of John and Julia Gardner Tyler. New York 1963 and Henry W. Howe, Passages from the Life of Henry Warren Howe, consisting of Diary and Letters Written During the Civil War (Lowell, Mass., 1899), 19-20.
17. Arthur and Weinert, 99.
18. Jensen, 16-17.
19. OR, Series I, Vol. II, 35-36, 870-871.
20. Edmond L. Pierce, "The Contrabands at Fortress Monroe," Atlantic Monthly (November 1861), 626-627.
21. OR, Series I, Vol. II, 649-650.
22. Pierce, 628.
23. Edwin M. Stanton, "Letter From the Secretary of War: Africans in Fort Monroe Military District, dated 25 March 1862" (Washington, D.C.: 1862), 1-14; Pierce, 628; Benjamin F. Butler, Butler's Book: A Review of His Legal, Political and Military Career (Boston, 1892), 258-259; and OR, Series I, Vol. II, 52-54.
24. OR, Series I, Vol. II, 54.
25. William H. Osborne, History of the Twenty-ninth Regiment of Massachusetts (Boston, 1877), 60.
26. Arthur and Weinert, 101.
27. West, 44-51.
28. Ibid., 49
29. OR, Series I, Vol. II, 871, 888.
30. West, 55-60.
31. Garland C. Hudgins and Richard B. Kleese, Recollections of an Old Dominion Dragoon: The Civil War Experiences of Sgt. Robert S. Hudgins II Co. B., 3rd Virginia Cavalry (Orange, Virginia: 1993), 18.
32. John Curry, "The Warwick Beauregards" (Fort Eustis Historical and Archaeological Association Historical Series Fact Sheet 2.2A, February 1993), 1.
33. Jensen, 32-40.
34. OR, Series I, Vol. II, 891.

Chapter 4

1. OR, Series I, Vol. 2, 817, 865.
2. Paul D. Casdorph, Prince John Magruder: His Life and Campaigns, (New York, 1996), 1-79.

3. George Ballentine, Autobiography of an English Soldier in the United States Army Comprising Observations and Adventures in the United States and Mexico (New York, 1853), 215.
4. U. S. Congress, Senate 1 (1848), 263.
5. John Esten Cooke, Stonewall Jackson: A Military Biography (New York, 1866), 14-15.
6. William Booth Taliaferro Papers, Earl Gregg Swem Library, College of William and Mary.
7. Ibid.
8. The Constitution of the Aztec Club of 1847 and the List of Members, 1893 (Louisville, KY, 1980), 1-3.
9. William L. Haskin, The History of the First Regiment of Artillery from its Organization in 1821, to January 1st 1876 (Portland, Maine, 1879), 321.
10. Casdorph, 84-109.
11. A. L. Long, "Memoir of General John Bankhead Magruder," Southern Historical Society Papers, 12 (1884), 105-106.
12. Ibid.
13. New York Times, 23 May 1870.
14. Laura Virginia Hale, Four Valiant Years (Front Royal, VA, 1986), 247.
15. OR, Series 1, Vol. 2, 37.
16. OR, Series 1, Vol. 2, 38.
17. Ibid.
18. OR, Series 1, Vol. 2, 39.
19. OR, Series 1, Vol. 2, 917-918.
20. OR, Series 1, Vol. 2, 888.
21. John Bell Hood, Advance and Retreat: Personal Experiences in the United States and Confederate Armies (New Orleans, 1880), 17-18.
22. OR, Series 1, Vol. 2, 883.
23. Hal Bridges, Lee's Maverick General (Lincoln, 1961), 27-28.
24. Ibid., 28.
25. OR, Series 1, Vol. 2, 876.
26. Bridges, 28; Kendall J. King, "Bold, But Not Too Bold," America's Civil War, (March 1993), 45 and Arthur and Weinert, 4.
27. Philip Corell, History of the Naval Brigade 99th, New York Volunteers, Union Coast Guard (New York, 1905).
28. Alfred Davenport, Camp and Field Life of the Fifth New York Volunteer Infantry (Duryea Zouaves), (New York, 1879), 41-48 and OR, Series 1, Vol. 2, 93-94, 213, 913.
29. Bridges, 28.
30. Butler, 267.
31. William J. Kimball, "The Little Battle of Big Bethel," Civil War Times Illustrated, VI (June 1967), 28; and Arthur and Weinert, 103-104.
32. King, 45-46.
33. Bridges, 28.
34. OR, Series 1, Vol. 2, 84.
35. Davenport, 48.
36. Butler, 269 and OR, Series 1, Vol. 2, 93-95.
37. OR, Series 1, Vol. 2, 97.
38. OR, Series 1, Vol. 2, 103.
39. Davenport, 50.
40. Walter Brown, Jr., ed., "Benjamin Huske's Letter from Bethel," Civil War Times Illustrated (October 1981), 30; Davenport, 50 and King, 47.
41. OR, Series 1, Vol. 2, 101-102.
42. OR, Series 1, Vol. 2, 95; New York Times, 14 June 1861; Brown, 30; Jensen, 27 and Butler, 268-269.
43. New York Times, 14 June 1861.
44. James Dinkins, "The Battle of Big Bethel, VA," Confederate Veteran 26 (1918), 291.
45. Bridges, 29.
46. B. M. Hord, "The Battle of Big Bethel, VA," Confederate Veteran 26 (1918), 419.
47. New York Times, 14 June 1861.

48. Heitman, 573 and OR, Series 1, Vol. 2, 104.
49. OR, Series 1, Vol. 2, 95.
50. Butler, 269.
51. King, 49.
52. Gary W. Gallagher, ed., Fighting for the Confederacy: Personal Recollections of General Edward Porter Alexander (Chapel Hill, 1989), 44.
53. OR, Series 1, Vol. 2, 91.
54. Ibid.
55. Ibid., 92.
56. Lynda Laswell Crist and Mary Seaton Dix, eds., The Papers of Jefferson Davis, 1861 (Baton Rouge, 1992), Vol. 7, 420.
57. OR, Series 1, Vol. 2, 925.
58. Baker P. Lee, "Magruder's Peninsula Campaign in 1862," Southern Historical Society Papers 19 (1891), 64.
59. Ibid., 63.
60. Richmond Dispatch, June 24, 1861, 1.
61. OR, Series 1, Vol. 2, 682-686.
62. Richmond Dispatch, June 26, 1861, 3.
63. Richmond Dispatch, July 10, 1861, 3.
64. Patricia L. Faust, ed., Historical Times Illustrated Encyclopedia of the Civil War (New York, 1986), 468.
65. Douglas Southall Freeman, Lee's Lieutenants (New York, 1942), XXXIV.

Chapter 5

1. Jensen, 28.
2. Frank Leslie's Illustrated Newspaper, August 10, 1861, 193-194.
3. Faust, 659.
4. OR, Series 1, Vol. 2, 709.
5. Jensen, 29.
6. OR, Series 1, Vol. 2, 41 and 43.
7. Jensen, 32-40.
8. Casdorph, 135 and Jensen, 29-30.
9. OR, Series 1, Vol. 2, 708-709.
10. Jensen, 29.
11. Charles F. Johnson, The Long Roll (East Aurora, NY, 1911), 25.
12. Charles W. Cowtan, Services of the Tenth New York Volunteers (National Zouaves) in the War of the Rebellion (New York, 1882), 44-45 and OR, Series 1, Vol. 2, 576-577.
13. OR, Series 1, Vol. 2, 960-961.
14. OR, Series 1, Vol. 2, 188-192.
15. Jensen, 41.
16. Richard M. McMurry, John Bell Hood and the War for Southern Independence (Lexington, 1982), 26.
17. Hood, 18.
18. OR, Series 1, Vol. 2, 297-298.
19. Ibid., 297.
20. Ibid., 295-296.
21. Ibid., 301, 307.
22. John Emmet O'Brien, Telegraphing in Battle (Scranton, 1910), 18-35.
23. F. Stansbury Haydon, Aeronautics in the Union and Confederate Armies (Baltimore, 1941), Vol. I., 85-95.
24. Ibid., 95-97.
25. Chester D. Bradley, "The Fanny: First Aircraft Carrier" (Fort Monroe, 1968), 2.
26. OR, Series 1, Vol. 2, 761 and Davenport, p. 89-90.
27. OR, Series 1, Vol. 2, 763-64.
28. Ibid., 765.
29. OR, Series 1, Vol. 4, 753.

30. Thomas P. Nanzig, 3rd Virginia Cavalry (Lynchburg, 1989), 10 and Jensen, 42.
31. OR, Series 1, Vol. 4, 567.
32. Ibid., 567-570.
33. Joseph R. Haw, "The Burning of Hampton," Confederate Veteran (October 1924), 389.
34. The Richmond Examiner, 12 August 1861, 4.
35. OR, Series 1, Vol. 4, 570-572.
36. Hudgins and Kleese, 32-33.
37. Jensen, 45.
38. OR, Series 1, Vol. 4, 573.
39. New York Times, August 9, 1861, 4.
40. David W. Blight, ed., When This Cruel War is Over; The Civil War Letters of Charles Harvey Brewster (Amherst, 1992), 106.
41. OR, Series 1, Vol. 4, 573.
42. Jensen, 44.

Chapter 6

1. "Camp Butler at Newport News," The New York Illustrated News, 14 October 1861.
2. OR, Series 1, Vol. 4, 600-602.
3. William R. Trotter, Ironclads and Columbiads (Winston-Salem, North Carolina, 1989), 33-41.
4. Faust, 843.
5. OR, Series 1, Vol. 4, 602-603.
6. Arthur and Weinert, 118, 124.
7. OR, Series II, Vol. 1, 596-597.
8. Arthur and Weinert, 118.
9. West, 49-51.
10. Butler, 258-259.
11. Pierce, 628 and Edwin M. Stanton, "Letter From the Secretary of War: Africans in Fort Monroe Military District," dated 25 March 1862 (Washington, D.C., 1862), 1-14.
12. Stanton, 5.
13. Chester D. Bradley, "Highlights of Black History At Fort Monroe," (Fort Monroe, VA: The Casemate Papers, N.D.), 5.
14. Stensvaag, 98.
15. Arthur and Weinert, 116.
16. OR, Series 1, Vol. 4, 612-613.
17. OR, Series 1, Vol. 4, 672-674.
18. Official Records of the Union and Confederate Navies in the War of the Rebellion, Series II, Vol. 2, 697, 767, 793, hereinafter cited as ORN.
19. ORN, Series 1, Vol. 6, 273.
20. William Clark Corson, My Dear Jennie: A Collection of Love Letters From a Confederate Soldier to his Fiancee During the Period 1861-1865 (Richmond, 1982), 34.
21. Jensen, 46.
22. OR, Series 1, Vol. 2, 970-971.
23. Ibid., 445-446.
24. William S. White, A Diary of the War, Or What I Saw of It (Richmond, 1983), 110-111.
25. Jensen, 49.
26. OR, Series 1, Vol. 2, 970-971.
27. Ibid., 972.
28. OR, Series 1, Vol. 51, 185-186.
29. OR, Series 1, Vol. 4, 680-681.
30. ORN, Series II, Vol. 6, 717.
31. OR, Series II, Vol. 51, 256.
32. OR, Series II, Vol. 4, 640-641.
33. Emma-Jo L. Davis, "Mulberry Island and the Civil War, April 1861 - May 1862," (Fort Eustis, VA, March 1968), 13.
34. OR, Series II, Vol. 4, 644-645.
35. Davis, 14.

36. OR, Series II, Vol. 4, 668-670.
37. Ibid., 670.
38. Ibid., 676.
39. Ibid., 680-681.
40. Ibid., 702.
41. Ibid., 717.

Chapter 7

1. Corson, 34-35.
2. Quarstein and Rouse, 54.
3. Corson, 35 and Jensen, 46.
4. Walter Clark, ed., Histories of the Several Regiments and Battalions From North Carolina in the Great War 1861-1865, 15 Vols., (Raleigh, 1901), Vol. 1, 47.
5. White, 111.
6. Ibid.
7. ORN, Series I, Vol. 6, 759.
8. OR, Series II, Vol. 4, 430-431.
9. White, 112.
10. Davis, 21-28.
11. Ibid., 23.
12. Stephen W. Sears, George B. McClellan, The Young Napoleon (New York, 1988), 95.
13. Faust, 456.
14. Sears, McClellan, 50-67.
15. Faust, 633.
16. Boatner, 524-525.
17. Stephen W. Sears, ed., The Civil War Papers of George B. McClellan (New York, 1989), 70.
18. Sears, McClellan, 123-125.
19. Ibid., 147-151.
20. Sears, The Civil War Papers of George B. McClellan, 162-171.
21. Sears, McClellan, 149-155.
22. Joseph E. Johnston, Narrative of Military Operations During the Civil War (New York, 1990), 96.
23. OR, Series 1, Vol. 9, 32-33.
24. Stephen W. Sears, To the Gates of Richmond (New York, 1992), 5-9.

Chapter 8

1. Gustavus V. Fox, The Confidential Correspondence of Gustavus V. Fox (New York, 1919), 1, 244.
2. ORN, Series I, Vol. 6, 543.
3. William C. Davis, Duel Between the First Ironclads (Baton Rouge, 1975), 68-70 and William N. Still, Jr. Iron Afloat (Columbia, 1985), 29.
4. John S. Long, "The Gosport Affair," Journal of Southern History, 23 (May 1957), 155-72.
5. Richmond Daily Enquirer, April 22, 1861.
6. Edward E. Barthill, Jr., The Mystery of the Merrimack (Muskegon, MI, 1959), 29-30.
7. Long, 155-72.
8. ORN, Series II, Vol. 2, 67-69.
9. Boatner, 503-504.
10. John M. Brooke, "The Virginia or Merrimac: Her Real Projector," Southern Historical Society Papers, 19 (1891), 3-34, John M. Brooke, "The Plan and Construction of the "Merrimac," Battles and Leaders of the Civil War (New York, 1887), Vol. 1, 715-716 and ORN, Series II, Vol. 2, 784.
11. ORN, Series II, Vol. 2, 77-79.
12. W. A. Wise to Edward Everett, June 19, 1861, Everett Collection, Massachusetts Historical Society.
13. Still, 18.
14. ORN, Series II, Vol. 1, 783-784; Richmond Examiner, April 3, 1862, Brooke, 14-15 and John

W. H. Porter, A Record of Events in Norfolk County, Virginia (Portsmouth, Virginia, 1892), 350.
15. ORN, Series I, Vol. 6, 742.
16. Porter, 331.
17. ORN, Series II, 1, 785-786 and Brooke, II, 769.
18. Brooke, II, 808.
19. William R. Cline, "The Ironclad Ram Virginia," Southern Historical Society Papers, 32 (1904), 244.
20. S. B. Beese, C. S. Ironclad Virginia, with Date and References for a Scale Model (Newport News, 1937).
21. Brooke, 799.
22. Ibid., 31.
23. John Taylor Wood, "The First Fight of Iron-clads," Battles and Leaders, 1, 719.
24. Still, 23-24.
25. Ibid.
26. Boatner, 94.
27. ORN, Series I, Vol. 6, 776-777.
28. Ibid., 803.
29. Dinwiddie B. Phillips, "The Career of the Iron-clad Virginia," Collections of the Virginia Historical Society, 6 (1887), 201.
30. Hardin B. Littlepage, "Statement of Midshipman Littlepage," Southern Historical Society Papers, 11 (1883), 33.
31. Wood, "The First Fight of Iron-clads," 696.
32. OR, Series 1, Vol. 51, pt. 2, 480.
33. OR, Series 1, Vol. 9, 14.
34. Ibid.
35. William Tindall, "True Story of the Virginia," Virginia Magazine of History and Biography, 31 (January 1923), 36-37.
36. Charles Lee Lewis, Admiral Franklin Buchanan: Fearless Man of Action (Baltimore, 1929), 184.
37. Henry Reaney, "How the Gun-Boat 'Zouave' Aided the 'Congress', " Battles and Leaders, 1, 714.
38. ORN, Series 1, Vol. 6, 661.
39. George F. Amadon, Rise of the Ironclads (Missoula, Montana), 39.
40. Reaney, 714-715.
41. H. Aston Ramsay, "Wonderful Career of the Merrimac," Confederate Veteran, 25 (July 1907), 311.
42. William H. Parker, Recollections of a Naval Officer, 1841-1865 (New York, 1883), 257 and John R. Eggleston, "Captain Eggleston's Narrative of the Battle of the Merrimac," Southern Historical Society Papers, 41 (September 1916), 170.
43. Thomas O. Selfridge, Jr., Memoirs of Thomas O. Selfridge, Jr.: Rear Admiral, U.S.N. (New York, 1924), 50.
44. Wood, 698.
45. Catesby ap R. Jones, "Services of the Virginia," Southern Historical Society Papers, 11 (January 1883), 68.
46. Ramsay, 311 and Jones, 68.
47. Littlepage, 202.
48. Moses S. Stuyvesant, "How the Cumberland Went Down", War Papers and Personal Reminiscences: 1861 - 1865, Vol. 1 (Wilmington, NC, 1992), 117.
49. Selfridge, 50.
50. Jones, 69.
51. Quoted on "The Sinking of the Cumberland by the Ironclad Merrimac off Newport News, VA. March 8th 1862, (New York, Currier & Ives, 1862).
52. Reaney, 716; Parker, 254-56; ORN, Series 1, Vol. 7, 7-24; and Wood, 698.
53. F. S. Alger, "Congress and the Merrimac," New England Magazine, 14 (February 1899), 681-693; Parker, 258-59; and Eggleston, 172-73.
54. OR, Series I, Vol. 9, 78.

55. Parker, 260.
56. To Kell, March 8, 1862, quoted in John M. Kell, Recollections of a Naval Life (Washington, D.C., 1900), 282-283.
57. Eggleston, 173.
58. Jones, 72.
59. Eggleston, 173.
60. Jones, 73.
61. Kell, 283.
62. Boatner, 560-561.

Chapter 9

1. Madeleine V. Dahlgren, Memoir of John A. Dahlgren (Boston, 1882), 359-360.
2. Gideon Welles, Diary of Gideon Welles Secretary of the Navy Under Lincoln and Johnson, ed., Howard K. Beale (New York, 1960), Vol. 1, 51-52.
3. Still, 35.
4. The U.S.S. Princeton was the first American steam, screw propelled man-of-war. The vessel was designed by John Ericsson as were several heavy caliber guns on board. One of the twelve-inch guns was designed by the Princeton's promoter and commander, Captain R. F. Stockton. The Princeton was a huge success, but during a demonstration of her heavy guns, an event attended by President Franklin Pierce and other high officials, in the Potomac, Stockton's gun exploded killing Secretary of State Abel P. Upshur, Secretary of the Navy T. W. Gilmer and others. Ericsson was blamed for the disaster and never received his full fee for his work on the Princeton. Bern Anderson, By Sea and By River, The Naval History of the Civil War (New York, 1989), 7-8.
5. Anderson, 67-68.
6. Welles, 39.
7. William C. Church, The Life of John Ericsson (New York, 1890), Vol. 1, 249.
8. Welles, 41-47.
9. William C. Wells, The Original United States Warship Monitor (New Haven, Conn., 1899), 17.
10. Amadon, 29.
11. Boatner, 948-949.
12. ORN, Series 1, Vol. 6, 516-17.
13. John Ericsson, "The Building of the Monitor," Battles and Leaders, Vol. 1, 735.
14. S. B. Beese, U.S.S. Monitor, with Data and References for a Scale Model (Newport News, 1937).
15. Ibid.
16. ORN, Series II, Vol. 1, 148.
17. Gideon Welles, "The First Iron-Clad Monitor," Annuals of the War (Philadelphia, 1879), 19-20.
18. Robert W. Daly, ed., Aboard the U.S.S. Monitor, 1862: The Letters of Acting Paymaster William Frederick Keeler (Annapolis, 1964), 8.
19. Louis N. Stodder, "Aboard the U.S.S. Monitor," Civil War Times Illustrated, 1 (January 1963), 31.
20. Samuel Lewis, "Life on the Monitor," in William C. King and William P. Derby, eds., Camp-Fire Sketches and Battlefield Echoes of 61-5 (Springfield, Mass., 1888), 258.
21. David R. Ellis, The Monitor of the Civil War (privately printed), 19.
22. ORN, Series 1, Vol. 25, 757.
23. Amadon, 31.
24. Alban C. Stimers, "An Engineer Aboard the Monitor," Civil War Times Illustrated, 9 (April 1970), 29.
25. Samuel Dana Greene, "In the Monitor Turret," Battles and Leaders, 1, 720-21, and Samuel Dana Greene, "I Fired the First Gun and Thus Commenced the Great Battle," American Heritage, 8 (June 1957), 11-13.
26. Ibid.
27. Ibid.
28. Ibid.
29. Daly, 31.

30. ORN, Series I, Vol. 7, 5 and Greene, "I Fired the First Gun," 102.
31. Greene, "I Fired the First Gun," 102 and Greene, "In the Monitor Turret," 722.
32. Thomas W. Rae, "The Little Monitor Saved Our Lives," American History Illustrated, 1 (July 1966), 34.
33. Greene, "In the Monitor Turret," 722.
34. Phillips, "The Career of the Iron-Clad Virginia," 206-7.
35. Eggleston, 174; Davis, 117; Porter, 361; and Jones, 71.
36. Ramsay, "Most Famous of Sea Duels," 12.
37. Eggleston, 175-76.
38. Ramsay, 12.
39. Daly, 39.
40. Daly, 50, Stimers, 35, Stodder, 34, and Greene, 105.
41. Ramsay, "Most Famous of Sea Duels," 13.
42. Daly, 64 and Ramsay, 13.
43. Davis, 130.
44. Greene, "I Fired the First Gun," 104 and Wood, 692.
45. Asher Williams, "Letters From a Soldier in the Union Army," The Staten Island Historian (Apr.-June 1961), 15.
46. ORN, Series 1, Vol. 7, 83.
47. Still, 35.
48. ORN, Series 1, Vol. 7, 225.

Chapter 10

1. Johnston, Narrative of Military Operations During the Civil War, 102-104.
2. Sears, To the Gates of Richmond, 16-18 and Sears, The Civil War Papers of George B. McClellan, 201-207.
3. Sears, The Civil War Papers of George B. McClellan, 215.
4. ORN, Series 1, Vol. 7, 100.
5. Ibid., 780-81.
6. OR, Series II, Vol. 8, 570.
7. Sears, The Civil War Papers of George B. McClellan, 168.
8. OR, Series II, Vol. 3, 53.
9. Sears, The Civil War Papers of George B. McClellan, 217.
10. OR, Series 1, Vol. 9, 14.
11. OR, Series 1, Vol. 51, 499-500.
12. Forrest Conner, ed., "Letters of Lieutenant Robert H. Miller to His Family, 1861-1862," Virginia Magazine of History and Biography 70 (January 1962), 64.
13. OR, Series 1, Vol. 51, 499-500.
14. OR, Series 1, Vol. 11, 389.
15. OR, Series 1, Vol. 9, 66-68.
16. OR, Series 1, Vol. 11, 405.
17. OR, Series 1, Vol. 11, 389.
18. Ibid.
19. OR, Series 1, Vol. 9, 422.
20. Ibid., 53-54.
21. OR, Series 1, Vol. 4, 389.
22. OR, Series 1, Vol.11, 406.
23. Edmund Patterson, Yankee Rebel: The Civil War Journal of Edmund Dewitt Patterson (Chapel Hill, 1966), 17.
24. George B. McClellan, McClellan's Own Story (New York, 1887), 254.
25. Casdorph, 146.
26. Sears, The Civil War Papers of George B. McClellan, 223.
27. Alexander S. Webb, The Peninsula (New York, 1881), 27.
28. Sears, The Civil War Papers of George B. McClellan, 215.
29. Webb, 36-44.
30. OR, Series 1, Vol. 9, 358.

31. Emil and Ruth Rosenblatt, ed., Hard Marching Every Day: The Civil War Letters of Private Wilbur Fisk, 1861-1865 (Lawrence, 1992), 17.
32. OR, Series 1, Vol. 9, 358.
33. Blight, 109.
34. Oliver Willcox Norton, Army Letters: 1861-1865 (Dayton, 1990), 57.
35. OR, Series 1, Vol. 9, 300.
36. Ibid., 17.
37. Quarstein and Rouse, 47.
38. OR, Series 1, Vol. 9, 300.
39. Ibid., 404.
40. Patterson, 17.
41. J. W. Minnish, "Reminiscences Relating to the Siege of Yorktown," Virginia War Museum, 4.
42. C. Vann Woodward, ed., Mary Chesnut's Civil War (New Haven, 1981), 401.
43. Sears, The Civil War Papers of George B. McClellan, 215.
44. Patrick Lyons, A Soldier's Log (Providence, 1988), 26.
45. A. B. Weymouth, ed., A Memorial Sketch of Lieut. Edgar M. Newcomb, of the Nineteenth Mass. Vols. (Malden, 1883), 54.
46. Lyons, 26.
47. William F. Smith, Autobiography of Major General William F. Smith, 1861-1864 (Dayton, 1990), 33-35.
48. Sears, The Civil War Papers of George B. McClellan, 254.
49. Ibid., 234.
50. Ibid., 245.

Chapter 11
1. Jubal Anderson Early, Narrative of the War Between the States (New York, 1991), 59.
2. Jensen, 59.
3. Sears, The Civil War Papers of George B. McClellan, 216.
4. Thomas B. Leaver Diary, May 2, 1862, New Hampshire Historical Society, Concord, New Hampshire.
5. Gilbert Thompson Diary, Manuscript Division, Library of Congress, Washington, D.C.
6. OR, Series 1, Vol.11, 307-308.
7. James Montgomery Holloway Papers 1861-1905, Virginia Historical Society, Richmond, Virginia.
8. Early, 59.
9. G. Moxley Sorrel, Reflections of a Confederate Staff Officer (New York, 1905), 63.
10. Early, 61.
11. W. H. Andrews, Footprints of a Regiment, A Recollection of the 1st Georgia Regulars, (Atlanta, 1992), 32-33.
12. ORN, Series 1, Vol. 7, 219-225.
13. Rosenblatt, Hard Marching Every Day, 56.
14. Andrews, 33.
15. William S. Smedlund, History of the Troup Artillery (unpublished manuscript), np.
16. Henry R. Berkley, Four Years in the Confederate Artillery (Chapel Hill, 1961), 64.
17. Andrews, 34.
18. Patterson, 17.
19. Blight, 113, 118.
20. Sears, The Civil War Papers of George B. McClellan, 217.
21. G. G. Benedict, Vermont in the Civil War, 2 Vols., (Burlington, 1886), Vol. 1, 258.
22. Jensen, 184 and Quarstein and Rouse, 43.
23. Berkley, 14.
24. Robert Hunt Rhodes, ed., All for the Union: The Civil War Diary and Letters of Elisha Hunt Rhodes (New York, 1991), 55.
25. OR, Series 1, Vol. 11, 421.
26. Otis F. R. Waite, Vermont in the Great Rebellion (Claremont, 1869), 122.

27. OR, Series 1, Vol. 11, 406.
28. Benedict, 253.
29. Webb, 64.
30. Ibid.
31. Benedict, 253.
32. Benedict, 254 and Waite, 123.
33. John E. Balzar, ed., Buck's Book, A View of the 3rd Vermont Infantry Regiment (Bolingbrook, 1993), 28.
34. Walter Clark, ed., Histories of the Several Regiments and Battalions From North Carolina in the Great War 1861-1865, 47.
35. Benedict, 254.
36. OR, Series 1, Vol. 11, 408.
37. Elizabeth Whitley Roberson, ed., Weep Not For Me, Dear Mother: The War Experiences of Private Eli Pinson Landers of the 16th Regiment, Georgia Volunteers, the Flint Hill Grays (Washington, 1991), 72-73.
38. Balzar, 30.
39. Ibid., 31.
40. Waite, 125.
41. Roberson, 72-73.
42. Benedict, 253.
43. Ibid., 261.
44. Waite, 126.
45. Albert C. Eisenberg, ' "The 3rd Vermont has won a name:' Corporal George Q. French's Account of the Battle of Lees Mills, Virginia," Vermont History, 49 (Fall, 1981), 225.
46. Ibid., 227.
47. New York Times, May 2, 1862, 3.
48. Rosenblatt, 19.
49. Webb, 66.

Chapter 12

1. Minnish, 4.
2. OR, Series 1, Vol. 11, 366.
3. Johnston, 111.
4. OR, Series 1, Vol. 11, 473.
5. Freeman, Lee's Lieutenants, 150-151.
6. Johnston, 116.
7. Coner, 79.
8. Andrews, 33.
9. R. Channing Price Papers, Virginia Historical Society, Richmond, Virginia.
10. Early, 62.
11. Patterson, 17.
12. Early, 63.
13. Judith N. McArthur and Orville Vernon Burton, eds., A Gentleman and An Officer, A Military and Social History of James B. Griffin's Civil War (New York, 1996), 199.
14. Norton, 68.
15. Blight, 111.
16. Patterson, 18.
17. McArthur and Burton, 199.
18. Andrews, 33.
19. David Herbert Donald, ed., Gone for a Soldier, The Civil War Memoirs of Private Alfred Bellard (Boston, 1975), 55.
20. Robert E. Lewis Papers, Private Collection, Williamsburg, Virginia.
21. History of the Twenty-Third Pennsylvania Volunteer Infantry, Birney's Zouaves (Philadelphia, 1903-1904), 32.
22. Donald, 56.
23. Blight, 114.

24. John M. Carroll, Custer in the Civil War, His Unfinished Memoirs (New York, 1976), 144-145.
25. Robert Stiles, Four Years Under Marse Robert (New York, 1903), 76.
26. Early, 60-61.
27. Minnish, 15-16.
28. G. B. Noyes, ed., "Letters written by Sgt. George B. Noyes, Co. K, 11th Regiment Maine Volunteers During the Civil War," Island Advantages, Vol. 27, No. 34 (July 1962), 2.
29. Ida Bright Adams, ed., "Letter of James Rush Holmes," Western Pennsylvania Historical Magazine, Vol. 22, No.2 (June 1961), 116.
30. William B. Styple, ed., Letters From the Peninsula: The Civil War Letters of General Philip Kearny (Kearny, 1988), 51-52.
31. Coner, 121.
32. Tom D. Crouch, The Eagle Afloat, Two Centuries of the Balloon in America (Washington, 1983), 375-376.
33. Carroll, 147.
34. Randolph Bryan, "Balloon Used for Scout Duty," Confederate Veteran, Vol. 22 (April 1914), 4, 162-163.
35. Robert V. Bruce, Lincoln and the Tools of War (New York, 1956), 199.
36. Lyons, A Soldier's Log, 30.
37. Freeman, Vol. 1, 127.
38. OR, Series 1, Vol. 11, 446.
39. ORN, Series 1, Vol. 7, 765-766.
40. OR, Series 1, Vol. 11, 462.
41. J. W. Reid, History of the Fourth Regiment of S. C. Volunteers (Greenville, 1892), 74-77.
42. McArthur and Burton, 200-201.
43. Jensen, 59-61, 187.
44. Bridges, 7.
45. ORN, Series 1, Vol. 7, 223-224.
46. Webb, 67-68.
47. Sears, The Civil War Papers of George B. McClellan, 251.
48. McArthur and Burton, 203.
49. H. T. Douglas to S.T.C. Bryan, 29 February 1909, St. George T. C. Bryan Papers, Brockenbrough Library, Museum of the Confederacy, Richmond, Virginia.
50. George T. Stevens, Three Years in the Sixth Corps (New York, 1870), 47.
51. History of the Twenty-Third Pennsylvania Volunteer Infantry, 39.
52. Boatner, 470.
53. History of the Twenty-Third Pennsylvania Volunteer Infantry, 128.
54. Milton F. Perry, Infernal Machines: The Story of Confederate Submarine and Mine Warfare (Baton Rouge, 1965), 27.
55. Weymouth, 58.

Chapter 13
1. OR, Series 1, Vol. 11, 302.
2. Benjamin P. Thomas, Abraham Lincoln (New York, 1952), 319.
3. ORN, Series 1, Vol. 7, 228-338.
4. OR, Series 1 Vol. 11, 634-635.
5. Wood, "First Fight," 710; Jones, "Services of the Virginia," 73; and ORN, Series 1, Vol. 7, 336-337.
6. Ramsay, "Most Famous of Sea Duels," 12.
7. Boatner, 948.
8. Ibid., 241-242.
9. Richard P. Weinert, "Longstreet's Suffolk Campaign," Civil War Times Illustrated, 7 (January 1969), 31-39.
10. Arthur and Weinert, 140-142.
11. Ibid., 143.
12. Dictionary of American Fighting Ships (Washington, 1970), 567.
13. Confederate Veteran, Vol. 21 (June 1913), 307, New York Sun, Feb. 28, 1897 and Richard N.

Current, ed., Encyclopedia of the Confederacy, Vol. 2 (New York, 1993) 447-448.
14. Hunter Davidson, "Torpedoes in Our War," U. S. Naval Institute Proceedings, Vol. 24 (June 1898), 352.
15. ORN, Series 1, Vol. 6, 603.
16. John C. Spencer, "A Page from the Old Navy," U. S. Naval Institute Proceedings, Vol. 86 (May 1960), 155 and ORN, Series 1, Vol. 6, 603.
17. Davidson, "Torpedoes in Our War," 353.
18. Ibid.
19. Hunter Davidson, "The Electric Submarine Mine," The Confederate Veteran, Vol. 14 (September 1906), 458.
20. ORN, Series 1, Vol. 6, 745.
21. Samuel G. Margolin, "Civil War Legacy Beneath the James," Archaeology 40 (September/October 1987), 53-54.
22. Ibid.
23. Justin G. Turner, "Hampton Roads Conference," Civil War Times, Vol. 3 (January 1962), 12-16.
24. OR, Series II, Vol. 8, 505.
25. Ibid., 689.
26. Ibid., 692-693.
27. Ibid., 508-509, 692-693.
28. Ibid., 1000-1003.
29. Arthur and Weinert, 147-158.
30. W. H. T. Squires, Unleashed at Long Last (Portsmouth, VA, 1939), 39.
31. A History of Lebanon Church of Christ (Newport News, n.d.), 1.
32. Charles A. Wainwright, A Diary of Battle (New York, 1962), 50.
33. Blight, 110.
34. Williams, "Letters From a Soldier in the Union," 15.
35. Ibid.
36. West, 43.
37. Williams, "Letters From a Soldier in the Union," 15.
38. Quarstein and Rouse, 244.

Bibliography

Manuscripts

John B. Cary letter book, May 16 - August 3, 1861. Eleanor S. Brockenbrough Library, The Museum of the Confederacy.

H. T. Douglas to S. T. C. Bryan, 29 February 1909, St. George T. C. Bryan Papers, Brockenbrough Library, The Museum of the Confederacy.

Benjamin Stoddert Ewell Papers, Earl Gregg Swem Library, The College of William and Mary.

"History of the Virginia Peninsula." Newport News Main Street Library.

James Montgomery Holloway Papers 1861-1905. Virginia Historical Society.

James Barron Hope Papers, Earl Gregg Swem Library, The College of William and Mary.

Thomas B. Leaver Diary. May 2, 1862. New Hampshire Historical Society.

Robert E. Lewis Papers, Private Collection.

Minnish, J. W. "Reminiscences Relating to the Siege of Yorktown." Virginia War Museum.

R. Channing Price Papers, Virginia Historical Society.

"The Sinking of the Cumberland by the Ironclad Merrimac Off Newport News, VA. March 8th 1862." Currier & Ives Lithograph Text.

William Booth Taliaferro Papers, Earl Gregg Swem Library, College of William and Mary.

Gilbert Thompson Diary. Manuscript Division, Library of Congress.

Smedlund, William S. History of the Troup Artillery.

W. A. Wise to Edward Everett. June 19, 1861. Everett Collection, Massachusetts Historical Society.

Diary of Captain Edward Rush Young, M.D. Private Collection.

Books

Amadon, George F. Rise of the Ironclads (Missoula, 1989). Anderson, Bern. By Sea and By River, The Naval History of the Civil War (New York, 1989).

Andrews, W. H. Footprints of a Regiment, A Recollection of the 1st Georgia Regulars (Atlanta, 1992).

Arthur, Robert and Weinert, Richard P., Jr. Defender of the Chesapeake: The Story of Fort Monroe (Shippensburg, 1989).

Ballentine, George. Autobiography of an English Soldier in the United States Army Comprising Observations and Adventures in the United States and Mexico (New York, 1853).

Balzar, John E., Ed. Buck's Book, A View of the 3rd Vermont Infantry Regiment (Bolingbrook, 1993).

Barthill, Edward E., Jr. The Mystery of the Merrimack (Muskegon, 1959).

Beese, S. B. C. S. Ironclad Virginia, with Date and References for a Scale Model (Newport News, 1937).

Beese, S. B. U.S.S. Monitor, with Data and References for a Scale Model (Newport News, 1937).

Benedict, G. G. Vermont in the Civil War. Volume I (Burlington, 1886).

Berkley, Henry R. Four Years in the Confederate Artillery (Chapel Hill, 1961).

Blight, David W. Ed. When This Cruel War is Over: The Civil War Letters of Charles Harvey Brewster (Amherst, 1992).

Boatner, Mark Mayo, III. The Civil War Dictionary (New York, 1959).

Bridges, Hal. Lee's Maverick General (Lincoln, 1961).

Brooke, John M. "The Plan and Construction of the Merrimac." Battles and Leaders of the Civil War. Volume 1. (New York, 1887).

Brown, Alexander C., Ed. Newport News' 325 Years: A Record of Progress of a Virginia Community (Newport News, 1946).

Bruce, Robert V. Lincoln and the Tools of War (New York, 1956).

Butler, Benjamin F. Butler's Book (Boston, 1892).

Campbell, Charles. History of the Colony and Ancient Dominion of Virginia (Philadelphia, 1860).

Carroll, John M. Custer in the Civil War, His Unfinished Memoirs (New York, 1976).

Casdorph, Paul D. Prince John Magruder: His Life and Campaigns (New York, 1996).

Church, William C. The Life of John Ericsson, Volume 1 (New York, 1890).

Clark, Walter, Ed. Histories of the Several Regiments and Battalions From North Carolina in the Great War 1861- 1865. 15 Volumes (Raleigh, 1901).

The Constitution of the Aztec Club of 1847 and the List of Members, 1893 (Louisville, 1980).

Cooke, John Esten. Stonewall Jackson: A Military Biography (New York, 1866).

Corell, Philip. History of the Naval Brigade 99th New York Volunteers, Union Coast Guard (New York, 1905).

Corson, William Clark. My Dear Jennie: A Collection of Love Letters From a Confederate Soldier to his Fiancee During the Period 1861-1865 (Richmond, 1982).

Cowtan, Charles W. Services of the Tenth New York (National Zouaves) in the War of the Rebellion (New York, 1882).

Craven, John J. Prison Life of Jefferson Davis (New York, 1866).

Crist, Lynda Laswell and Dix, Mary Seaton, Eds. The Papers of Jefferson Davis, 1861 (Baton Rouge, 1992).

Crouch, Tim D. The Eagle Afloat, Two Centuries of the Balloon in America (Washington, DC, 1983).

Current, Richard N., Ed. Encyclopedia of the Confederacy. Volume 2 (New York, 1993).

Curry, John. The Warwick Beauregards (Fort Eustis, 1993).

Curtis, Richard. History of the Great Naval Engagement Between The Iron-Clad Merrimac, C.S.N., And The Cumberland, Congress and The Iron-Clad Monitor, U.S.N. March the 8th and 9th, 1862, As Seen By A Man At The Gun (Hampton, 1957).

Dabney, Virginius. Virginia: The New Dominion (New York, 1971).

Dahlgren, Madeleine. Memoirs of John A. Dahlgren (Boston, 1882).

Daly, Robert W. Abroad the U.S.S. Monitor, 1862: The Letters of Acting Paymaster William Frederick Keeler (Annapolis, 1964).

Davenport, Alfred. Camp and Field Life of the Fifth New York Volunteer Infantry (New York, 1879).

Davis, William C. Duel Between the First Ironclads (Baton Rouge, 1975).

Dictionary of American Fighting Ships (Washington, DC, 1970).

Donald, David Herbert, Ed. Gone for a Soldier, The Civil War Memoirs of Private Alfred Bellard (Boston, 1975)

Early, Jubal Anderson. Narrative of the War Between the States (New York, 1991).

Ellis, David R. The Monitor of the Civil War (privately printed).

Ericsson, John. "The Building of the Monitor." Battles and Leaders of the Civil War. Volume 1. (New York, 1887).

Faust, Patricia, L., Ed. Historical Times Illustrated Encyclopedia of the Civil War (New York, 1986).

Flourney, H. W., Ed. Calendar of Virginia State Papers, 1808-1835 (Richmond, 1892).

Fox, Gustavus V. The Confidential Correspondence of Gustavus V. Fox (New York, 1919).

Freeman, Douglas Southall. Lee's Lieutenants (New York, 1942).

Gallagher, Gary W., Ed. Fighting for the Confederacy: Personal Recollections of General Edward Porter Alexander (Chapel Hill, 1989).

Hale, Laura Virginia. Four Valiant Years (Front Royal, 1986).

Haskin, William L. The History of the First Regiment of Artillery from its Organization in 1821, to January 1st 1876 (Portland, 1879).

Haydon, F. Stansbury. Aeronautics in the Union and Confederate Armies (Baltimore, 1941).

Heitman, Francis B. Historical Register and Dictionary of the United States Army (Washington, DC, 1903).

A History of Lebanon Church (Newport News, n.d.).

History of the Twenty-Third Pennsylvania Volunteer Infantry, Birney's Zouaves. (Philadelphia, 1904).

Hood, John Bell. Advance and Retreat: Personal Experiences in the United States and Confederate Armies (New Orleans, 1880).

Howe, Henry W. Passages from the Life of Henry Warren Howe, Consisting of Diary and Letters Written During the Civil War (Lowell, 1899).

Hudgins, Garland C. and Kleese, Richard B. Recollections of an Old Dominion Dragoon: Civil War Experiences of Sgt. Robert S. Hudgins, II Co. B., 3rd Virginia Cavalry (Orange, 1993).

Jensen, Les. 32nd Virginia Infantry (Lynchburg, 1990).

Johnson, Charles F. The Long Roll (East Aurora, New York, 1911).

Johnston, Joseph E. Narrative of Military Operations During the Civil War (New York, 1990).

Jones, Catesby ap Roger. "Services of the Virginia." Southern Historical Society Papers. Volume 11 (January 1883).

Journals of the House of Burgesses (Richmond, 1905-1915).

Kell, John M. Recollections of a Naval Life. (Washington, DC, 1900).

Lewis, Charles Lee. Admiral Franklin Buchanan: Fearless Man of Action (Baltimore, 1929).

Lewis, Samuel. "Life on the Monitor." King, William C. and Derby, William P., Eds. Camp Fire Sketches and Battlefield Echoes of 61-5 (Springfield, MA, 1888).

Lyons, Patrick. A Soldier's Log (Providence, 1988).

McArthur, Judith N. and Burton, Orville Vernon, Eds. A Gentleman and An Officer, A Military and Social History of James B. Griffin's Civil War (New York, 1996).

McClellan. George B. McClellan's Own Story (New York, 1887).

McMurry, Richard M. John Bell Hood and the War for Southern Independence (Lexington, 1982).

Martin, Joseph. A New and Comprehensive Gazetter of Virginia and the District of Columbia: Containing a Copious Collection (Charlottesville, 1835).

Maxwell, William, Ed. Virginia Historical Register and Literary Advisor (Richmond, 1973).

Moore, Robert H., II. Miscellaneous Disbanded Virginia Light Artillery (Lynchburg, 1997).

Nanzig, Thomas P. 3rd Virginia Cavalry (Lynchburg, 1989).

Norton, Oliver Willcox. Army Letters: 1861-1865 (Dayton, 1990).

O'Brien, John Emmet. Telegraphing in Battle (Scranton, 1910).

Official Records of the Union and Confederate Navies in the War of the Rebellion (Washington, DC, 1889-1901).

Osborne, William H. History of the Twenty-ninth Regiment of Massachusetts (Boston, 1877).

Parker, William H. Recollections of a Naval Officer, 1841-1865. (New York, 1883).

Patterson, Edmund. Yankee Rebel: The Civil War Journal of Edmund Dewitt Patterson (Chapel Hill, 1966).

Perry, Milton F. Infernal Machines: The Story of Confederate Submarine and Mine Warfare (Baton Rouge, 1965).

Porter, John W. H. A Record of Events in Norfolk County, Virginia (Portsmouth, 1892).

Quarstein, John V. and Rouse, Parke S., Jr. Newport News: A Centennial History (Newport News, 1996).

Rhodes, Robert Hunt, Ed. All for the Union: The Civil War Diary and Letters of Elisha Hunt Rhodes (New York, 1991).

Robertson, Elizabeth Whitley, Ed. Weep Not For Me, Dear Mother: The War Experiences of Private Eli Pinson Landers of the 16th Regiment, Georgia Volunteers, the Flint Hill Grays (Washington, 1991).

Rosenblatt, Emil and Ruth, Eds. Hard Marching Every Day: The Civil War Letters of Private Wilbur Fisk, 1861-1865 (Lawrence, 1992).

Seager, Robert, II. and Tyler Too, A Biography of John and Julie Gardner Tyler (New York, 1963).

Sears, Stephen W., Ed. The Civil War Papers of George B. McClellan (New York, 1989).

Sears, Stephen W. George B. McClellan, The Young Napoleon (New York, 1988).

Sears, Stephen W. To the Gates of Richmond (New York, 1992).

Selfridge, Thomas O., Jr. Memoirs of Thomas O. Selfridge, Jr.: Rear Admiral, U.S.N. (New York, 1924).

Smith, William F. Autobiography of Major General William F. Smith, 1861-1864 (Dayton, 1990).

Sorrel, G. Moxley. Reflections of a Confederate Staff Officer (New York, 1905).

Squires, W. H. T. Unleashed at Long Last (Portsmouth, 1939).

Stensvagg, James T., Ed. Hampton: From the Sea to the Stars (Virginia Beach, 1985).

Stevens, George T. Three Years in the Sixth Corps (New York, 1870).

Stiles, Robert. Four Years Under Marse Robert (New York, 1903).

Still, William N., Jr. Iron Afloat (Columbia, 1985).

Stith, William. History of the First Discovery and Settlement of Virginia (Williamsburg, 1747).

Stuyvesant, Moses, S. "How the Cumberland Went Down." War Papers and Personal Reminiscences: 1861-1865. Volume 1 (Wilmington, NC, 1992).

Styple, William B., Ed. Letters From the Peninsula: The Civil War Letters of General Philip Kearny (Kearny, 1988).

Tarleton, Banistre. History of the Campaign of 1780 and 1781 in the Southern Provinces of North America (London, 1787).

Thomas, Benjamin P. Abraham Lincoln (New York, 1952).

Trotler, William R. Ironclads and Columbiads (Winston-Salem, NC, 1989).

Tyler, Lyon G. History of Hampton and Elizabeth City County, Virginia (Hampton, 1922).

Tyler, Lyon G., Ed. Narratives of Early Virginia, 1606-1625 (New York, 1966).

Wainwright, Charles A. A Diary of Battle (New York, 1962).

Waite, Otis F. R. Vermont in the Great Rebellion (Claremont, 1869).

War of the Rebellion: A Compilation of the Official Records of the Union and Confederate Armies (Washington, 1880-1901).

Warner, Ezra. Generals in Gray (Baton Rouge, 1959).

Webb, Alexander S. The Peninsula (New York, 1881).

Welles, Gideon. Diary of Gideon Welles, Secretary of the Navy Under Lincoln and Johnson. Howard K. Beale, Ed. Volume 1 (New York, 1960).

Wells, William C. The Original United States Warship Monitor (New Haven, CT, 1899).

West, George Benjamin. When the Yankees Came (Richmond, 1977).

Weymouth, A. B., Ed. A Memorial Sketch of Lieutenant Edgar M. Newcomb, of the Nineteenth Mass. Vols. (Malden, 1883).

Whichard, Rogers Dey. The History of Lower Tidewater (New York, 1959).

White, William S. A Diary of the War, Or What I Saw of It (Richmond, 1983).

Wood, John Taylor. "The First Fight of Iron-clads." Battles and Leaders of the Civil War. Volume 1 (New York, 1887).

Woodward, C. Vann, Ed. Mary Chesnut's Civil War (New Haven, 1981).

Periodicals
Adams, Ida Bright, Ed. "Letter of James Rush Holmes." Western Pennsylvania Historical Magazine. Volume 22 (June 1961).

Alger, F. S. "Congress and the Merrimac." New England Magazine. Volume 14 (February 1899).

Bradley, Chester D. "The Fanny: First Aircraft Carrier." (Fort Monroe, 1968).

Bradley, Chester D. "Highlights of Black History At Fort Monroe." Casemate Papers (Fort Monroe, VA, n.d.).

Bradley, Chester D. "President Lincoln's Campaign Against the Merrimac." Journal of the Illinois Historical Society. Volume 51 (Spring 1958).

Brooke, John M. "The Virginia or Merrimac: Her Real Projector." Southern Historical Society Papers. Volume 19 (1891).

Brown, Walter, Jr., Ed. "Benjamin Huske's Letter from Bethel." Civil War Times Illustrated (October 1981).

Bryan, Randolph. "Balloon Used for Scout Duty." Confederate Veteran. Volume 22 (April 1914).

Cline, William R. "The Ironclad Ram Virginia." Southern Historical Society Papers. Volume 32 (1904).

Confederate Veteran. Volume 21 (June 1913).

Conner, Forrest, Ed. "Letters of Lieutenant Robert H. Miller to His Family, 1861-1862." Virginia Magazine of History and Biography. Volume 70 (January 1962).

Davidson, Hunter. "The Electric Submarine Mine." The Confederate Veteran. Volume 14 (September 1906).

Davidson, Hunter. "Torpedoes in Our War." U. S. Naval Institute Proceedings. Volume 24 (June 1898).

Davis, Emma-Jo L. "Mulberry Island and the Civil War, April 1861 - May 1862." Quarterly Bulletin, Archaeological Society of Virginia. Volume 26 (March 1972).

Dinkins, James. "The Battle of Big Bethel, VA." Confederate Veteran. Volume 26 (1918).

Eggleston, John R. "Captain Eggleston's Narrative of the Battle of the Merrimac." Southern Historical Society Papers, Volume 41 (September 1916).

Eisenberg, Albert C. " 'The 3rd Vermont has Won a Name': Corporal George Q. French's Account of the Battle of Lees Mills, Virginia." Vermont History, Volume 49 (Fall, 1981).

The Farmer's Register, Vol. 3, No. 4, August 1835.

Frank Leslie's Illustrated Newspaper. August 10, 1861.

Greene, Samuel Dana. "I Fired the First Gun and Thus Commenced the Great Battle." American Heritage. Volume 8 (June 1957).

Greene, Samuel Dana. "In the Monitor Turret." Battles and Leaders of the Civil War. Volume 1 (New York, 1887).

Haw, Joseph R. "The Burning of Hampton." Confederate Veteran (October 1924).

Hord, B. M. "The Battle of Big Bethel, VA." Confederate Veteran, Vol. 26 (1918).

Jones, V. C. "The Sack of Hampton, Virginia." American History Illustrated, Vol. 9 (June 1983).

Kimball, William J. "The Little Battle of Big Bethel." Civil War Times Illustrated, Vol. VI (June 1967).

King, Kendall J. "Bold, But Not Too Bold." America's Civil War (March 1993).

Lee, Baker P. "Magruder's Peninsula Campaign in 1862." Southern Historical Society Papers, Vol. 19 (1891).

Littlepage, Hardin B. "Statement of Midshipman Littlepage." Southern Historical Society Papers. Volume 11 (1883).

Long, A. L. "Memoir of General John Bankhead Magruder." Southern Historical Society Papers. Volume 12 (1884).

Long, John S. "The Gosport Affair." Journal of Southern History. Volume 23, (May 1957).

Margolin, Samuel G. "Civil War Legacy Beneath the James." Archaeology. Volume 40 (September/October 1987).

New York Illustrated News. 14 October 1861.

New York Sun. 28 February 1897.

New York Times. 14 June 1861.

New York Times. 9 August 1861.

New York Times. May 2, 1862.

"News From Warwick County." Tyler's Quarterly Historical and Genealogical Magazine. Volume 7 (1926).

Noyes, G. B., Ed. Letters Written by Sgt. George B. Noyes, Co. K, 11th Regiment Maine Volunteers During the Civil War." Island Advantages. Volume 27 (June 1962).

Phillips, Dinwiddie. "The Career of the Iron-clad Virginia." Collections of the Virginia Historical Society. Volume 6 (1887).

Pierce, Edmond L. "The Contrabands at Fortress Monroe." Atlantic Monthly (November 1861).

Rae, Thomas W. "The Little Monitor Saved Our Lives." American History Illustrated. Volume 1 (July 1966).

Ramsay, H. Aston. "Wonderful Career of the Merrimac." Confederate Veteran. Volume 25 (July 1907).

Reaney, Henry. "How the Gun-Boat Zouave Aided the Congress." Battles and Leaders of the Civil War. Volume 1 (New York, 1887).

Richmond Daily Examiner. 22 April 1861.

Richmond Dispatch. June 24, 1861.

Richmond Dispatch. June 26, 1861.

Richmond Dispatch. July 10, 1861.

The Richmond Examiner. 12 August 1861.

Richmond Examiner. 3 April 1862.

Spencer, John C. "A Page from the Old Navy." U. S. Naval Institute Proceedings. Volume 86 (May 1860).

Stanton, Edwin M. "Letter From the Secretary of War: Africans in Fort Monroe Military District." (Washington, DC, 1862).

Stimers, Alban C. "An Engineer Aboard the Monitor." Civil War Times Illustrated. Volume 9 (April 1970).

Stodder, Louis N. "Aboard the U.S.S. Monitor." Civil War Times Illustrated. Volume 1 (January 1963).

Tindall, William. "True Story of the Virginia." Virginia Magazine of History and Biography. Volume 31 (January 1923).

Turner, Justin G. "Hampton Roads Conference." Civil War Times. Volume 3 (January 1962).

Virginia Gazette. 17 March 1781.

Virginia Gazette. 16 February 1854.

Weinert, Richard P. "Longstreet's Suffolk Campaign." Civil War Times Illustrated. Volume 7 (January 1969).

Welles, Gideon. "The First Iron-Clad Monitor." Annuals of War (Philadelphia, 1879).

William and Mary Quarterly. 1st Series, Volume 15 (July 1906).

Williams, Asher. "Letters From a Soldier in the Union Army." The Staten Island Historian. Volume 15 (April-June 1961).

Index

-A-

Abbott and Company; 98.
Adriatic; 49, 55.
Alabama, 9th; 120.
Albany Iron Works; 105.
Albertson, Williams; 144.
Algernon, Lord; 1.
Amanda; 105.
American Missionary Association (AMA); 65, 66.
Anderson, George Thomas "Tige"; 137.
Anderson, Robert B.; 8.
Andrews, W. H.; 130, 131, 132, 142, 144.
Anglo-Dutch War; 3.
Annapolis, M.D.; 80, 84, 88.
Appomattox; 161.
Army of the Peninsula; 47, 56, 67, 77, 114, 118, 119.
Army of the Potomac; 78, 79, 80, 112, 113, 130.
Arnold, Benedict; 4.
Aroostock War; 31.
Atlantic Monthly; 44.
Ayres, Romeryn B.; 134.
Aztec Club; 32.

-B-

Back River; 1, 35, 39, 49, 50, 56.
Back River Road; 54.
Bahia, Brazil; 160.
Baker's California Regiment; 56.
Ballentine, George; 31.
Balling, Ole Peter; 61.
Baltimore; 32, 63, 89, 98.
Baltimore & Ohio; 79.
Baltimore Riots; 20, 22.
Bankhead, James; 31.
Baptist Church; 59.
Baptists; 14.
Barlett, Washington A.; 38.
Barlett's Naval Brigade; 38.
Barnard, John G.; 113, 120, 125.
Barron, Samuel; 3.
Bartwistle, James; 158.
Beaufort; 63.
Beaufort, C.S.S.; 90, 92, 93, 94, 149.
Beckwith, Sir Sidney; 6.
Bellard, Alfred; 144.
Bendix, John E.; 39, 40.
Bennett, R. E.; 10.
Berdan's Sharpshooters; 144.
Berkley, Henry; 132, 133.
Bermuda Hundred Campaign; 157.
Bernard, Simon; 6.

Berry, Albert; 151.
Bethel; 38, 114.
Big Bethel; 14, 37, 38, 39, 40, 42, 43, 44, 45, 47, 48, 49, 51, 54, 59, 61, 67, 72, 73, 122, 123, 142.
Big Bethel Church; 35.
Birney's Zouaves; 144, 151.
Black Hawk War; 7.
Blackbeard's Point; 6.
Blair, Francis P.; 161.
Blunt, Humphrey; 2.
Boyenton, Edward C.; 32.
Brandywine; 83.
Brazil; 160.
Brest, France; 160.
Brewster, Charles Harvey; 60, 123, 132, 143, 144, 164.
Brick House Creek; 77.
Brick Kiln Creek; 35, 39, 41.
Britain; 5.
Brooke gun; 87, 92, 109.
Brooke, John Mercer; 84, 85, 87.
Brooks, W. T. H.; 133, 134, 137.
Brown, J. Thompson; 40.
Brown, John; 17.
Bryan, John Randolph, 147.
Buchanan, Franklin; 87, 88, 89, 90, 91, 92, 93, 94, 95, 96, 99, 105, 111.
Buchanan, James; 155.
Buck, Erastus; 135, 137.
Buena Vista, Battle of; 62.
Bull Run; 78, 96, 145.
Burnside, Ambrose E.; 63, 76, 77.
Burnt Chimneys; 131.
Burwell's Bay; 19, 68.
Bushnell, Cornelius; 96, 97.
Butler, Benjamin Franklin; 10, 20, 21, 23, 24, 25, 26, 28, 30, 38, 44, 45, 46, 47, 49, 54, 55, 56, 58, 60, 61, 64, 155, 157.

-C-

Cabell, H. C.; 124, 125.
Calhoun, John C.; 7.
California; 32.
Cambridge; 83.
Cameron, Simon; 57, 63.
Camp Butler; 26, 27, 28, 31, 38, 39, 49, 54, 56, 57, 61, 62, 63, 65, 66, 67, 82, 114, 155, 161, 166.
Camp Hamilton; 22, 38, 40, 54, 56, 63, 155.
Camp Troy; 22.
Campbell, John A.; 161.
Camtuck; 102.

Cape Henry; 104.
Capes, Battle of; 5.
Carrick's Ford; 79.
Carrieville; 160.
Carroll Hall; 163.
Carter, Hill; 68.
Cary, Colonel Miles; 3.
Cary, John Baytop; 13, 22, 23, 24, 27, 47.
Casey, Silas; 8.
Castle Calhoun; 7, 38.
Celey's Plantation; 6.
Chapel of the Centurion; 14.
Chapultepec; 31.
Charles City Southern Guard; 71.
Chase, Salmon; 153.
Chasseurs Britaniques; 6.
Chesapeake and Albemarle Canal; 77.
Chesapeake Bay; 1, 5, 80, 111, 113, 130, 154.
Chesapeake Female College; 13, 14, 66.
Chesnut, Mary; 126.
Clark Farm; 18, 19.
Clarke, John J.; 115.
Clinton, Sir Henry; 5.
Cobb, Howell; 137, 146.
Cobb's Legion; 137, 138.
Cockburn, Sir George; 5, 6.
College Creek; 31, 48, 68.
Columbiads; 19, 26, 68, 151.
Commissary-General of Prisoners; 162.
Committee on Naval Affairs, U.S.; 84.
Commodore Barney; 158.
Commodore Jones; 158.
Concord; 4.
Concordia Rifles; 142.
Congress, U.S.; 6, 62, 96.
Congress, U.S.S.; 82, 91, 92, 93, 94, 95, 96, 105.
Conscription Act; 149.
Constitution (balloon); 147.
Continental Iron Works; 98.
Contraband of War; 24.
Contrabands; 25, 64, 65, 66.
Cooper, Samuel; 8.
Copeland, Ralph; 29.
Coppens, George; 48.
Cornwallis, Lord; 4, 5, 7, 122.
Corson, William; 67, 74.
Cosnahan, Joseph B.; 124.
Court Street; 59.
Crafford House; 115, 116.
Craney Island; 20, 83, 90, 91, 130, 154.
Craney Island, Battle of; 6.
Craven, John J.; 163.
Crawford's House; 71, 76.
Crickett Hill; 4.

Crimean War; 96.
Crutchfield, Major Stapleton; 6.
Cumberland, U.S.S.; 18, 82, 91, 92, 93, 94.
Cummings, Alfred; 124.
Curtis, Daniel Prentis; 10.
Curtis, Humphrey Harwood; 28, 29, 52, 67, 73.
Curtis, Maria; 75.
Curtis, Richard; 53.
Curtis, Robert G.; 29.
Curtis Store; 51.
Curtis, Thomas Glanville Harwood; 29.
Curtis, William H.; 29.
Custer, George A.; 144, 147.
Cutshaw, Lieutenant; 22.

-D-

Dahlgren gun; 82, 87, 100, 106.
Dam No. 1; 127, 130, 131, 132, 133, 134, 139, 140, 141, 144, 145, 152.
Daniel Webster (Devil Dan); 79.
David-class; 157.
Davidson, Hunter; 105; 157; 158; 159; 160.
Davidson, J. Ham; 162.
Davidson, John W.; 135.
Davis, Captain James; 2.
Davis, Charles H.; 96, 97.
Davis, Jefferson; 45, 77, 81, 116, 141, 142, 148, 160, 161, 163.
Davis, Varina; 163.
Day's Point; 69, 77.
de Grasse, Comte; 5.
de Joinville, Prince; 134.
de Molina, Diego; 2.
de Paris, Comte; 134.
De Russy, Rene; 7, 18.
Declaration of Independence; 88.
Deep Creek; 1, 68, 72.
Delamater, Cornelius; 96.
Denbigh Court Day; 17.
Denbigh Plantation; 29.
Dennison, William; 79.
Department of Annapolis (Union); 20.
Department of the East (Union); 62.
Department of Ohio; 79.
Department of Virginia (Union); 20, 61, 66.
Department of Virginia and North Carolina; 155.
Dimick, Justin; 18, 19, 21.
Disciples of Christ; 14.
District of Eastern Virginia; 155.
Dix, John A.; 155.
Douglas, Hugh Thomas; 151.
Downing Street; 100.
Dragon; 109.
Dreux, William D.; 50, 51.

Dunmore, Lord; 4.
Dupont, Samuel F.; 63.
Duryea, Abram; 40, 41.
Duryea's Zouaves; 38, 40, 41.

-E-
Early, Jubal; 8, 128, 129, 142, 145, 146.
Eastern Military Department; 155.
Eaton Charity School; 13.
Eggleston, John R.; 95, 106.
Elizabeth City County; 1, 9, 12, 13, 14, 15, 17, 19, 35.
Elizabeth River; 83, 101.
Ellis, David R.; 102.
Endview Plantation; 11, 28, 29, 75.
England; 158.
Episcopal Church; 14.
Ericsson, John; 96, 97, 98, 100, 101, 102, 106.
Ewell, Benjamin Stoddert; 19, 20, 21, 23, 29, 30, 33, 35, 48, 68.
Express, 67.

-F-
Fanny; 49, 55.
Farragut, David; 63.
First Artillery; 31.
First Corps; 126.
Fisk, Wilbur; 123, 131.
Florida; 84.
Florida, C.S.S.; 160, 161.
Forno, Henry; 67.
Fort Adams; 32.
Fort Algernourne; 2.
Fort Boykin; 68.
Fort Calhoun; 9, 18, 47, 66.
Fort Charles; 2.
Fort Crafford; 148.
Fort Crawford; 76, 77, 115.
Fort Delaware; 78.
Fort Donaldson; 145.
Fort Fisher; 157.
Fort George; 3.
Fort Henry; 2.
Fort Macon; 63.
Fort Monroe; 6, 7, 8, 9, 10, 17, 18, 19, 20, 21, 23, 24, 25, 26, 29, 31, 33, 34, 37, 38, 44, 47, 48, 56, 58, 61, 77, 150, 153, 154, 155, 157.
Fort Pickens; 18, 98.
Fort Sumter; 17, 29, 33.
Fort Wool; 130, 154.
Foster, John G.; 155.
Fourth Corps; 122, 123, 124.
Fox, Gustavus V.; 82, 101, 113.
Fox Hill; 38.

Fox Hill Academy; 13.
France; 96.
Franklin, William B.; 150.
Free State of Warwick; 17.
French, Forrest; 85.
French, George Q.; 140.
Fugitive Slave Law; 23, 24.

-G-
Galena, U.S.S.; 96, 141, 150.
Garnett, Richard S.; 19.
Garnett, Robert S.; 79.
Garrow Family; 133.
Garrow, John Toomer; 133.
Garrow's Chimneys; 144.
Garrow's Field; 132, 133.
Garrow's Ford; 131.
General Assembly; 11, 12, 13, 16.
Georgia Regiment,
    1st; 131, 142.
    6th; 50.
    7th; 137.
    8th; 137.
    11th; 137.
    16th; 137.
Georgia; 62.
Germantown, U.S.S.; 88.
Gilmore, Q. A.; 157.
Gloucester Point; 19, 33, 34, 68, 113, 120, 122, 126, 148.
Goldsboro, N.C.; 135.
Goldsborough, Louis M.; 63, 65, 82, 91, 120, 153.
Gorgas, Josiah; 116.
Gosport Navy Yard; 18, 19, 20, 82, 83, 84, 85, 89, 154.
Governor's Advisory Council; 33.
Grant, U. S.; 157.
Great Bridge; 4.
Great Britain; 5.
Great Dismal Swamp Canal; 77.
Greble, John T.; 36, 41, 44.
Green, Benjamin H.; 11.
Green Mountain Boys; 135.
Green Point; 100.
Greene, Samuel Dana; 99, 102, 103, 104, 105, 108, 109, 110.
Greenpoint, NY; 98.
Greensville Guard; 71.
Griffin, James B.; 142, 143, 149, 151.
Griffith, Big Bill; 145.
Griswald, John; 97.

-H-

Half-Way House; 122, 124, 148.
Hampton; 1, 5, 6, 13, 14, 17, 20, 22, 23, 25, 27, 28, 30, 31, 33, 35, 37, 38, 40, 43, 54, 55, 56, 57, 58, 59, 60, 61, 62, 65, 66, 73, 123.
Hampton Academy; 13.
Hampton Church; 60.
Hampton Creek; 53.
Hampton Creek Bridge; 22, 23, 58.
Hampton Grays; 48.
Hampton Military Academy; 13.
Hampton River; 2, 4, 38, 40.
Hampton Roads; 1, 2, 5, 6, 7, 8, 9, 61, 62, 63, 67, 73, 76, 81, 82, 83, 88, 89, 91, 92, 95, 96, 101, 102, 103, 105, 108, 110, 111, 112, 113, 130, 152, 153, 157, 160.
Hampton Roads Peace Conference; 161.
Hampton's Legion; 142.
Hampton-York Highway; 15, 41.
Hampton-York Road; 38, 122.
Hancock, Winfield Scott; 121, 127, 135.
Hanover Artillery; 132.
Harden's Bluff; 68; 72.
Harney, William S.; 31.
Harrington, Fernando C.; 135, 137, 140.
Harris Creek; 50.
Harwood, "Big" Humphrey; 11.
Harwood's Mill; 56, 68, 72, 118.
Hatteras Inlet; 61, 62, 63.
Hawkins Family; 28.
Hawkins Zouaves; 51.
Heintzelman, Samuel P.; 122, 123.
Henderson, NY; 55.
Hill, Daniel Harvey; 36, 37, 38, 39, 40, 41, 43, 44.
Hill, D. H.; 148, 150.
Hodges, James G.; 58, 71.
Hollins, George N.; 69.
Holloway, James Montgomery; 129.
Holmes, James Rush; 145.
Hood, John Bell; 37, 43, 51, 54, 155.
Hopkins, David; 150.
Hopkins, Edward; 150.
Hopkins, James P.; 68.
Hord, B. H.; 43.
House of Burgesses; 3, 11.
Howard, Samuel; 105.
Howard's Bridge; 38, 68, 120.
Hudgins, Robert; 59.
Hudgins, Robert Scott II; 28.
Huger, Benjamin; 88, 154.
Hunter, Robert M. T.; 161.
Hurt, Benjamin; 162.
Hutchinson, Alonzo; 136, 137.
Hyde, Brad N.; 133.

Hygeia Hotel; 8.

-I-

Illinois Central Rail Road; 79.
"Intrepid"; 126, 147.
Irwinville, GA; 163.
Isherwood, B. F.; 84.

-J-

Jackson, Andrew; 8.
Jackson, Thomas J.; 32.
James City Artillery; 48.
James City County; 11, 19.
James Rifles; 26, 154.
James River; 2, 3, 4, 5, 10, 12, 17, 19, 25, 27, 33, 34, 35, 49, 61, 67, 68, 69, 70, 71, 72, 76, 77, 81, 87, 90, 111, 112, 113, 114, 118, 122, 129, 149, 150, 152, 154, 158, 160.
James River Road; 51.
James River Squadron; 91.
Jamestown; 19, 30, 31, 33, 71, 72.
Jamestown, C.S.S.; 72, 91, 95, 122, 130, 149.
Jamestown Island; 19.
Japan, 88.
Johnston, Joseph E.; 8, 80, 112, 141, 142, 146, 148, 149, 152.
Johnston, Robert; 56.
Jones, Catesby ap Roger; 19, 85, 86, 87, 92, 95, 99, 105, 106, 107, 109.
Jones, J. Pembroke; 156.
Jones, Jesse Simpkins; 52.
Jones, William B.; 125.

-K-

Kansas; 32.
Kearny, Philip; 145.
Kecoughtan Indians; 2.
Keeler, William F.; 101, 103, 104, 107, 108, 109.
Keyes, Erasmus Darwin; 121, 122, 124, 125, 129.
Kilpatrick, Judson; 40, 41.
King Street; 23, 59.
King's Wharf; 120.
1st Kentucky; 145.

-L-

La Mountain, Jack; 55.
Land's End; 70, 76, 77.
Landers, Eli Pinson; 137, 139.
Leaver, Thomas B.; 128.
Lebanon Church; 14, 75, 120, 164.
Lee Artillery; 29.
Lee, Baker Perkins; 45.

Lee, Francis Lightfoot (Frank); 53.
Lee, George Washington Custis; 7.
Lee Guards; 48.
Lee Hall; 10, 71, 147, 148, 151.
Lee, Richard Decauter; 10, 34.
Lee, Robert E.; 7, 19, 30, 31, 33, 35, 45, 69, 77, 115, 116, 118, 119, 141, 149, 150.
Lee's Mill; 16, 119, 124, 125, 126, 127, 131, 144, 145, 147, 148, 149, 151.
Letcher, John; 19.
Lewis, Robert E.; 144.
Lexington; 4.
Lincoln, Abraham; 17, 23, 33, 79, 80, 81, 82, 96, 97, 112, 113, 126, 127, 132, 140, 150, 153, 154, 155, 161.
Lincoln gun; 113.
Little Bethel; 37, 38, 40.
Little Bethel Church (Chapel); 39, 40.
Littlepage, Hardin B.; 89, 92.
Logan; 33.
Long, Armistead E.; 32.
Long Bridge; 33.
Longstreet, James; 148.
Lords of the Admiralty; 100.
Louisiana,
    2nd; 114, 133.
    5th; 67.
Louisiana Battalion; 50.
Louisiana Zouaves; 48.
Lowe, Thaddeus; 126, 147.
Lumpkin, Edward; 131.
Lyons, Patrick; 126, 147.

-M-

Macy, William D.; 68.
Macy's Sawmill; 68.
Maffitt, John Newland; 156, 160.
Magruder, John Bankhead; 27, 31, 32, 33, 34, 35, 36, 37, 39, 40, 44, 45, 46, 47, 48, 49, 50, 51, 54, 56, 57, 58, 65, 67, 68, 69, 70, 71, 72, 73, 76, 77, 81, 88, 89, 90, 114, 115, 116, 118, 119, 120, 122, 124, 125, 126, 128, 129, 131, 134, 135, 140, 141, 145, 146, 147, 148, 149, 151, 152, 153, 164.
Maine,
    11th; 145.
Mallory, Charles K.; 17, 18, 21, 24.
Mallory, Colonel Francis; 4.
Mallory, Stephen R.; 84, 85, 88, 89, 160.
Manassas; 26, 56, 79, 80.
Mansfield, John; 91, 94.
Marrow Family; 28.
Marston, John; 82, 91, 104.
Maryland; 20, 88.

Massachusetts Regiments,
    3rd; 18.
    4th; 18, 26, 39.
    10th; 123.
Massachusetts troops; 43.
Matthews, Captain Samuel; 3.
Maury, Matthew F.; 158.
McAllister, Lieutenant Julian; 14.
McCauley, C. S.; 83, 84.
McClellan, George B.; 78, 79, 80, 81, 96, 112, 113, 114, 120, 121, 122, 123, 125, 126, 127, 128, 129, 130, 132, 133, 134, 140, 141, 143, 150, 153, 164.
McClellan Saddle; 78.
McDowell, Irwin; 79, 126.
McGraw, John; 144.
McKinney, William; 135.
McLaws, Lafayette; 48, 120, 121, 137, 139.
Mecklenburg Cavalry; 58, 164.
Mecklenburg Grays; 75.
Medal of Honor; 139.
Merrimack; 84, 85, 86, 90, 91, 92, 93, 94, 96, 101, 110, 113, 157, 166.
Merrimack, U.S.S.; 83.
Merry Oaks; 133.
Methodists; 14.
Mexican War; 7, 18, 78.
Mexico; 31, 32.
Mexico City; 31, 78.
Miles, Nelson A.; 163.
Militia; 4.
Mill Creek; 18.
Mill Creek Bridge; 22.
Miller, Robert H.; 114, 142, 147.
Miller, Joaquin; 166.
Miner's Farm; 77, 148, 149.
Minnesota, U.S.S.; 65, 82, 91, 95, 105, 106, 107, 108, 109, 110, 158, 159, 160.
Minnish, J. W.; 126, 141, 145.
Minor, R. D.; 94, 95, 105.
Monitor, U.S.S.; 96, 100, 101, 102, 103, 104, 105, 106, 107, 108, 109, 110, 111, 113, 115, 150, 166.
Monroe, James; 3.
Montague, Edgar B.; 37, 41.
Montague's Battalion; 45.
Morris, Charles N., 160.
Morris, George U.; 93.
Mott, Thaddeus P.; 133.
Mulberry Island; 10, 28, 35, 68, 69, 70, 71, 75, 76, 77, 115, 116, 118, 119, 120, 128, 129, 148, 149.
Mulberry Island Church; 14.
Mulberry Island Point; 34, 69, 70, 71, 72, 73, 77, 115, 148, 149.
Mulberry Island Point Battery; 76, 115.

Mulberry Island Road; 148.
10th Massachusetts; 143.
19th Massachusetts; 126, 152.
18th Mississippi; 129.

-N-

Nansemond River; 4, 25.
Napier, Sir Charles; 6.
Nash, Virginius; 29.
Nat Turner's Rebellion; 7, 11.
Naugatuck, U.S.S.; 154.
Navy Department; 102.
Nelson Guards; 48.
New Bern; 63.
New Hampshire; 128.
New Market Bridge; 37, 39, 40, 56, 58, 66.
New Orleans; 63.
New York; 9, 87, 95, 98, 102, 104.
New York Battery,
    3rd; 133.
New York Regiments,
    1st Mounted Rifles; 94.
    2nd ; 41.
    3rd; 40, 41, 56.
    4th; 56.
    5th; 38, 40, 41, 49, 56.
    7th; 39, 40.
    10th; 49.
    56th; 147.
New York Times; 43.
New York Tribune; 57.
Newcomb, Edgar N.; 126, 152.
Newmarket Creek; 1.
Newport, RI; 32.
Newport News; 1, 10, 25, 49, 50, 72, 77, 89, 90, 114, 115, 116, 166.
Newport News Point; 2, 4, 5, 6, 9, 13, 25, 26, 27, 28, 30, 37, 39, 40, 50, 54, 56, 57, 65, 66, 67, 71, 82, 89, 90, 91, 93, 94, 95, 161, 166.
Newport News POW Camp; 161; 162.
Niagara; 18.
Norfolk; 1, 6, 13, 25, 49, 55, 62, 77, 82, 83, 86, 111, 116, 120, 142, 150, 153, 154, 159.
North Atlantic Blockading Squadron; 82, 161.
North Carolina; 63, 75, 77, 91.
North Carolina Military Institute; 37, 40.
North Carolina Regiments; 50.
    1st; 37, 41, 43, 44.
    15th; 75.
Northampton, C.S.S.; 67.
Norton, Oliver W.; 123, 143.
Novelty Iron Works; 98.
Noyles, E. M.; 134.

-O-

Ocean View; 154.
Office of Ordnance and Hydrography; 158.
Ohio Volunteers; 79.
Old Dominion Dragoons; 28, 57, 58.
Old Point Comfort; 1, 2, 3, 5, 6, 7, 8, 54, 62, 63, 95, 153, 161.
Old Point Lighthouse; 113.
Oliver, John; 66.
Ordnance of Secession; 17, 23.
Osborne, Private William; 26.
Oysters; 16.

-P-

Parker, William; 93, 94.
Parrish Family; 28.
Parrott gun; 128.
Patrick Henry, C.S.S.; 66, 71, 72, 91, 95, 105, 106, 149, 158.
Patriot; 4.
Patterson, Edmund Dewitt; 120, 125, 132, 142, 143.
Patton, J. M.; 71.
Paulding, Hiram; 96, 102.
Pawnee, U.S.S.; 25, 84.
Peake, Mary; 13, 66.
Peck, John J.; 129.
Peninsula; 1, 2, 4, 5, 8, 10, 12, 13, 14, 16, 17, 19, 23, 27, 28, 29, 33, 34, 35, 37, 48, 49, 54, 56, 59, 61, 62, 63, 67, 68, 69, 72, 73, 81, 112, 113, 114, 116, 125, 141, 142, 148, 151, 153, 155, 157, 163.
Peninsula Artillery; 29, 48, 124.
Pennsylvania,
    23rd; 151.
    61st; 145.
    83rd; 123.
Pensacola Bay, FL; 98.
Percy; George; 2.
Perry, Matthew C.; 88.
Persimmon Ponds Bridge; 28.
Petersburg; 154, 157.
Phelps, J. Wolcott; 22, 23, 26, 28, 50.
Philadelphia; 78.
Phillips, Dinwiddie B.; 89, 105.
Phillips, Jefferson Curle; 53, 58.
Pickett, George; 155.
Pierce, Ebenezer W.; 38, 40, 43, 44.
Pig Point; 25, 26, 55.
Pingree, Samuel E.; 136, 137, 140.
Pinkerton, Allan;
Plattsburg; 62.
Pleasant Point; 10.
Pope, Alexander Franklin; 131, 133.
Poppy; 158.
Poquoson River; 68.

Port Royal, VA; 31.
Porter, David Dixon; 102.
Porter, Fitz-John; 147.
Porter, John L.; 85, 87.
Portsmouth, VA; 1, 13, 85, 154.
Potomac River; 80, 88, 96, 104, 112.
Presbyterians; 14.
Price, Richard Channing; 142.
Princeton, U.S.S.; 96.
Provisional Army; 33.

-Q-

Quaker Guns; 112.
Queen Street; 23.
Queen's Creek; 31, 48, 68.
Queenstown Heights; 62.

-R-

Radical Republicans, 80.
Rae, Thomas; 105.
Rains, Gabriel J.; 146, 151.
Raleigh, C.S.S.; 90, 93, 130, 149.
Ramsay, H. Ashton; 91, 92, 106, 107, 108, 109, 154.
Randolph, George W.; 37, 41, 44, 45, 141.
Rappahannock River; 80, 81.
Ratchford, J. W.; 39.
Ratcliffe, Captain John; 2.
Reaney, Henry; 91.
Red River; 78.
Reid, Jesse; 149.
Religion; 14.
Rennsselaer Works; 98.
Revolutionary War; 5, 14.
Rhode Island; 32.
Rhode Island,
    2nd; 126, 147.
Rich Mountain; 79.
Richmond; 9, 10, 17, 26, 27, 30, 33, 37, 62, 63, 67, 69, 71, 72, 76, 80, 83, 84, 90, 105, 111, 112, 113, 116, 118, 141, 150, 152, 153, 154, 155, 157.
Richmond and Danville Rail Road; 116.
Richmond Howitzers; 19, 39, 41, 57, 75, 142.
Rip-Raps; 7, 8, 25, 38, 47, 63, 111.
River Queen; 161.
Rives, Alfred; 48, 115.
Roanoke, U.S.S.; 49, 82, 83, 91, 95, 104.
Roanoke Island; 76.
Rochelle, James H.; 106.
Rocketts Navy Yard; 158.
Rodman gun; 128.
Rosecran, William S.; 79.
Royal Marines; 5.
Royal Navy; 4.

-S-

St. John's Church; 14, 58, 59.
St. Lawrence, U.S.S.; 91, 95.
St. Louis; 55.
Sachem; 102.
Salter's Creek; 6, 57.
San Antonio, TX; 62.
Saragossa; 20.
Sawyer Gun; 38, 47.
Sawyer, Sylvanus; 47.
Sawyer Rifle; 26, 154.
Scott, Julian; 136, 137, 140.
Scott, William; 136, 140.
Scott, Winfield; 18, 20, 22, 25, 31, 49, 56, 60, 62, 78, 79.
Seaboard and Roanoke Rail Road; 86.
Sebastopol; 127.
Secession Convention; 17.
Segar Farm; 22.
Selfridge, Thomas O.; 92, 93.
Seminole War; 7, 18, 31.
Seth Low; 102, 103.
Seward, William; 161.
Sewell's Point; 25, 27, 38, 55, 83, 91, 95, 110, 153, 154.
Sewell's Point Battery; 47.
Sherwood; 67.
Ship's Point; 68.
Signal Point; 94.
Skiffes Creek; 148.
Slabtown; 65.
Slaves; 12, 23, 29.
Smith, Captain John;
Smith, G. W.; 148.
Smith, Joseph B., Commodore; 96, 98.
Smith, Joseph B., Lt.; 93.
Smith, Nelson; 50, 51, 54.
Smith, William F. "Baldy"; 120, 122, 124, 127, 132, 133, 134, 135, 137, 138, 139, 141, 157.
Smith, William H.; 75.
Sorrel, Moxley; 128.
South Carolina; 62.
South Carolina,
    4th; 149.
Southampton County; 12.
Spanish; 2.
Squires, W. H. T.; 163.
Stanton, Edwin; 80, 96, 141, 153, 163.
Stephens, Alexander H.; 161.
Stiles, Robert; 144.
Stimers, Alban C.; 102.
Stodder, Louis N.; 101.
Stores, William J.; 51, 59.
Stoughton, Edwin H.; 133, 139.
Stringham, Silas H.; 61, 62, 70, 82.

Stuart, William D.; 37, 40, 41.
Stuyvesant, Moses S.; 93.
Suffolk, 26, 77, 155.
Sumner, Edwin Vose "Bull"; 122.
Sunset Creek; 6.
Susquehanna, U.S.S.; 88.
Swash Channel; 70.
Syms Free School; 13.

-T-

Talcott, Andrew; 19.
Taliaferro, William Booth; 32.
Tarleton, Lieutenant Colonel Banastre; 4.
Tarrant, Cesar; 12.
Tattnal, Josiah N.; 111, 150, 154.
Taylor, Zachary; 62.
Teaser, C.S.S.; 67, 72, 91, 94, 105, 122, 149.
Ten Corps; 157.
Terry, Alfred H.; 157.
Texas; 32.
Third Corps; 123.
Thirteenth Corps; 157.
Thompson, Gilbert; 128.
Torpedo, C.S.S.; 158.
Torpedo Division; 158.
Townsend, Frank; 39, 40, 41.
Tredegar Iron Works; 86.
Troop Artillery; 131, 134.
Truscott, Peter; 102.
Tyler, John; 8, 17, 22, 66.
Tyler, Julia; 22.

-U-

U. S. Army; 18, 65.
U. S. Artillery,
    5th; 134.
U. S. Cavalry,
    5th; 122.
U. S. Colored Cavalry,
    1st; 162.
U. S. Colored Light Artillery,
    2nd; 162.
U. S . Colored Troops,
    122nd; 162.
U. S. Military Academy; 19.
U. S. Naval Academy; 88, 157.
U. S. Navy; 17, 20, 65, 66, 77, 82, 83, 85, 88, 96, 98, 100, 101, 102, 126, 158, 160.
Union; 17, 19, 33.
Union Gun; 47, 113.
United States; 14.
University of Pennsylvania; 78.
University of Virginia; 31.
Upsher, H. H.; 158.
Urbanna; 81, 112.

Urbanna Plan; 80, 81.

-V-

Van Brunt, Gershon; 105, 106, 107, 110.
Vermont Brigade; 133, 140.
Vermont Regiments,
    1st; 18, 22, 23, 39.
    2nd; 123.
    3rd; 133, 135, 140.
    4th; 133, 134, 139.
    6th, 139.
Vermont Volunteers; 25, 43, 133, 134, 137.
Villa Margaret; 22.
Virginia; 1.
Virginia, C.S.S.; 86, 87, 88, 89, 90, 91, 92, 93, 94, 95, 96, 101, 104, 105, 106, 107, 108, 109, 110, 111, 112, 113, 114, 118, 122, 126, 130, 142, 149, 150, 152, 153, 154, 157, 158.
Virginia,
    3rd; 37, 41, 43.
    14th; 58, 70, 71.
    32nd, 29, 48, 149.
    115th Militia; 5, 24.
Virginia State Navy; 4, 19.
Von Kapft, Henrietta; 32.

-W-

Wachusett, U.S.S.; 160.
Wainwright, Charles S.; 164.
War of 1812; 5, 6, 13.
Warren, Sir John Borlase; 5.
Warwick Beauregards; 28, 29, 47, 48, 54, 58, 75, 133, 149.
Warwick County; 1, 4, 8, 11, 12, 13, 14, 15, 16, 17, 19, 28, 149, 164.
Warwick Court House; 14, 15, 50, 57, 67, 122, 125, 147, 164, 165.
Warwick Line; 68, 118, 120, 140, 141, 148, 149.
Warwick River; 1, 15, 19, 34, 68, 69, 70, 71, 72, 74, 76, 77, 90, 118, 119, 123, 125, 127, 128, 129, 131, 133, 135, 137, 140, 141, 142, 148, 149, 154.
Warwick Road; 15, 47, 50, 54, 116, 122.
Warwick-Yorktown Line; 141, 142.
Washburn, Peter T.; 39.
Washington, DC; 20, 26, 32, 33, 56, 78, 79, 80, 88, 97, 104, 114, 120.
Washington, George; 122.
Washington Artillery; 48.
Washington Navy Yard; 87.
Waters Creek; 4, 55, 122.
Waterview; 10.
Watkins, Lieutenant James; 4.
Webb, William A.; 94.

Weldon, NC.; 86.
Wells, Gideon; 65, 88, 91, 96, 97, 100, 101, 104, 111.
West Family; 28.
West, George Benjamin; 9, 12, 13, 16, 27, 64.
West, Parker; 13, 27.
West Point, VA; 120.
West Point (USMA); 18, 31, 37, 44, 78.
West Virginia; 79.
Wheeler, Charles C.; 134.
Whitaker, Richard; 52.
White, Robert T.; 53.
White, William; 75, 76.
White House; 82.
Whitney's Store; 56.
Whittemore, Robert D.; 137.
Wilcox, Cadmus; 129.
William and Mary, College of; 13.
William P. Clyde; 163.
Williams, Asher; 110, 165.
Williamsburg; 14, 28, 29, 30, 31, 33, 48, 57, 68, 69, 71, 148, 151, 153.
Williamsburg Junior Guard; 19, 48.
Williamsburg Line; 29, 33, 48.
Williamson, William P.; 85.
Wilmington, NC; 157.
Winslow, John; 97.
Winthrop, Theodore; 38, 43, 44.
Wise, Lieutenant; 85.
Wood, John Taylor; 87, 92, 109, 122.
Woodson, Harrison; 162.
Wool, John Ellis; 61, 62, 63, 64, 66, 73, 91, 94, 113, 116, 153, 155, 156.
Worden, John Lorimer; 98, 99, 101, 102, 103, 105, 106, 108, 109.
Wormley Creek; 150.
Wright, Thomas Sr.; 13.
Wyatt, Henry L., Pvt.; 36, 44.
Wynne's Mill; 119, 129, 131, 133, 142, 145, 147.
Wythe Rifles; 29, 43, 48, 50.

-X-Y-Z-

Yankee; 19.
Yeo, Colonel Leonard, 3.
York County; 19, 150.
York Rangers; 48, 58, 59.
York River; 1, 17, 19, 31, 34, 35, 68, 74, 113, 118, 120, 136, 130, 141, 150, 152.
York-Hampton Road; 123.
Yorktown; 5, 19, 27, 30, 31, 33, 34, 35, 49, 50, 68, 71, 113, 116, 118, 119, 120, 122, 123, 125, 126, 127, 128, 132, 141, 147, 148, 150, 153.
Yorktown, C.S.S.; 67.
Yorktown Road; 14, 75.
Yorktown-Williamsburg Road; 124.
Young Family; 10.
Young, Dr. Edward Rush; 15.
Young, William G.; 29, 47, 52.
Young's Mill; 15, 47, 48, 50, 54, 55, 66, 67, 68, 114, 118, 120, 122, 123, 124.
Zouave; 91, 93, 95.